ALSO BY WILLIAM S. COHEN

Of Sons and Seasons

SENATOR WILLIAM S. COHEN

ROLL CALL

One Year in
the United States Senate

SIMON AND SCHUSTER   NEW YORK

Designed by Elizabeth Woll

Manufactured in the United States of America

1   3   5   7   9   10   8   6   4   2

Library of Congress Cataloging in Publication Data
Cohen, William S
Roll call.
1. United States. Congress. Senate. I. Title.
JK1161.C63   328.73'071   80-22233
ISBN 0-671-25142-2

The author gratefully acknowledges permission to quote from the following:
    "The New Faces" from *Collected Poems* by William Butler Yeats. Copyright 1928 by
Macmillan Publishing Company, Inc., renewed 1956 by Georgie Yeats.
    Poem by Archibald MacLeish on page 213 is reprinted by kind permission of the author
and Houghton Mifflin, Inc.
    Zen and the Art of Motorcycle Maintenance by Robert M. Pirsig. Copyright © 1974 by
Robert M. Pirsig. Reprinted by permission of William Morrow & Company, Inc.

To Diane,
the rose who has lived with the thorn

Let the new faces play what tricks they will
  In the old rooms; night can outbalance day,
  Our shadows rove the garden gravel still,
  The living seem more shadowy than they.

—William Butler Yeats

ROLL CALL

INTRODUCTION

THERE IS, perhaps, no group that has been the object of more public esteem or criticism than that of politicians. It is an interesting paradox in our society that permits the public to heap adulation upon individual public officials while condemning them as a class.

Criticism of our system of government since our fiery birth as a nation has been as constant as the sunrise. Indeed, words such as "disenchantment," "disillusionment," "discontent," and "alienation" can be found as readily in the yellowed pages of yesteryear as they can in current Gallup or Harris statistical surveys.

But political observers tell us that during the 1970s, we began to experience a disconcerting new phenomenon: the day of the empty polling booth, the decade of the nonvoter, the age of the positive apathetic.

It is frustrating for those who consider public service a noble calling to witness the withering away of our national spirit, the triumph of a secular fatalism which harbors in its dark core the conviction that no one can significantly alter the riptide rush of events; which concludes that life, bad as it may be, is as good as it's going to be. So why bother to fight or change it?

But there is more than one exit lane to the boneyard of indifference.

If the people of this country are losing faith in the future, it should come as no surprise that an increasing number of politicians are doing the same. They are resigning, "dropping out"—in numbers proportionate to those of the citizens who register their contempt or apathy by not voting. Their reasons for doing so ring with near unanimity: too many demands and pressures; too little time to reason and reflect; too much criticism of their efforts; the hair-trigger presumption of guilt that is pulled at the slightest whisper of impropriety; the schizophrenia of a public that wants less government spending, more government services, and lower taxes; the unyielding demands of proliferating single-issue constituencies ("No, Congressman—there is no other issue that is as important to us as citizens and constituents. This is the vote that will determine whether we will support or oppose you. . . ."). And so they are leaving, discouraged and depleted.

As a participant in the daily drama of trying to reconcile the competing interests of a vast and diverse nation, I rationalize that the general public does not fully comprehend the dimensions and limitations of the political process. And yet, I concede that the public intuitively knows enough to know that something is wrong with the process, that it no longer seems capable of coping with contemporary stresses and that too often hypocrisies are shrouded in a fog of rhetoric about high-minded ideals.

Perhaps time is not on our side. History reveals that democracies enjoy short, happy lives. They are predisposed to dissolve in the acid of spiritual sloth and economic flaccidity. Over the centuries liberty has been lost through an insufficiency of self-discipline, self-restraint, and self-respect. Alistair Cooke has observed that in America, "a country in which I see the blandest cynicism and the most persistent idealism, the race is on between its vitality and its decadence."

On January 15, 1979, nineteen men and one woman raised their hands in the Chamber of the United States Senate and took a solemn oath. I was among those who stood in that historic room and shared the silent conviction that we could help lift the weight of world history and move it forward.

But even as I repeated the oath, I could not clear my thoughts of a conversation I had had a short time before with a well-known journalist; his questions were not new, but they seemed more intense and imperative now.

"Is Congress obsolete? Is it too factionalized, parochial and petty? Has its reach exceeded its grasp—particularly in the field of foreign policy? What can *you* do to change the direction, the policies, the System? What *will* you do?"

I had no answers to these questions. Some opinions, yes. But no answers.

I had completed three terms in the House of Representatives. While my eyes were no longer wide with lofty aspirations or illusions about the promise and productivity of the legislative process, they were not yet leadened with a world-weariness and cynicism that blinks benignly at the perpetual call for change.

In six years I had witnessed some memorable events in the history of our government: a President forced to resign from office; the confirmation of two Vice Presidents under the Twenty-fifth Amendment to the Constitution; the adoption of the War Powers and Budget Control Acts—designed to restore a balance of power in our constitutional system; and a host of other important legislative triumphs.

But I also knew how narrow, small-minded and, yes, irresponsible Congress could be and had been. The final days of the 95th Congress' session will not be remembered as our "finest hour." A massive but virtually impotent energy bill was passed with only a few members having any knowledge of what the bill contained (I was not among the select few who were fully informed). A "tax cut" bill was gaveled into law. It was not a tax cut in fact, but a reduction in the net impact of a scheduled tax increase. Aside from the dubious label, the provisions of the bill remained incomprehensible to most members, who had only a few hours to digest its arcane and complex provisions before voting and consequently had to read about what we had done in *The Wall Street Journal* the following day. A Milky Way of watered-down bills were funneled through a wide trough as House members fought the torpor of 36 nonstop hours, playing a saxophone in the cloakroom, singing songs ("Auld Lang Syne"), cat-napping in chairs or on tables in the Speaker's lobby, begging the leadership to end the sessions so that planes could be caught and campaigns for reelection undertaken. . . .

On more than one occasion during those final moments as a Representative, I wondered why I wanted to continue to participate in this silliness and stupefaction. I also found myself being grateful that the proceedings were not being nationally televised—for surely our legislative performance was just cause for insurrection!*

There were of course compensations for the inevitable flurry of activity that comes at the end of every session. I had known moments of satisfaction in securing the passage of an amendment to a bill that would be beneficial to my state or in helping constituents receive reprieve and

---

* Proceedings in the House of Representatives are now televised on a daily basis. The Senate has, to date, refused to allow its proceedings to be broadcast by television or radio.

relief from the inscrutable indifference of some civil servant safely immune from electoral pressures or threat of a job loss. But I also burned with anger at the arbitrariness of a bureaucracy, which I helped to perpetuate, that sits behind a wall of marble reciting Dewey-decimaled codes and regulations as if they had been etched on Mt. Sinai. I was supposed to be in a position to control the behemoth, move it, shake it, and if necessary, kill it—and yet on many occasions I found it impenetrable, outrageous, and impervious to my anger.

In spite of my misgivings and doubts about my limitations in a limited process whose motion is mostly molecular, I wanted to continue to participate—but in the Senate. The Senate is different, I was told. There you are released from the procedural restraints that bind all the would-be Brobdingnagians of the House. In the Senate there is an opportunity to have a greater impact upon legislation, to be creative and persuasive on a larger scale. . . .

I had my wish.

I finished my oath with "So help me God" with the hope that the brooding thoughts that were leaping behind my eyes did not visibly contradict or diminish the sense of pride that I nonetheless felt at that moment. Pride and doubt, hope and skepticism filled my thoughts. I looked up to the balcony and saw my father, wife, and sons. Their eyes were glistening.

This was a new year, a new legislative body, a new beginning. It was the last time in my career that I would ever be a freshman.

I had decided to keep a journal, recording daily events and episodes, the shadows and fleeting nuances of human encounters that have a meaning of their own, but scatter and slip away under the jackhammer hum of a "Senator's busy schedule."

This journal is not a new version of an old theme—Mr. Smith Goes to Washington: I've been there too long. Nor is it the story about a young legislator's loss of innocence. From that blissful state of mind I was deflowered long ago. It is my hope that this book may serve as a lens, clouded as it is with prejudice and passion, that will allow the viewer to see the flowing metamorphosis of power, people, and events. Perhaps each of us will be in a better position to judge whether the American people demand too much from their political system or receive too little from their political representatives—and why politics as perceived and practiced seems to have become increasingly unsatisfactory to the governors and the governed.

CHAPTER 1

NOVEMBER 7, 1978

"ABC NOW PREDICTS William Cohen to be the new Senator from Maine." A roar went up from the supporters crowding into the Bangor Civic Center.

"Hey, Bill, ABC says you've won!"

"Well," I responded, "the night's still young. Let's wait a little before we celebrate."

This was not false modesty on my part. The returns from our largest cities were not in, and my instinct for caution simply would not concede what the ABC computers flatly declared.

A short time later, CBS issued the same pronouncement. Another roar went up. It was still only 9:30 P.M. I wasn't satisfied the networks were right. The entire day had been one of uncertainty.

I awoke that morning at 6:45 A.M. to catch the morning newscasts and wondered whether any of the major networks would make predictions on the elections. No forecasts other than the weather were offered.

I was confident that I was going to win—every survey showed me comfortably ahead—but an indefinable doubt fluttered about my mind. There were too many imponderables. A last-minute surge by the incumbent Senator, William D. Hathaway; the savage attacks by one of the independent candidates (there were three); President Carter's two trips to Maine; Teddy Kennedy's three appearances; reports that I had peaked too soon and had lost the momentum; my loss of voice with severe laryngitis during the last eight days of the campaign . . . There was no way of telling.

A network prediction, I thought, just might change a few votes. . . . I snapped off the television set and ordered breakfast for Diane and myself. During the final weeks of the campaign we found there was virtually no privacy left in our lives. It was practically impossible to start or finish a meal without friends or constituents coming to our table to offer early congratulations or a word of encouragement. It was what every politician thrives on and, of course, wants to hear, but it becomes frustrating when you try to secure the few moments for conversation and mutual reinforcement with the person who not only shares in the glory of victory, but also suffers the hidden lacerations inflicted by solitude and neglect along the long road of a political campaign.

And so in the final days when we saw so little of each other, we ate in hotel rooms. Often the coffee came in plastic cups and the eggs or French toast were as cold as the orange juice was warm, but we needed the time together to sort out what was happening in and to our lives.

When we arrived at the polls, I experienced a sudden sinking feeling in my stomach. The voting machines were not properly aligned for the punch cards, and one of the ballot clerks had been giving the wrong instructions for correcting the misalignment.

I followed her instructions while she looked over my shoulder. I checked the ballot and discovered I had voted for one of my opponents. At this point, I panicked.

I returned to my campaign headquarters to report my discovery about the ballots and to inquire whether other polling places had the same problem. Then I called Lew Vafiades, a prominent trial attorney and staunch supporter, and asked him to meet me at the City Clerk's office to launch a protest. We insisted, over the Clerk's objections, on making an on-site ballot inspection to demonstrate how confusing the misaligned ballot was to the average voter (I placed myself in that category). The Clerk finally conceded that it might be somewhat confusing but there was little that could be done other than identifying by time checks those ballots which had already been cast and making a slight modification in the machines for the balance of the day.

By this time, that gray moth of doubt in my mind had ballooned into a terrifying pterodactyl whose razored jaws were shredding what remained of my confidence. I saw 14 months of campaigning, $650,000, thousands of hours of staff and volunteer effort all geared to reach the high pitch of perfection on election day sliding into the dark swamp of defeat.

Diane and I returned to the campaign office, but I succeeded only in passing on my anger and pessimism to the staff. We left and went to a new shopping center to window-shop and have lunch. As we were on our way through the fast-service line, the young manager cautioned me against campaigning on the premises. Diane was as offended as I was (and said curtly, "We came here to eat, not to shake hands"), because we have always made it a point never to intrude upon people's privacy in restaurants.

The manager was embarrassed about his remark and came to our table to apologize, explaining that so many candidates had come in recently that they interrupted the ability of the waitresses to serve the patrons. Although we tried to eat our lunch without looking up or around, we were interrupted at least five or six times by people who came over to congratulate us. Although we were somewhat embarrassed, because we produced the exact effect the manager was concerned about, we were also reassured by the sincerity of our well-wishers.

That evening at a private dinner in the back room of the Red Lion, a prominent restaurant in Bangor, we entertained the Chairwoman of my volunteers along with a number of key supporters—the people who raised the money for the campaign and stood behind me even when I cast some votes with which they strongly disagreed. I tried to be pleasant and gracious, but my heart wasn't in it. My doubt about victory by that time was all-consuming, but I did not want to burden them with it.

We finally arrived at the Civic Center and moved into the wave of our supporters.

"Hey, Bill, Harry Reasoner said he's going to read your poetry tonight. . . ."

"Bill, would you sign this for my daughter?"

Hugs. Kisses. Handshakes. Klieg lights from television crews.

After it became clear that I had won, I mounted a stage, stopped the band from playing, and expressed my gratitude for the love, the labor and the support that had been showered upon me. I then proceeded to call each member of my family to the stage:

"I didn't have Jimmy Carter campaigning for me. I had someone far more formidable—my father, Ruby Cohen."

"I didn't have 'Miz Lillian' appearing on my behalf, I had my mother, Clara Cohen."

"I didn't have Rosalynn, I had Diane. . . ."

I continued in this fashion, stringing out the parallels with my brother, Bob, and sister, Marlene, just to emphasize that my support came from within my family and the State, not from the Washington power structure.

We then boarded a plane and headed for Lewiston, a strongly Democratic city, but one that had supported me over the years. Mayor Lillian Caron, a courageous and strong-willed woman, had announced her support for me and campaigned in my behalf all over the State. Georgette Berube, a popular Democratic State Representative, ran the risk of political retribution by her party when she endorsed me a year before the election. So I stopped to thank them and share the excitement of victory.

Finally, we arrived in Portland about 12:30 A.M. and joined our teen-age sons, Kevin and Chris, who had flown up separately from Washington. We didn't want them traveling with us on the small private plane. The memory of our friends Jerry and Sharon Litton, who died in a fiery crash with their children on the eve of a Senatorial primary victory in Missouri in 1976, was seared forever in our minds.

Click. Whirr. Click. Whirr. The flashes popped. The automatic cameras advanced their film, sounding like metallic crickets. Another speech. More interviews. Congratulatory calls were coming in from all over the country. Finally, the evening ended at 3:45 A.M.

NOVEMBER 8, 1978

WE BOARDED a Delta Airlines flight back to Washington, weary but still flushed with the warm feeling of victory.

My joy was enhanced by the news I had received during the night that Senator Charles Percy of Illinois had been re-elected to a third term in the Senate. Chuck had been one of my strongest supporters while I was a member of the House. He had held two fund-raisers for me during my Senate race and had even encouraged his major contributors to give me priority over his own campaign. Several weeks before the election, he had fallen victim to a negative, but effective, advertising campaign by his opponent and was in serious danger of being defeated. Only a major effort on his part managed to pull him over the public-opinion polls to victory.

In Boston, Senators Edward Brooke of Massachusetts and Thomas McIntyre of New Hampshire entered and sat in the first-class section of the plane. I walked up front to express my condolences over their defeats.

Brooke offered me congratulations, and said, "Bill, I feel as if a great burden has been lifted from my shoulders. I have never given up on any challenge in my life, and I didn't on this campaign. But now that it's over, I feel a great burden has been lifted."

Mrs. McIntyre turned to me and said, "You're a young man and you have to have the energy to be in politics today. Make sure you get on the Appropriations Committee. That's where the power is; that's where you can help your State the most."

I thanked her for the advice and went to the back of the plane. I knew what Brooke meant when he said how free he felt now that he was out of the eye of the storm, the *Boston Globe,* and the glass jar he had been living in for the past year.

DECEMBER 13, 1978

THE FRESHMAN RUSH BEGAN. Five weeks had elapsed since the euphoric night of victory. I had spent the time leisurely reading novels, poetry and magazines, making a deposit into an intellectual bank that had practically run dry during the past year. I had reintroduced myself to Diane, and our sons. I had promised them that if they could just endure one more long year of my absences, life would improve. There would be time for dinners at home, the gym and movies on weekends. It was a promise that I kept.

In a moment of weakness, I had also promised to grow a mustache. I really didn't relish the idea, but the boys wanted to add a little dash to my life. I needed time away from public appearances so that I would not be caught in grubby mid-growth. My plan didn't work. A speech earlier in the month delayed the start of my new look. When the new members of the Senate gathered for the orientation program, I was in the awkward stage of having random red-blond hairs splayed across my upper lip that prompted every person I encountered to ask, "Cohen, are you trying to grow a mustache?"

It was exactly the impression I did not want to make during my first days. But Diane and the boys held firm. "Since when were you concerned what other people thought about you? They're interested in what's in your head, not what's on your lip."

"But what's on my lip is diverting their attention from what's in my head," I countered weakly. It was no use. They put me in the cardboard box of the young man in a gray flannel suit, with no internal courage to challenge convention.

We gathered in a large room on the first floor of the Dirksen Building. A large blue three-ring loose-leaf notebook was furnished to each new member. The notebook contained information on the Senate rules and regulations regarding office accounting, payroll allowance and benefits. One section was devoted to the reports and disclosure statements that Senators are required to file. Another discussed the various computer-center services, office equipment and facilities that were available to us. In short, it was a handy guide to the Senate, designed to alert the new members to the practical, day-to-day problems of managing an office and to help us chart our way around Capitol Hill so that we would not appear to be looking for the men's room each time we walked down an unfamiliar corridor.

The Washington press corps was there in full force. Network television crews and photographers for weekly magazines and national newspapers were waiting to catch a shot of New Jersey Senator Bill Bradley towering over Robert Byrd of West Virginia or Howard Baker of Tennessee. We were seated at tables in a kind of classroom arrangement.

The only things that distinguished it from my college days were the lack of beanie caps and pledge cards.

Shortly after 9 o'clock, Senate Majority Leader Robert Byrd opened the proceedings with a speech. He was dressed in a gray vested suit, white shirt and striped red tie. His gray hair was swept back into a high arching pompadour of the '50s and feathered neatly in the back into a "duck's tail." He proceeded to quote from Daniel Webster, Aaron Burr and Gladstone. We were told that the period of the 1830s had been the most dignified in Senate history. Byrd turned to Baker and bowed slightly. "Senator Baker and I work closely together. He is considerate, cooperative, courteous and understanding [It sounded like the Boy Scout oath]. The members of the Senate are a body of equals. Let's all work together to keep this the most dignified body in the world."

It was Senate Minority Leader Baker's turn to speak. He began on a light note and then said:

"We do work together. Do not confuse the heated debate we might have with hostility, because we always maintain a degree of civility. It's nice to see your unsullied aspirations—you will get over it!

"There is no place like the Senate where you can let ideas flower into fruition and where you can ventilate new concepts. It's tedious work at times, but it is most rewarding. A word of caution. As Senator Aiken [of Vermont] once said, 'Don't get intoxicated with the smell of white marble.' "

After the introductory speeches that were clearly designed to instill a sense of the Senate's history, collegial respect and camaraderie among the new members, it was all downhill. We were told by various Senate officials in painful detail about the great characters who had left their marks in the Senate and their idiosyncrasies in our history books.

We were treated to a brief lecture on Senate ethics rulings (some 675 of them now existed), followed by a description of the health- and life-insurance benefits that were available.

Throughout the morning, appeals were made to a sense of history, tradition and civility—and the importance of being a Senator.

The initial instinct is to scoff at this or belittle its importance; but it is necessary to coat one hundred egos with the sugar of custom and institutional courtesy. The role of manners in the art of government is an important one.

After lunch, I returned for two more hours of indoctrination which rivaled the power of Sominex tablets. I finally had to leave before my boredom became blatant. I went home to rest before going on to Howard Baker's for an evening affair.

The dinner that night was for the Senatorial Trust Committee—those men and women who had contributed so generously to a campaign fund for the election of Republican Senators. Our presence was to show them what kind of Senators they had helped to elect.

Just before dinner, Howard Baker gave an impromptu speech and said that we were not only one of the largest, but one of the brightest classes ever to enter the Senate. I offered a muffled "Hear, hear" to that bit of obligatory puffery.

It reminded me of the time that Congresswoman Barbara Jordan and I had received an award from our law school, Boston University, for our efforts in Congress.

Shortly before we were scheduled to speak to a large audience, Barbara said, "Bill, I don't have a thing prepared. I'm not sure what to say today."

"Don't worry, Barbara. I'll spend my twenty minutes just praising you. You won't have to say anything."

I had never known Barbara to be unprepared for anything. She is an intimidating person to many, cold and intolerant of small talk or fools. As she rose to address the audience, she waited until the applause died down and began in her unique speaking idiom—a lyrical mixture of Southern Baptist cadence and High Oxford accentuation: "I assume [pronounced "asssummme"] that you think that I am something special. . . .[An in-

tolerably long pause; the audience waited.] Well, I *am* something special
—and if you did not think I am special, I would ask you to take back this
award today. . . ."

The alumni hesitated momentarily, then broke into a sustained ovation that was just short of standing. Only Barbara Jordan could have
made that statement and succeeded. Anyone else would have been considered supremely arrogant. Barbara was just absolutely confident and
candid about her efforts and accomplishments.

Tonight, we were again being told that we were something special—
equal parts representing the sum total of the nation.

I wondered how long it would be before each of us would adopt the
solemnity and demeanor that reflected the weight of our burden and responsibility.

DECEMBER 14, 1978

TWO DAYS of "freshman orientation" remained. The program undoubt-
edly was beneficial for the new members who had not served in the
House, but I felt fortunate that I was catching a plane to Scottsdale,
Arizona, to deliver a speech to the Traveling Salesmen of America.

I arrived in Phoenix early in the afternoon and was greeted by a
fellow graduate of Bowdoin College—my alma mater—who serves as
attorney for the organization, and ushered into a mile-long Cadillac. A
very heavy gentleman sat on my left in the back seat and a frail fellow
was on my right. In a sense, I was trapped during the ride from the airport
to the motel. The two individuals then proceeded to relay every grievance
they had against a government that was totally insensitive to their needs.
Gas rationing would extinguish their livelihood; they couldn't carry their
wares in a Volkswagen Rabbit; they should be treated as employees and
not independent contractors; they needed some relief from Congress so
that when they made their sales territory successful, their franchise
couldn't be revoked or divided at the whim of manufacturers. . . . Some
of their complaints had substantial merit.

When we arrived at the hotel, I declined an invitation to drive up into
the nearby mountains to a restaurant. I wanted to sit in the sun for a while
and think about what I was going to say to the group the following morning.

I sat on the patio outside my room, directly across from Camelback

Mountain. Barry Goldwater's home sits high up on the mountain. Out here against the dramatic backdrop of the vast desert and the spectacular mountains, it would be difficult for anyone to relate to the day-to-day desperation of urban dwellers in the decaying cities of the East.

That evening, I joined Taiwan's Ambassador to the United States, James C. H. Shen, and his wife for dinner at the China Inn in Scottsdale. We had a magnificent seven-course meal and toasted each other by calling for the maintenance of strong ties between our countries. The irony of the evening became apparent just twenty-four hours later.

After my speech to the salesmen the next morning, I boarded a plane back to Washington. Ed and Sheila Weidenfeld were giving a celebration party for Diane, me and my staff. A number of press people were there, and I learned for the first time that President Carter was holding a press conference at 9 P.M. to announce the formal recognition of the People's Republic of China. I was stunned, but most of those present reacted matter-of-factly. I didn't watch the press conference or offer any reaction to the announcement. I was thinking about the previous night and my exchange of good wishes with Ambassador Shen. "Here's to your health, Mr. Ambassador. May the bond between our countries remain strong."

On the evening of December 19, I read a memorandum written by my administrative assistant, Tom Daffron, who had once worked for Senator Charles Percy of Illinois. The memo indicated that first impressions in the Senate were critical to my reputation with my colleagues, that with the exception of Bill Bradley and possibly Nancy Kassebaum (of Kansas), I was the best-known of the freshman Senators.

Recognition, however, did not necessarily bring with it acceptance. Because of the inordinate national exposure I had received as a Congressman, I was expected to be arrogant, disdainful, and possibly anti-Republican as a result of my vote to bring impeachment proceedings against President Nixon. The Senate regulars, I was told, would be watching my attitude and performance with a critical eye. It did not matter what kind of legislative reputation I had as a member of the House. It was not transferable. I had to begin with a clean slate and chalk a new record all over again.

As I pondered the memo, the hair over my lip suddenly felt like walrus whiskers. I went to Kevin and Chris, who were in the upstairs bathroom, brushing their teeth and preparing for bed. "Boys," I said pleadingly, "I've got to break a promise. It's very important to my career in the Senate that people not get the wrong impression of me or my attitude. The only question people have been asking me is why I'm growing a mustache. They see it as a sign of brashness and arrogance. 'Like, what are you trying to prove, Cohen?' I don't want something that silly or insignificant to detract from the hard work that I intend to do as a Senator. You know what the editorial cartoonists will do—portray me as some evil villain with a waxed mustache or maybe even a Fu Manchu. . . ."

They couldn't understand my anxiety over what other people might say or think ("Dad, you're in the Senate now, you don't have to worry about how you look. . . ."), but they knew that I was going to break my promise and wanted their agreement so I would feel a little less guilty.

"Okay, Dad, it's all right. We understand." They let me off gently, knowing that they would not have to wait much longer before they could grow their own first insignia of manhood and independence.

I kissed them both, thanking them for being so understanding. After they went to bed, in a moment of self-contempt at my inability to perform such a small favor for my sons, I took a slightly dull razor to my upper lip.

CHAPTER 2

ONE DAY during the fall of 1978, Representative Tom Railsback of Illinois slapped me on the back and said, "Just remember when you get to the Senate, don't become like the rest of those bastards." This was an admonition that was repeated to me by at least a dozen of my House colleagues, and a sentiment that was shared by countless more. But coming from Tom Railsback, it was not just the shorthand expression of envy and contempt most members have for the Senate brethren and mask with a smile and a wink; it meant much more.

Tom Railsback is regarded as a moderate Republican who has sponsored some very progressive measures on the House Judiciary Committee, particularly in the field of penal reform.

During my first year on the House Judiciary Committee, Tom took me under his wing. When several reporters were experiencing jail conditions in America for refusing to disclose confidential sources, Tom and I helped draft a bill called the "Newsmen's Privilege Act of 1973." But in an act of uncommon generosity, Railsback allowed me to be the chief sponsor.

Tom's charity was indicative of a legislator who is mature and confident of his standing with his constituents and with his colleagues. It also reflected his genuine concern for helping younger members move up within the party itself.

We became close friends immediately and were almost always seen in tandem—in Congress, at evening events, and most importantly in the House gym, for there is a place that the strands of friendship are woven into an invisible bond that is carried into committee hearings and House debates (in the steam room, neither emperors nor committee chairmen wear clothes).

I had played basketball in high school and college, and Tom was sort of the hotshot of the Republican athletes who frequented the gym. He had a well-established reputation for making up his own rules in order to ensure victory, whether at basketball or at paddleball, the major sports in the gym.

Whenever he got a slight lead in either game, he would shout to spectators or participants in adjoining courts, "Okay. Get a buck on this one. I am going to get Cohen's ass. Get a buck!" And, of course, if he lost, he would simply cry foul and double the stakes for the next game. He always builds a sense of camaraderie, singing in the steam room or shower or socializing on the House floor.

He frequently will be seen having lunch with new Members, regardless of ideology. In fact, that is one of the nonsecrets of his success—his ability to rise above the pettiness and pugnacity of the political camps that cover the Capitol Hill landscape. His capacity not to take himself seriously also has endeared him to the general House membership. Even when on the wrong side of a party-line issue, he would pass his vote off lightly or pat a critic on the back and say, "Maybe you were right on that one—why did I do that?"

As a result, Tom is effective in his work. Frequently when he would offer an amendment to a bill being debated on the Floor, members would stream through the doors to answer a roll call asking, "What's this amendment?"

"It's Railsback's amendment to increase the appropriation for additional probation officers."

"Well, I think I'll give this one to Tom."

I was fascinated by Tom's personality and politics. Frustrated, too, because I was in many ways just the opposite. A loner, too serious and too rigid and academic in my approach to politics and people.

I recall saying, "Rails, you have got more moves than Gypsy Rose Lee." I said it with admiration and just a touch of envy.

I vowed to Tom and my other House colleagues that I would not forget them, that I would come back to the House frequently. I would not fall victim to the egomania of the Senate.

It seemed as if I were graduating from high school and on my way to college. The "Don't forget us" warnings and "Stay as you are" pleas. It is a ritual that is performed every year with every class. The wet-eyed promises inevitably are broken. Each party to the promises knows that they will be—but the ritual must be invoked, if only as a testament to the friendship that will dissolve under the pressure of distance and new demands.

Even as I was frequenting the House during the interim between the November election and the new session of Congress, I knew that I would be back on only a few occasions. Like the inevitability of the aging process, a transformation was taking place in my relations with people on Capitol Hill. The system ensures that it will and spits out a declarative: If you don't want the privileges and prestige that go with the Senate, then you shouldn't have reached for the prize.

The privileges and prestige come in small and various packages. The first night back in Washington, Diane and I took our sons to one of our favorite French restaurants, La Niçoise (described by the owners as the best French restaurant between R and S Streets on Wisconsin Avenue. Of course, there is only one French restaurant in that location), where the ladies are greeted with a kiss and the waiters whip around dervishly and devilishly on roller skates. The maître d', Jean-Louis, acknowledged my victory with a bottle of champagne.

A similar gesture took place a week later in another prominent restaurant. Small items, perhaps, but symbolic.

During the last six weeks of 1978, I received more invitations to speak than I had had during the entire two preceding years. I do not recall a commensurate increase in wisdom during that six-week period which justified new confidence in my judgment. In fact, I had even less confidence in my judgment.

The morning after President Carter recognized China, I received a call from a reporter from a major newspaper. She had eight questions concerning the decision to which she wanted my responses.

As a Member of the House, I would not have been called for my opinion. But it is implicitly assumed by the press, local as well as national, that a Senator does have an opinion—at the very least, should have—as to the political significance of such a dramatic foreign-policy move and the cosmic consequences that will follow.

The pressure of being considered some sort of font of wisdom, of course, has a salutary effect. Not wanting to appear uninformed or an intellectual dullard, you undertake more in-depth and serious reading that goes beyond the borders of your state and the latest sewer grant. Understanding Chairman Hua Quo-feng and Vice Chairman Teng Hsiao-ping's rise to power and geopolitical visions tends to overshadow your immediate concern for the latest request to speak at Saturday's bean-hole supper in a remote part of your state. The pressure of being knowledgeable about national and international affairs is thus a mind-expanding exercise on one's way up the ladder to statesmanship. If the exercise is all-consuming, however, it will lead to an intellectual narcissism that becomes immediately perceptible to one's constituents, who will conclude that "He's gone Washington"—a description that can prove and has proved fatal to rejoining the "Club" in the next election.

A balance must be struck between establishing a reputation for being thoughtful and informed and being a simple ombudsman for every parochial interest or grievance.

I chose my words too carefully in response to eight simplistically worded questions about the consequences of establishing diplomatic relations with China. "Well, I don't know what factors the President took into account in reaching his decision. It may be that he has information that would justify the recognition of China. It's my personal judgment that China needs us at this point more than we need China and that we should not have extended recognition without, at a minimum, securing a pledge of nonaggression against Taiwan or without guaranteeing Taiwan's security against a future attack. . . . I don't know whether the President has the constitutional power to terminate a treaty without the consent of Congress, but I don't think it would be wise for Congress to try to reverse the decision now that it has been made, since we would only inherit the contempt of both countries and the worst of both worlds. . . ."

The reporter picked up the hesitancy in my voice and the bland, qualifying nature of the answers immediately. "What's the matter, Bill? You never used to be so cautious when you were in the House."

The reporter wanted a pithy quote, but I didn't want to gain the reputation of shooting from the hip even before I was sworn into the Senate. Already I felt the weight of added responsibility from the press, and their presuming that I had an informed judgment on every major event of the day.

CHAPTER 3

IN THE SENATE, the seniority system is still the frame of reference for the selection of committee assignments and such minor but status-oriented matters as the location of office space.

When I first arrived in the House of Representatives in 1973, the seniority system was just coming under assault by reformers—those without power who were unwilling to wait for the accumulation of years to drop authority on their shoulders. I was among those reformers, brash and cocksure that leadership should be purchased with merit and not with the slow trickle of time.

Within my first three weeks in Washington, I ran head-on into the brick wall of the prevailing sentiment among the older members—where else but in the gymnasium?

During the organization days (usually the entire month of January and half of February), the House was in adjournment by 2 in the afternoon. I went to the gym to practice and to show off a two-handed set shot that I had perfected in high school and college basketball. It was an anachronism in the day of the jump shot. The equivalent of a silent movie in the era of the Betamax.

Each day I put on a shooting exhibition that had older members talking about "Old Doc" finally having met his match.

"Old Doc" was a not-so-old former college All-State player from South Carolina. He used to chew on a dry cigar and just watch me shoot for the first couple of weeks.

One day when everybody was in a betting mood, he said, "Okay, Cohen. Let's see what you can do."

I was feeling cocky as hell and said, "Okay, but I'm not playing unless we shoot from at least thirty feet out."

Doc looked at me with a sort of gun-sighting squint in one eye and said, "How long did you say you've been here?"

"About three weeks," I replied naively.

"Then who the hell are you to be telling me what the rules of the game are going to be?"

With that, he turned and walked off the court and left me with my jaw hanging. It was my first lesson about the seniority system and the unspoken rule that freshmen should walk a little more lightly around the seasoned stalwarts.

While power in the House has been diffused and democratized with the virtual elimination of the seniority system, the Senate has held fast to tradition.

On December 14, I received a letter from the Republican leadership outlining the seniority system in the Senate:

> Briefly, the procedure generally works like this: after the election the total number of Republicans and Democrats are compared to determine a ratio. That ratio is then applied to each of the various committees, and adjustments in the size of the committee and the Republican/Democrat ratio are made.
>
> The vacancies caused by the election results, plus any changes in the number of seats each party controls, provide the actual number of vacancies for the next Congress. A list of all committees and vacancies is compiled. Each Republican Senator and Senator-elect is asked to notify the Committee on Committees as to their preferences for committee assignment. Incumbent Senators may indicate that they wish to retain their current committee assignments, or they may want to move from one committee to another. If they want to change, they indicate in writing the committee(s) they wish to relinquish and their preferences, in order of priority, for new assignment. Newly elected Senators indicate, in order of priority, their desired assignments.
>
> These letters are all compiled, through the use of a computer, into a list indicating each Senator, beginning with the most senior member, and on down the line, with his or her committee preferences.
>
> When the Committee on Committees meets, after the reorgani-

zation of the Republican leadership, the two lists are compared. The Committee looks at the letter from the most senior Senator. If he requests any changes they look to the list of committees and, if the assignments he requests are available, they are made. The positions he is giving up are then reflected as vacancies on whatever committees he has relinquished, and the Committee turns to the next Senator, and so on through all incumbent Senators.

After each incumbent Senator is given his committee assignments, the Committee turns to the most senior freshman Senator. Each freshman Senator is allowed to make one committee selection before the most senior freshman senator is permitted to make two committee selections. . . .

I wish you every success in obtaining the committee assignments in which you feel you can contribute most and participate with the greatest degree of enthusiasm. I look forward to the prospect of serving with you in the important work of the legislative committees.

Sincerely,

In other words, the assignment to committees would be done by the numbers.

I started to receive several inquiries from the press about which committee assignments I would seek. I usually tried to deflect the questions by saying I hadn't really decided or alternatively listed some that looked interesting. There were several reasons for this: First, I had absolutely no control over which committees I would ultimately serve on. If I specified one that I wanted and then failed to secure it, that would be read as an initial setback or failure in the Senate. Secondly, I was under bombardment by various supporters in and out of Maine urging me to seek a position on a committee of their special interest. I didn't want to spend weeks explaining my rationale for any particular committee choice or answering why an alternative would not be better for my state. Most importantly, I was truly in doubt about the direction I should take in the Senate. I was simply resigned to accepting whatever the spin of the roulette wheel produced, and I knew that chance was to play an even larger role than choice once the "lame duck" members of the Senate started to resign a day or two early so as to allow their successors to gain seniority over the other new members. Because of my past experience in the House, I was originally listed as number 87 on the Senate membership scale of 100. By the time of the official swearing-in ceremony, I had dropped to 91, because my opponent refused to resign early. I became even more cavalier in my attitude about committee assignments.

But chance has always been a lodestar in my life. Few things have ever happened to me by design. As a Latin major in college, I meant to teach. As a high school and college jock, I considered a fling at professional basketball. Somehow, I gravitated instead, like so many in my aimless generation, into law school. The practice of law proved, on occasion, to be stimulating. I received particular satisfaction in reversing more than 100 years of precedent in personal-injury law before the Supreme Court of Maine.

But the truth is that I went into politics because I became bored and dissatisfied with the day-to-day resolution of personal conflicts. The "in box" became a flood tide of divorce and criminal cases that was washing my soul with cynical acid. I had to look too many times into the face of death during autopsies that I had to attend while serving as an assistant county prosecutor. I had watched the thin line between love and hate dissolve in divorce cases while children were used as bargaining chips to gain the divorce or reduce the support and alimony payments. My law practice was starting to thrive, but I was turning sour inside.

I drifted into local politics initially as a means of advertising my talents as a lawyer, but ultimately as an escape from the practice of law itself.

I was serving as Mayor of the City of Bangor when the opportunity presented itself to run for Congress. The incumbent Congressman had had enough of service in the House of Representatives and decided to run against Senator Margaret Chase Smith. The odds against my winning in a primary fight for my party's nomination, not to mention a general election, were heavy. I surprised nearly everybody in the State, including myself, by winning in both.

Following the election, I was invited to attend an experimental four-week course at Harvard's John F. Kennedy Institute of Politics. It was there that I was given some very practical advice on how I should go about trying to secure a seat on the committees of my choice. "If you want to serve on a particular committee, don't list it first, list it last" came the seasoned voice of the program chairman.

I thought it was a peculiar, topsy-turvy way of doing business, but I followed the free advice. Out of five possible choices, I listed the Judiciary Committee as the last in my list of priorities—and that's exactly what I got. Every knowledgeable person on Capitol Hill advised me not to seek a seat on the Judiciary Committee, because there was no political mileage to be gained there, nothing that could translate into visible and tangible benefits for my constituency. I would toil endlessly in the vineyard of legal technicalities and niceties without notice or political benefit and have nothing to show to my constituents as a reason for sending me back to Washington when my contract was up for renewal in two very short years.

Even though the arguments were compelling, I rejected the advice. Fate played its ultimate trick on me and turned my assignment to the Judiciary Committee into a rendezvous with history.*

The roulette wheel was spinning again. On December 20, following a meeting at the Capitol in the office of the Secretary of the Senate, the Secretary of the Senate Republicans, Bill Hildenbrand, asked me if I wanted to go on a trip. I thought he meant back to his office for some personal advice and said, "Sure." I then realized he had something else in mind. "I mean, how would you like to go to China? There is a Pacific Study Group that is going to the Far East—Philippines, Thailand, China, Japan and Korea. John Tower will be in Russia with Baker and we would like a Republican to go with Sam Nunn, Gary Hart and John Glenn." I told him that I was interested, but would have to check at home to see if I could work it out.

The idea was exciting to me, but I was in the middle of packing up the accumulations of six years in the House, making an office selection in one of the Senate buildings and then moving. The trip was not coming at a convenient time. Also, I didn't relish leaving Diane and the boys for eleven days.

But they didn't hesitate. They knew it would be an invaluable experience and urged me to go.

---

* On October 20, 1973, President Richard Nixon ordered U.S. Attorney General Elliot Richardson to fire the Watergate Special Prosecutor, Archibald Cox. Richardson refused the order and instead resigned his office. Nixon then fired Richardson's assistant, William Ruckelshaus. The purge was labeled as the "Saturday Night Massacre." A "fire storm" of protest erupted throughout the country and within the Congress. Resolutions calling for Richard Nixon's impeachment were filed in the House of Representatives. On February 6, 1974, the House, by a vote of 410 to 4, adopted a resolution that directed the Judiciary Committee to fully investigate whether sufficient grounds existed to impeach Richard Nixon. On July 27, 1974, the Committee voted, 27 to 11, in favor of Article I of an impeachment resolution. Two other articles were subsequently adopted. Richard Nixon resigned from office on August 9, 1974.

The next day, I picked up a copy of Mao Tse-tung's poetry at a local bookstore and began my study of the land of the golden vase.

Diane and I usually take the boys to Maine during the Christmas holiday season for a week of skiing. Last year our trip turned out to be a disaster. Diane, in addition to having a severe case of strep throat, came down with the flu and passed it on to Kevin. They spent the entire week in the beds of friends with whom we stayed. It was a long drive back to Washington, with two of the four occupants in our small car disabled.

This year we decided to spend the time together in the Washington area. This would enable me to continue to pack up my books and papers at the office in preparation for the big move, since I would be gone during the first two weeks of January.

I had forgotten to give Kevin a check for his ski trip with the sophomore class. I drove to his high school and walked to the principal's office. It was an intimidating experience. During a class change, I came into physical contact with at least a thousand students. I felt like a country bumpkin on a Los Angeles freeway. Electricity and raw energy filled the hallways. Young, pretty girls clomped along awkwardly in high-heeled shoes, somewhat self-conscious and yet excited about being on the edge of womanhood. The boys were lean and athletic—and irreverent! I thought of Satchel Paige's admonition, "Don't look back, something may be gaining on you." I looked back and they were.

That evening we took Kevin and his first date to the American Film Institute to see a private showing of *Superman*. Senator Ed Muskie and his family were there, as well as Senator Gary Hart of Colorado. I spoke with syndicated columnist Charles Bartlett before the dinner. He made me promise not to start running for the Presidency before I got to the Senate, and to slow down and enjoy a few weekends at home with the boys. This was something we had talked about more than two years before when he was in Maine covering Bob Dole's quest for the Vice Presidency. "Charlie," I said, "I have absolutely no desire to be President or Vice President, but whenever I say that, no one believes me. So I just don't say anything anymore."

Superman was a total delight. A wonderful fantasy with the kind of hero that our childhood dreams were made of. I felt a spinal shiver as I watched the parents and their children cheer when Superman said, "I stand for Truth, Justice and the American Way." There was no mortal alive who could have produced that geyserlike reaction.

As we drove home, I grew silent as I thought about the significance of the evening. Our older son had chosen without self-consciousness to share his first date with his parents. Our younger son, Chris, sitting with Kevin and his date in the back seat of the car, sensed for the first time that the bond between brothers was being loosened by this young woman. Diane had to deal with the experience of sharing the affections of her son with another woman. And I—I had to endure the criticisms coming from the back seat about my driving ability's being less than adequate in the opinion of that man-child of mine. As I listened to his nonstop chatter (envying his lack of inhibition), I thought, He's falling victim to the fifteen-year-old male affliction of revealing too much of himself—even his James Bond collection!

JANUARY 3, 1979

THIS MORNING, the delegation heading for the Far East received a briefing from Admiral Stansfield Turner, the Director of the Central Intelligence Agency. We were given an updated report on the size of the North Korean troops near the DMZ.

Sam Nunn of Georgia, chairman of the delegation, made it clear that he did not want any written documentation furnished to us by the CIA and handed back his copy of the report to the officials. His reasoning became clear several days later.

At 2 P.M., we lifted off from Andrews Air Force Base in a military transport plane that had no windows. It was like being in a flying submarine without a periscope. Shortly after we were airborne, Dr. Freeman Cary, Attending Physician in the Capitol, gave me a gamma shot.

I sat across from Gary Hart at one of the four tables in the rear of the plane. He was dressed casually in a gray turtleneck sweater and slacks. Sam Nunn was diagonally across from me. Sam had on a plaid suit and a blue V-neck sweater. John Glenn of Ohio was directly across the aisle from me on my left. He was wearing a military-brown sport shirt with a brown sport coat over it.

We had an informal meeting shortly after takeoff to discuss some general strategy and ground rules on the visit to Peking.

I spent most of the time reading the three loose-leaf notebooks filled with information on each country we would be visiting, biographical notes on each of the foreign dignitaries we would be meeting, synopses of their political backgrounds, philosophy, public statements and private assessments. But China dominated my thoughts. I disagreed with the way in which the new relationship with China had been established, but I tried to shake and sift my personal opinions through a screen of reason and self-doubt. I have learned that running at full speed on the fresh scent of one's emotions can lead into a brick wall instead of an open door. Things are not as simple as they might appear or as we would like them to be. China was an unguarded railroad crossing. I would pause, look and listen before proceeding.

We arrived in Alaska twenty minutes ahead of schedule. The airstrip is surrounded by beautiful, breathtaking mountains. The temperature was cold, but no colder than that in Maine. A bus picked us up and transported us from the flying submarine to the officers' club, where we waited while the plane was being refueled. After socializing at the officers' club for about an hour and fifteen minutes, we returned to the plane. I studied for two or three more hours and then decided to sleep. There were six bunks on the plane. I took the one next to the floor. After two and a half hours of rest, I got up and started reading more briefing materials.

Around 4:30 A.M., the flight steward brought me breakfast. Everyone else but the crew was asleep. I read from Mao Tse-tung's poetry for an hour and drafted a toast for Teng Hsiao-ping that I might find an occasion to use.

Later that morning, Sam asked me what I thought of Mao's poetry.

"It's difficult for me to tell because it's translated into English. Most of the poems contain war or political themes, but he uses images of the seasons well. Of course, I am not one to judge Mao, since he sold forty million copies and I've sold less than ten thousand."

We arrived in Manila at approximately 10:30 P.M. It was 80 degrees. The air was heavy with humidity. A long caravan of small limousines took us to the Manila Hotel. We had a briefing in the control room about our plans for the following day. Then Gary Hart and I went down to the cocktail lounge for a beer before we retired.

JANUARY 5, 1979

I WOKE UP at 6 A.M. It was 5 P.M. January 4 in Washington. We had crossed the international date line. I was tired, but the bells in my mind were going off at the wrong time. I was completely disoriented.

A wake-up call came an hour later. I tried to do some exercises, but the immunization shots I had received had numbed the muscles in my arms.

An "American breakfast" arrived about a half hour later—scrambled eggs, ham, orange juice, assortment of rolls and coffee. Price: 30 pesos. I read the two morning newspapers that were slipped under the door. The major stories were: General Haig to leave Army. Iranian civil government approved, leader pledges liberalization. Cleveland property taxes seized to pay pension debt. A terrorist (FALN) sues New York City for $1.2 million charging it confiscated his fingers for evidence after they were blown off in a bomb-factory explosion instead of taking them to a hospital so they might be surgically reattached. Military governor of Madrid shot and killed.

We arrived at the American Embassy at approximately 9:30 A.M. We were led through a series of security doors into a large, high-ceilinged paneled room. There were portraits of Presidents hanging on the walls from FDR to Gerald Ford. The one of Ford seemed almost amateurish. The briefing began. There were three areas to cover: (1) the strategic importance and mission of the Clark and Subic bases located in the Philippines; (2) the state of our negotiations to retain access to and use of the bases; and (3) economic and political questions concerning the entire region. The briefing was conducted by Ambassador Richard W. Murphy. Ambassador Murphy is a tall, lanky man who speaks with a mocking self-assurance. He must have been bored with having to entertain yet another Congressional delegation, but he gave the impression that he was simply delighted to see us. "Senator Cohen, how are things in Bangor?" It was obvious that he had reviewed the profile that the State Department had prepared on each of us. It was a small flattery that he sent fluttering by, just to let me know that he had spent time learning about my background. He has a facile mind and verbal fluency to match it. He reviewed the status of the negotiations that were about to be concluded on Clark and Subic and the nature of the statements that President Ferdinand Marcos would probably make once the agreements were concluded.

It became clear as Murphy talked that the language of diplomacy is a delicate dance which allows for a lot of local strutting and chest beating while preserving our self-interest.

Following the review of the negotiations and our intelligence-gathering capabilities, we were given a long routine slide presentation of the missions of the bases—their strategic locations, functions and justifications.

I wondered during the presentation how one could translate the significance of all this to our constituents. The fact is that it can't be done. The value of Diego Garcia, the strategically located island in the Indian Ocean, is meaningless to a poor family in Presque Isle, Maine, or Wheeling, West Virginia, who want an increase in food stamps or Social Security and point an angry finger at the waste in the defense budget.

All the military strategies and diplomatic niceties are lost during a congressional debate. The function of a representative government is to have leaders who inform themselves and make assessments and judgments and hope that they can convey the value of the priorities established for the security and well-being of the nation. This is principally why the United States is in such grave danger today, at least from my perspective: the people at home have lost confidence in the honesty and goals of their government, and our allies are witnessing a retreat in the commitment to leadership in world affairs.

At 3, we arrived at the Presidential Palace and were escorted directly to the second floor. A seventy-five-foot-long rug with blue trim and an off-white center that had been made in Madrid covered the dark teak floors. The hall was ringed with portraits of Filipino generals or presidents. At the end of the hall were large portraits of Marcos on the left, dressed in a white military uniform. On the right was his wife, Ymelda—striking, mysterious, like an Asian cat.

After about a ten-minute wait, we were taken to meet Marcos. He had not aged since I had seen him in 1973. He has high cheekbones and thick black hair that is slicked back in a high pompadour. His nails are manicured. His face is virtually unlined, although there is a little puffiness under his eyes. He was wearing a barong tagalog, the traditional white dress shirt of the Philippines. He sat upright behind a mahogany desk with the presidential seal carved in front. There were two microphones lying openly on his desk. It was obvious that our conversation would be recorded. Six years before, he had had our delegation meeting video-taped.

He was smooth and articulate—just as I remembered him. He chose his words cautiously. We proceeded with questions tentatively to see how far we could go. The talk ranged from his assessment of the Vietnam-ese invasion of Cambodia, normalization of U.S. relations with China, human rights, and martial law—the torture of prisoners—to economic plans and the new agreement on the Clark and Subic bases.

John Glenn tried to impress upon him the continuing interest on the part of the United States in pressing for human rights. Glenn had handed him a copy of a recent *Washington Post* editorial. I followed up Glenn's questions concerning human rights and pointed out that it was not just the *Post* editorial but the special presentation telecast by ABC and the na-tional media in general that questioned our policy of supporting dictator-ships. I noted that conditions in the Philippines in 1972 which had justified his imposition of martial law were different now. Now there was no threat of insurrection, there were no student uprisings, no civil disorders, and yet martial law still existed. His argument that the Muslims in the south were being supported by Libya and were being infiltrated by communists could always be used as an excuse to maintain his current policy. So I suggested that it would be very helpful if he showed some positive and public signs of changing his policies to fit the times. John noted that I had served in the House and perhaps I might provide some insight as to how the House might view the new agreements.

I indicated that the agreements would have more difficulty in the House after the *Washington Post* editorial and the recent ABC special program which had been highly critical of Marcos' imposition of martial law, and that the Senate would not be as difficult as the House and Republicans not as difficult as Democrats.

Actually, I believed that the agreements would fly through Congress with a minimum of opposition just because Congress was aware of how badly we were handling our foreign policy and it would not want to jeopardize our bases in the Philippines. But I thought we should give Marcos a little incentive to loosen up his domestic policies.

After the meeting, we were served lemonade and hors d'oeuvre. We then departed for the airport. Outside the palace, as we drove off, I noticed for the first time that a thirty-foot tinsel Christmas tree was stand-ing in the middle of the lawn. Somehow, in this land of martial law, it seemed to be an obscene gesture rather than a symbol of the Christmas season and spirit.

Beyond the gates of the palace, some of the poverty in Manila became dramatically visible—ramshackle housing, beggars, children with distended bellies, young boys hawking cigarettes to stopped cars.

I couldn't be too critical. There had been significant economic progress made under Marcos' rule. Besides, you can see almost the same conditions just a few blocks beyond the periphery of the Capitol or in any of the major urban centers in America. Splendor surrounded by squalor.

Gary Hart, in his soft voice, said when we reached the plane, "No matter what country I'm visiting, I'm always glad to see that plane that says USA sitting on the runway."

By 8 that evening, we had arrived in Bangkok. We were bused to the President Hotel preceded by a police escort with a flashing red dome light.

Bangkok is a noisy and impoverished city. The streets are lined with shops that are little more than hovels. Sidewalks are littered with debris, glass, junk. The people appeared to be even poorer than those of Manila. The Filipinos wore jeans and T-shirts, but they were stylishly cut and clean. On the strip between the airport and the hotel, the people that I saw were unconcerned or could not afford to be concerned about style. As we arrived at the hotel, we were greeted by young Thai girls who hung leis around our necks while photographs were taken. After checking into our rooms, we all met for a drink in the open cocktail lounge. Glenn was reading the Asian *Wall Street Journal,* and a trio was singing "I Left My Heart in San Francisco."

We went to a small French restaurant just around the corner from the hotel. It had not more than ten tables downstairs and about the same number on the second floor. The proprietor looked like a Peter Lorre character out of a war movie. Someone mentioned that he probably had served in the war and then retired to become a restaurateur. We learned later that he had flown 163 missions over Dien Bien Phu and that he had been the military adviser to the Saigon Air Force. He thought that Thailand was in serious jeopardy from the Communists in Vietnam.

The prices in the restaurant were incredibly low: chateaubriand, 110 Thai dollars, which was little more than $5 in American money. I had a beer, French soup and chateaubriand and paid a total of $10 for the evening.

During the dinner, a young American woman came over to me and said, "Senator Cohen, my name is Ann Rosenblatt. My husband and I used to work in Bangor [he was a reporter briefly for the *Bangor Daily News* and is now with the State Department and stationed in Bangkok]. I just wanted to say hello. I've read a lot about you."

I told her I would stop by and say hello to her husband before I left. I turned a few moments later to Gary Hart and said, "What a damned small world this is when you can go from Bangor to Bangkok and still run into people you know."

JANUARY 6, 1979

AT 6 A.M., a wake-up call came. I was careful in the shower not to swallow any water, since it was not potable.

At 9 A.M. we arrived at the American Embassy. We were escorted to a large conference room where approximately thirty men and two women were sitting around several large teakwood tables that had been placed together. The purpose of the meeting was to give our ambassadors to the Southeastern Asian nations an opportunity to review the strategic, military, political and economic interest and importance of the nations to which they were respectively assigned. This was the first time any members of Congress had been invited to participate in the conference.

The moderator who gave the initial presentation was a consummate diplomat. He was the stereotype that we see caricatured in the *New Yorker* magazine cartoons: gray suit, white shirt, balding, horn-rimmed glasses, prissy and precise. (He told me, during dinner that evening, that he was being attacked by one hostile newspaper as the "prattling Ambassador.") Above all, he was exceptionally competent. In his overview he discussed the political forces and dynamics at work in Korea, Japan, Taiwan and the ASEAN nations (Association of Southeastern Asian Nations) as a result of our recognition of China.

"Our relations with China seem to be in a state of flux between romantic intoxication and open hostility. We will need to take a lot of cold showers along the way. . . ."

Of growing concern to the ambassadors was the threat Vietnam posed to Thailand and the other countries of Indochina. If Cambodia fell, then the Thais were in a very difficult situation. They would be faced with a choice of rolling over and allowing Vietnam to take over or being compelled to set up some sort of protective shield and thus engage in open hostilities.

The moderator then turned to the "refugee problem." There are anywhere from a half a million to a million people who are living in virtual starvation conditions.

"I would recommend that more refugees be admitted to the United States with an expedited process. I recognize that the more we let in, the more will come out, but we can't just sink their ships. . . ."

As I listened to his presentation, I thought how easy it was for our ambassadors to sit in an air-conditioned teak-walled room in humid Bangkok discussing the intrigues of diplomacy, the needs of Eastern nations and the desire of refugees to seek a new life free of terror and oppression in the United States. Policy. Programs. Abstractions. What they didn't seem to realize was that foreign aid has a small and diminishing constituency in the United States. A few of the major newspapers might editorialize in favor of an enlightened foreign-aid program, several peace or liberal-oriented groups might undertake a letter-writing effort to Congressmen, but it would be virtually impossible to increase foreign assistance at a time when the President, the Congress and the country were calling for less federal spending and more balanced budgets. The point, if considered by the ambassadors, could not be fully appreciated in the heady world of State Department cables, intelligence memos—the secret and intriguing world of high-level diplomacy.

It is easy to understand why Presidents and ambassadors prefer to deal with global and foreign-policy issues. A little progress here to alleviate pressures, a little concession there, a little intellectual fine tuning—without ever having to confront the reality of dealing with people. "Mr. Cohen, I can't survive on the $180 a month I get from Social Security. The price of oil is going up. What are you going to do for me?" How do we explain macroeconomics, trade imbalances, the need for open trade with Third World nations to those who are having a difficult time surviving in our own country? The drought of double-digit inflation was causing the deep river of American compassion and humanitarianism to run dry. Our diplomatic representatives did not appear to appreciate the dark mood that was developing in our country.

There was a presentation by a high-level Central Intelligence Agency official. During his presentation, I was handed by a State Department official a draft of a cable to Washington summarizing our agreement with Marcos on the Subic and Clark bases. The cable had a line saying that we agreed to the financial terms as being very reasonable. I struck the word "very."

I was suspicious of the manner in which the official was circulating the cable during the briefing and concluded that the department was trying to secure senatorial support for its negotiations and slip some words into our mouths which we might find difficult to retract at a later time.

A treaty or agreement always tends to look more enlightened, responsible, fair-minded, and reasonable when one is in the country that is to benefit from the agreement in some tangible or significant way. Undoubtedly the Panama Canal Treaty seems more responsible in Panama City than in Peoria, Illinois. Any agreement that will cost the American taxpayers more money tends to look less reasonable or responsible the closer one gets to Washington, D.C.

During lunch, a State Department official pointed out to me that there was general concern on the part of Japan and other nations that we not go overboard with this new recognition of China. "Congressional delegations are always anxious to go over to Peking, and they come back rather overwhelmed. In Russia, they mostly come back mad." In response to my question as to how the ASEAN nations would react to a rejection of SALT II, the official said, "The problem is, who do you like better, Marilyn Monroe or Golda Meir?"

"Marilyn Monroe," I laughed.

"It all depends. For example, you may get roughed up in the Senate by Russell Long and not like it, but you still have to do business with him. The same is true of the Soviet Union."

The afternoon session was devoted to a discussion of trade issues. One Ambassador bemoaned the fact that the United States could not compete because we were tied down by Western concepts of morality that simply did not apply in the real world of business. John Glenn stopped the drift of the complaint before it picked up any momentum.

"Be realistic. We are not about to draw down our criminal laws to compete with foreign corruption."

Gary Hart then put to rest the argument that some of our major corporations could not compete unless they engaged in new alliances. "The fact is that they have more than enough capital to invest but they are unwilling to take any risk."

A midafternoon break occurred around 3. Hart and I were all "briefed out" and decided to go with Captain John McCain to visit the famous Temple of the Reclining Buddha.

That evening we attended a reception and dinner at Ambassador Morton Abramowitz' residence, a spectacular colonnaded, high-ceilinged building. We met informally in the study with Thailand's Defense Minister. The Prime Minister had been delayed on his return from Laos. The meeting was interrupted several times by either phone calls or a courier bringing a brown envelope to Abramowitz that contained the most up-to-date State Department cables.

After the dinner and the obligatory toasts, Gary and I decided to walk back to the hotel. On the way, we speculated on the futility of much of our efforts.

Hart has been described as *"un homme sérieux."* He is a thoughtful man with strong convictions, which he expresses in a soft and understated manner.

"You know, it's hard to accept the reality of the fact that events often control men and not men, events. What Napoleon had for breakfast may have had as much to do with history as his brilliance. . . ."

"Gary," I responded, "I am not sure about whether I want to make a career out of politics, but I do know that I wouldn't want to spend my life waiting for the arrival of a brown envelope with the latest cables reporting on some shift in the tide of insurgency or some updated analysis of the kaleidoscopic events in the world and what it all means to us.

"It's probably not much different from what we do in Congress. But I am really concerned about the things that are taking place now— the cynicism, the distress. I think we are passing through a ten-year period of negativism where elected leaders will not be in a position to take more than a narrow or parochial view without being punished at the polls. . . ."

JANUARY 7, 1979

WE ARRIVED at the airport at 9 A.M. Everyone seemed to be in good spirits. The Thais provided us with hot coffee, and someone said it was "great and reputed to cure anything you might have contracted in Thailand." Someone jokingly replied, "In that case, I'll have three cups. Just pour it over my head."

At 4 that afternoon, we arrived in Peking. As we stepped off the plane, the first thing I noticed was a film of haze that permeated the atmosphere. It came from the burning of coal. We went to a control room at the airport, where we were served tea that was slightly flavored hot water. After a half-hour wait, we boarded a bus and headed for the Peking Hotel. The route was a long and narrow road and nearly an hour's ride. On both sides of the road were acres of orchards, thousands of rows of trees all neatly lined up. The fields were gray and barren. There were people everywhere on bicycles. Many challenged the bus driver at intersections and were nearly hit, but they seemed to know that the driver would yield. I saw a number of children playing in the trees and was reminded of Robert Frost's poem about being a child and swinging in birch trees.

As we turned from the airport access road onto the main street in Peking, we hit 5 P.M. traffic—bike traffic! There were hundreds of thousands of them, and yet it seemed more orderly (and safer) than the Los Angeles freeways.

Glenn and Hart observed that the women were wearing brightly colored scarves and just starting to wear makeup. This was a sharp departure from just one year ago.

Their clothing was not just one color. Some people wore green and others blue-gray or a combination. The suits were bulky, padded and quiltlike. It made all the people look fat, but kept them very warm.

We checked into the new section of the Peking Hotel. The rooms were quite modest, with blond, stark furniture of the 1950s era. We had a brief meeting with our Chinese hosts which proved to be quite unsatisfactory. We gave them a list of people whom we wanted to see while in Peking, and they indicated they would try to make the arrangements, but there was no guarantee that we would even see Deng Xiaoping. It appeared to us that they were simply playing games.

We then went for a walk to some of the local stores. We seemed to be relatively unnoticed by the Chinese people, except that they occasionally stared at our shoes. According to Glenn and Hart, there are remarkable changes taking place in Peking. Crowds of people were standing and gawking at the latest fashions in clothing, which were the equivalent of styles in the '50s in the United States. But it was a sharp departure from the traditional Mao suit.

In the stores, whenever we inquired about a specific item on a shelf, crowds quickly gathered around us to watch what we might buy. It was disconcerting to have as many as twenty or thirty people standing around and staring at you as you pulled out your wallet to pay for an item.

We returned to the hotel for dinner. Herb Horowitz, a State Department expert on China, advised me, after I commented on a particularly savory course, that I had just eaten two helpings of horsemeat.

January 8, 1979

I woke up at 5 A.M. I decided that I would watch the sunrise coming up over T'ien An Men Square. At 6 A.M. it was still pitch-dark outside. I did not realize at the time that the sunrise would not occur until 7:45. There was motion everywhere—bicycles; people running to work on the sidewalks, in the streets with the bicycles and buses. They were all moving together with the complexity and ease of fish in the sea.

The buses were traveling with only their parking lights on and on rare occasions would flash them to high beam to avoid bicyclists and runners. Occasionally the drivers would honk their horns, more frequently as the sunlight chased away the darkness.

The bicycles were all one-speed and moved without noise. Runners moved quietly, so that only occasionally you could hear a soft plop of shoes hitting the sidewalk.

There was physical activity everywhere. Off the sidewalks were groups of men and women, young and old, who were going through a series of exercises as deliberate and musical as a ballet. A squadron of Chinese soldiers were running in perfect double time into T'ien An Men Square.

What was striking about the morning was the motion and the quiet. It was as if every sound were softened by a large sheet of gauze.

At 11 A.M., we met with officials at the Institute of Foreign Affairs. We were the first Senate delegation to visit China since our formal recognition, and as such, we received a formal welcome. "The Chinese people are happy. The American people are happy. People all over the world are happy. . . ."

During the meeting, it became obvious that the Chinese do not confide in others easily or quickly. Much of the conversation was ceremonial in nature, deliberately ambiguous, and laced with homilies or metaphorical expressions.

We inquired about the threatened fall of Cambodia to Vietnam.

"The Cambodian people will fight to the end. They have decided they will wage a people's war and win final victory. It is possible that Phnom Penh has fallen. But the loss of land or one place is insignificant.

He who laughs last laughs best. . . . There will be twists and turns and half-struggles, but the final victory will be won by Cambodia.''

And how, we wondered, will you assist Cambodia?

"We will assist them in the future as we have in the past."

Is there any potential, we asked, for conflict between China and the Soviet Union on the border?

"A conflict is possible, yes. If the Soviet Union invades or provokes us on the border on a massive scale. If the Soviet Union thinks they are strong and China is weak, they may act. But if they do, they will not get out. . . . We always take defensive measures, not offensive. We will not be courteous. We will annihilate them. . . .

"When one man goes mad, he cannot think clearly. If Vietnam is victorious in Cambodia, it may turn and attack China. Since the United States did not conquer Vietnam, why should Vietnam win in Cambodia? The Vietnamese are not thinking according to common sense. Since they are insane, you cannot expect them to think rationally. The Vietnamese are trying to sabotage efforts at normalization. Therefore, we have to prepare for the worst and pray for the best.

"It would be easy for the Soviet Union to put a base in Cam Ranh Bay—like picking your pocket. What is available to the Vietnamese is now available to the Soviet Union. . . .''

The meeting ended at 11:30 A.M. and we were bused back to the hotel, where a luncheon was being held for us by Hao Deqing, the President of the Institute of Foreign Ministry. The luncheon was much less formal than our morning meeting. There was a great deal of interplay among the Chinese generals and official personnel at our tables. Again, the conversation turned to Vietnam.

"The Vietnamese cannot eat lunch at 2 and then have dinner at 2:05.''

John Glenn picked up on the theme of gluttony. "You mean that if the Vietnamese tried to go from lunch to dinner and the Cambodians fight back, they may very well experience indigestion."

"No," Hao responded, "not indigestion. Cambodia will stick like a bone in their throats."

At one point, Nunn asked how Hao wanted to be referred to. Hao said, "Old." Sam responded almost instinctively, "You're not old, you're—" but he was interrupted by the interpreter. "He prefers 'old' because old is respected and it refers to wisdom."

At 3:30 P.M. we attended a meeting with officers of the General Staff of the People's Liberation Army. It was not a productive session. They opened up the meeting with a statement of welcome and then launched into a long diatribe against the Soviet Union. One general outlined China's strategic policies, which seemed rather anachronistic in the nuclear age. He had been talking without interruption (through an interpreter) for nearly an hour.

I slipped a note to Nunn: "Now I know what they mean by a Chinese torture."

A young man came into the room carrying hot tea. The serving of tea did not break the general's stride.

"Throughout the twenty-five years of war, we used inferior weapons to defeat those with superior weapons. But we admit our weapons are inferior, and therefore we want to modernize. It's not a matter of one or two years, but hopefully three to five. We should try to postpone the outbreak of a new world war, but it's not a matter of man's will. History is full of war maniacs: for example, Hitler. [The tea man returned.] If war should come, China will go forward to meet it—one heart, one mind, to fight to victory. We'll have to sacrifice a lot of human and material resources. The Russians adjusted themselves to meet the Germans during World War II, and they suffered many losses until they turned the tide. Therefore China expects to suffer great losses. Any time we can secure to modernize our army, we will need. But if the Soviets attack, the PLA will give due punishment to the Soviet Union. . . ."

A few minutes later, Sam sent my note back: "This is just a warm-up for the U.S. Senate."

JANUARY 9, 1979

AT 10 A.M., we gathered in the Great Hall to meet the Vice Premier. The meeting was held in a large conference room, where we posed for official photographs. Teng is a small man (four feet eleven inches), but quite youthful and vigorous-looking at the age of seventy-four.

The initial salutations began rather formally and somewhat cautiously. Just about a half hour after the meeting had begun and right in the middle of one of Sam Nunn's questions, Teng cleared his lungs, leaned over and launched some phlegm into a brass spittoon. Then he casually lit up another cigarette (he is a chain smoker). The problem was that there was a microphone hookup with amplifier, and when he coughed up the phlegm, it was amplified to a decibel level that really rattled our eardrums. Nunn remained seemingly unperturbed, although his eyes widened slightly and his speech pattern wavered like the ink on an electrocardiogram. Teng was completely unabashed about his great expectoration. He repeated the process approximately three times during the course of two hours. Each time, he lit up a cigarette immediately after clearing his lungs.

Prior to our arrival in Peking, we had tried to divide up the area of questioning of the Vice Premier. Each of us had suggested a number of questions that he would like to have included, and then we had had the State Department people as well as the staff put them in some sort of order and appropriate language. State Department representatives cautioned against the use of certain language or certain questions as being inappropriate; however, there were no restrictions placed upon any member of the delegation.

I ended up with questions concerning Cambodia and also human rights. During the course of Teng's discussion, it became obvious to me that there would be very little time for me to engage in any sort of long exchange on these issues, as we had to go through an interpreter on each and every question. I knew that time was fading rapidly, as the questions and answers were pretty much consuming the two-hour time limitation. When Sam Nunn finally recognized me for questions, I decided to put the Vice Premier on notice as to my objections to the way in which the new relationship had been established.

"Mr. Vice Premier, as you can see, I am a relatively young man, and I am not as skilled with the use of metaphor as Chinese are, nor am I as skilled in the use of diplomatic language as my colleagues from the Senate. And so I will have to speak to you as candidly and directly as possible.

"As Senator Glenn has indicated, there are many members of the Congress and many people in our country who desire peace, peace throughout the world, but are skeptical about the way in which this new relationship with China has been established. I personally objected to the way in which the relationship was established not only because Congress was not consulted, but because I believe that our obligation to an ally is of equal value to China's claim to sovereignty and that we throw our reliability into question with other allies who will see that our pledges are simply paper promises and can be ignited overnight. This does not enhance the prestige of the United States but diminishes it.

"So I would say that I am skeptical, but it is a healthy skepticism,

and my reservations may be eliminated over a period of time as I observe
whether words of peace will be matched with deeds of peace. I would
point out that I am a member of the same party as Senator Goldwater,
although I am regarded, I guess, as a moderate. I am not sure exactly
what that means. I notice that the Vice Premier considers himself to be a
moderate smoker; perhaps there is some analogy. . . .''

I touched upon the fate of Cambodia and also upon the new breeze
of democracy that was flowing through the streets of Peking. Teng reacted
quite abruptly with me when I asked whether or not he would discuss
human rights, if not now, then at any time in the future. He made it very
clear that on his trip to the United States under no circumstances would
the subject of human rights be on the agenda.

The meeting ended at 12 sharp, and we proceeded to walk over to
Teng and have photographs taken once again with him. He said to me in
Chinese, ''The fact that we disagree does not mean we cannot still shake
hands.''

At 5:30 P.M. we left for the Great Hall of the People. This hall, in
which a banquet was held to celebrate the new relationship, can accommodate ten thousand people. The widow of Chou En-lai was the guest of
honor. A magnificent spread of food dominated every table. As the only
Republican Senator in the delegation, I was strategically placed at a table
with four former generals of the Nationalist Army of Chiang Kai-shek and
one Tibetan. None of the generals could speak English, but the language
of hospitality and good cheer needed little translation. Each general
would stand up with chopsticks in hand, lean into the center of the round
table, and pick up food from each one of the many courses and place it
on my plate. I washed the food down with beer that was warm and bitter
and periodically toasted my five hosts with a glass of Mai Tai—an incen-
diary libation that rivals the paralyzing power of a jellyfish sting. I scrupulously avoided the Chinese custom of consuming the small glass of Mai
Tai at the conclusion of each long and wordy toast, to the cry of ''Kan-
pei, kan-pei'' (meaning a dry glass, or our equivalent of ''bottoms up'').
Had there been only one toast, I would have followed protocol. But I had
been forewarned that the toasts have a way of multiplying, and so I just
sipped the Mai Tai as inconspicuously as possible.

During dinner, a Chinese band played some favorite old American
songs—''Home on the Range,'' ''Shenandoah,'' ''Chicken in the Hay,''

"Billy Boy," "She'll be Comin' Roun' the Mountain," and "America the Beautiful."

We left the banquet early to attend the Peking Opera. The Opera was not reserved for cultural elitists, but for the general population. I was impressed by the exuberance shown by the actors and the audience, since it was the first time that I had seen any sign of emotion in the Chinese people. During the final act, there was an incredible display of panto-mime, acrobatics, karate, and self-defense, with all of the actors in brilliant costumes and masks. At the conclusion of the act, Captain John McCain joked, "That's the most fun I've had since my last interrogation!" McCain was a Navy fighter pilot during the Vietnam war who was shot down during a mission over Hanoi. He spent six years as a prisoner of war. He was beaten and tortured regularly during his residence in a windowless and unventilated shed, but he remained resolute and strong in his commitment to the United States and steadfastly refused to disclose any information. He bears his considerable wounds with an incomparable optimism and effervescence that is uplifting to all who surround him.

I later learned that the performers had appeared a year before at Wolf Trap Farm in Virginia. The tickets at Wolf Trap were $20. The price in Peking was 50 cents. The Chinese people had to wait months for tickets, some of them for more than a year. I regretted that we had displaced an entire row of people—particularly since we had missed the entire first act.

We left Peking at 9 o'clock the next morning and headed for Japan. Shortly after we were in the air, I called my son Chris in McLean, Virginia, via the communications hookup in the plane. His voice was barely audible, but I could hear him say that my father was definitely coming to Washington for the swearing-in ceremonies.

During the flight to Japan, I reflected on my impressions of China. Life in the capital of the People's Republic is not primitive now, but it is sparse and spartan—merely adequate as far as food and clothing are concerned, although there are reports that a hundred million people are on the verge of starvation. The housing is well below anything we would label as decent or standard.

In visiting almost any country for the first time, one is struck with the customs and life-styles of the people.

What is striking in China is the politeness of the people to each other.

We witnessed a bicycle accident; the two participants simply apologized to each other rather than expressing any sense of anger.

In China, what is most impressive is the very movement of masses of people, the sense of order, the absence of the pursuit of material wealth, and the tolerance and patience that the people show for each other under circumstances that might prompt fisticuffs in the United States.

But what seems to be missing from the lives of the Chinese is a sense of intellectual creativity, of experimentation, of challenge to established authority, of doubt, of debate—the very lifeblood of a democratic society. The State's control over the actions, if not the minds, of its people has produced a certain dull gray uniformity of dress and conduct, a stagnant and backward economy, a system of science and technology that is lacking in innovation and contemporaneity.

There is always the danger, of course, that China, in its desire to modernize its bleak, almost medieval society, will be buried in a wave of industrial waste if it modernizes too rapidly and without adequate planning. But for now, the Chinese people seem to be looking westward with great anticipation of improving themselves and bringing a far greater range of material comforts to their simple lives.

China's search for methods to bring itself into the 21st century may not accord with deep-seated cultural or social beliefs. History will have to judge whether modernization can be achieved in China by the year 2000 and whether the Chinese people are willing to pay the price of prosperity.

We arrived in Tokyo at 3 P.M. There was a perceptible change in the tempo. The city hummed like the proverbial beehive. In Peking I had been conscious of the swollen waves of people, but there had seemed to be a dull gray monotony that hung over their existence like the coal dust in the air.

In Tokyo there was an energy and dynamism that was exciting and invigorating. Polished automobiles moved quickly and efficiently through the streets without the horn-blowing that is endemic to New York City. Dramatic new buildings spiraled into the sky, white thoughts of an architect's mind. The age of electronics was evident on every city block.

We went directly to the Ohira Hotel, a beautiful structure with all the conveniences we had missed in Peking—even the phone in the bathroom.

After checking into the hotel, we went directly to the American Embassy compound to receive a briefing by our military and State Department personnel on current political issues and the military status of Japan. Afterward, we were escorted to Ambassador Mike Mansfield's residence. Mansfield is a taciturn, pipe-smoking former Majority Leader of the United States Senate. Mike, while a Senator, made Gary Cooper seem loquacious. He has the lined and leathered face of a Montana cowhand He does not possess the stereotypic qualities that most people assume all ambassadors have—elegance, eloquence and the dash of a country squire —but he is well respected by the Japanese and obviously by the members of the Senate who had served with him.

That evening, Captain McCain, Gary Hart and I had dinner with a representative of Grumman Aircraft. We wanted to know the background behind a scandal that had erupted in Japan involving Grumman. The evening turned out to be quite unpleasant.

The Grumman representative was wallowing in the bitter aftertaste of our recognition of China and dumping of Taiwan. We then asked him about the scandal, and he gave some lame excuse that Grumman was not guilty, but was being set up as a scapegoat. The company had entered a consent decree to settle the case.

"That's the same as the nolo contendere plea that Spiro Agnew gave on tax evasion, and he was guilty as hell," I said.

John McCain wasn't far behind. "How could you plead nolo if the company was in fact not guilty?" McCain asked.

"Well, it costs a lot of money to fight these things, and we just couldn't continue to bear the legal expense in such a long and complicated case that would take years to litigate. . . ."

John would not concede. "Well, if in fact you were not guilty, then you should have stood your ground."

Under the circumstances, the dinner conversation deteriorated rapidly. We left our host at the hotel and took a cab to the famous Ginza district—an area lined with fashionable nightclubs and restaurants. Rows of black limousines with white interiors, driven by uniformed chauffeurs, were double-parked outside the clubs.

We watched in amazement as geisha girls escorted young Japanese businessmen, who obviously had consumed too many sakes, into their waiting limousines and bade them sayonara.

We stopped at some of the clubs to inquire about cover charges and the cost of drinks. They were all extremely expensive.

I walked into one lounge and was told abruptly, "Sorry, only Japanese allowed." I was tempted to ask the maître d' if he was an equal-opportunity employer, but concluded that the question would lose a lot in translation.

With that rejection, we tried to hail a cab, New York fashion. The cabdrivers completely ignored our whistles and waving arms. We finally found a police officer who could speak some English and were informed that we would have to walk several blocks to a designated pickup station. We finally arrived back at the hotel, weary and still disoriented by the time changes. I concluded the evening by watching a half hour of televised sumo wrestling—a grunting and rather grotesque display of flesh and flanks.

At 10 the next morning, we met with Japan's new Prime Minister Ohira in his office. "Welcome. I have been in office only about a month. I am happy with our security arrangement with the United States. Our people now have a better understanding of the importance of the treaty,* and there has been a distinct change in the opposition party's attitude about the treaty in that they are much less critical. . . ."

An assistant to the Prime Minister who wore a white patch over his eye sat across a low coffee table dozing. The Diet (Japan's Parliament) had been in session until 5 A.M.

Sam Nunn summarized our meeting with Teng Hsiao-ping and emphasized how critical our relations with Japan were to the security of the entire Asian area. Sam also wanted to check on Ohira's thoughts about the presence of American troops in South Korea.

The balance of the day was spent visiting with the Defense Minister and other officials to explore ways in which Japan could reorder its defense priorities and assume a greater percentage of the costs of its defense budget without stirring up domestic political controversy and conflict.

That evening, we attended a cocktail reception hosted by Japanese defense officials. Later, I had arranged to have dinner with two friends (one of whom had been educated at Harvard and was an officer with the Mitsubishi company). During the dinner, I said, "Okay, you sat through most of the meetings today. What do you really think of our country?"

* In November 1978, the United States and Japan concluded negotiations on Guidelines for Defense Cooperation. This agreement, designed to enhance our two countries' common defense efforts for Japan, called for a program of joint military planning which began the month of our visit.

"We think your country is a crippled giant, restrained on all sides by competing interest groups and no longer capable of making difficult decisions domestically or internationally. This is not just something the defense officials feel; the average Japanese believes that if Japan were attacked, the United States would never come to its rescue. . . ."*

Almost reflexively, I rushed to assure my friend that we would protect our allies. But there was little evidence I could point to that would indicate that the United States had recovered from the deep wound inflicted by our defeat in Vietnam.

JANUARY 12, 1979

AT 6 P.M. we arrived in Seoul. A crush of reporters greeted us, pushing, flashing their cameras. It seemed as if we were back in the United States.

Korea was an unreal world of my childhood and adolescence. It was a Warner Brothers production of tough-talking GIs being engulfed in waves of North Koreans and Chinese. Seoul remained fixed in my mind's eye as a small farming community. Thousands of Americans had died in battles to capture strategic locations. I could never understand why Pork Chop Hill was worth the letting of so much blood. But I believed it was the duty of Americans to help anyone who was being attacked in the world.

That night, my childhood memories ran into the rock wall of reality. The outline of Seoul's size emerged in a sea of lights along the Han River. That peasant village is a city of nearly seven and a half million people that is as modern as any in America. South Korea's economy has been booming for more than a decade. That economy has grown at an average rate of 10 percent for seventeen years. Last year, the growth rate was 12 percent. My childhood notions of allegiance and global obligation nearly dissolved in the scandal known as Koreagate. Allegations that the South Korean government, through businessman and sophisticated Washington socialite Tongsun Park, had bribed a number of Congressmen nearly unraveled our relationship. In fact, I had voted to terminate any further aid to South Korea unless South Korean President Chung Hee Park forced material witnesses to appear before congressional committees and a U.S.

---

* One year later, I spoke to a college audience in Maine following President Carter's decision to implement a draft-registration program in response to the Soviet invasion of Afghanistan. I asked the students how many would vote to assist Japan if it were attacked. Nearly 75 percent responded "No."

grand jury. The American blood that had stained the frostbitten hills and ravines of Korea had faded under the sulfurous stream of scandal.

We arrived at the Hyatt Regency and witnessed the tightest security that we had on the entire trip.

We were watched at all times. Our hotel floor was patrolled constantly by Korean security personnel in dark suits. Once I attempted to walk into an empty room on a dare by Captain McCain (who said it was filled with Korean agents) and a Korean stepped out and blocked the entrance. Embarrassed, I said "we were just looking around." We headed for the elevator, and he followed us into it and stayed with us until we entered the lobby and joined the rest of the American delegation.

That evening, McCain and I went to the top of the Regency to have a beer. The view was dramatic. We could have been overlooking New York City or San Francisco or any other large metropolitan area in the United States.

Just before we left, I noticed a very inebriated American being helped from his table and out of the lounge by two very attractive Korean women. He may have had love in his heart, but there was too much liquor on his brain. I concluded that he was about to be divested of his possessions.

JANUARY 13, 1979

WE BEGAN the morning with a briefing from Ambassador William Glystein and General J. W. Vessey, Jr., the Commander in Chief of the U.S. Command. We reviewed the current economic and political climate in South Korea; President Park's steps to relax his harsh rule; the South Korean attitude toward our recognition of China; and whether the South could fight and win a battle with the North—particularly if the United States continued its pullout of troops.

At 10 A.M. we met with South Korea's Prime Minister Choi Kyu Ha in a long and angular room. The furniture, while ornately carved, was low; the ceiling, high. The emphasis was on simplicity of lines and a lack of clutter. The table next to the Minister appeared to be wired for recording. I nudged John Glenn and pointed it out to him. It was an unnecessary warning. We operated on the premise that all of our conversations were being recorded during the trip.

At 10:30 A.M., we arrived at President Chung Hee Park's house. The security measures taken to protect Park made those at the White House look like an open door to a public museum. Several years ago, Park escaped an assassination attempt, but his wife was caught in the cross fire and killed.*

Park's office was by far the most elaborate we had seen. The furniture, again, was low and clean in its lines. The high ceiling had brass inlays. His desk was dark mahogany with hand carved floral designs. There was a portrait of Korean mountains hanging on one wall and one of Park consoling peasant women behind his ornate desk. Sterling silver and jade items decorated the long table around which we were seated.

Park was wearing a dark blue wool suit, pin-striped shirt, eel-skin loafer-style shoes and a polka-dot tie. He was a tightly knit little man, who was coiled like a spring. He would wring his hands as his interpreter translated his words into English to us. He held his arms folded across his chest and never looked directly at us while he talked or listened. He sat poised with the intensity of a mongoose.

Park was interested in learning what Teng Hsaio-ping had said to us, particularly about North Korea and its military buildup. Sam Nunn gave a brief review of our discussions with Teng and noted specifically that we had advised Teng that nothing would jeopardize our relations with China more than if North Korea should ever attack the South.

During Sam's recitation, I noticed that Park snapped his middle finger twice against his thumb. It was an unusual gesture; evidence, perhaps, of an inner tension that he is known to struggle to control. While John Glenn was talking, he snapped his fingers again. The click of Captain Queeg's metal balls in *The Caine Mutiny* flashed across my mind.

We had lunch with the Foreign Minister and then left by helicopter for the Demilitarized Zone (DMZ). There we visited the tunnels that were being dug by the North Koreans deep into the mountains under the DMZ itself. They were blasting through solid rock, tunnels fifty meters deep and wide enough to run three men side by side right under the lines guarded by American and South Korean forces.

In an effort to foil this tactic, we are using sophisticated listening devices and digging tunnels to interdict them and seal off their road network.

The climb back to daylight was wet and hot. The reason for the mandatory wearing of helmets became clear as all of us periodically smacked our heads against the jagged rock ceiling of the tunnel.

We then went to visit the crack troops of the 2nd Division. We

---

* On October 26, 1979, Park was assassinated by the head of his Intelligence Agency.

witnessed the riot-control unit in action. The squadron was a finely honed military unit whose members took a great pride in the precision of their movements.

It was bitterly cold out on the front line. In the warmth of a congressional office, war is an abstraction that we pray will never have to happen again. Out on the DMZ, the men sit on the cold hair trigger of extinction.

That evening we attended an elaborate dinner at the official residence of the Speaker of the Korean Assembly. We were then entertained by a concert pianist and an opera singer. We were each given a set of spoons as a gift.

The next day, General J. W. Vessey gave us a classified briefing on our state of readiness to repel an invasion by the North Koreans.

At 10:30, a press conference was held at the airport. I stated that Senator Glenn's report, filed the year before, advocating that we suspend the withdrawal of American troops from South Korea was a persuasive document and that I intended to lend my support to his position.

At 11:15, it was wheels up. Six hours and fifty-eight minutes later, we touched down in Elmendorf Air Force Base in Alaska. A red carpet was rolled out to greet us. I had never felt so happy to touch down on American soil in my life. And I had never felt prouder to be living in a free country.

As soon as we had refueled and were airborne again, I called Diane from somewhere over the northwestern United States to make sure that my father was coming to Washington. Then I sat back and thought about the men I had traveled with—Nunn, Hart, Glenn, McCain—and decided that I would seek a position on the Armed Services Committee if the opportunity presented itself.

CHAPTER 4

JANUARY 15, 1979, was a special day in my life. It was the moment I had spent fourteen months of campaigning to achieve. It was even more special because my father came to Washington for the first time in his life to see where I now lived and worked. He was reluctant to miss one day from his bakery in Bangor ("What will my customers do without bread?"). He also was apprehensive about flying on an airplane to come to Washington. Only after I had threatened never to visit him again did he manage to conquer his fear of flying and, for twenty-four hours, forget his customers.

Reuben Cohen is Jewish—dark, intelligent and hardworking. He rises at 11:45 P.M. six days a week and returns home at 6 P.M. the next day. (At the age of seventy-two he still works eighteen hours a day.) He is known almost to everyone in Bangor as "Ruby." He can be seen delivering rye bread and rolls in large brown bags to restaurants, grocery stores and supermarkets, his coat and trousers dusted with flour. In spite of the long hours of work, he maintains a quick sense of humor. He is self-deprecating and gregarious, a man of the Old Country, scarred by the Depression, wanting the best for his children. When I was young he always used to say, "Billy, why don't you become an orthodontist? Big money, easy hours, you wouldn't have to be a 'shlepper' like me."

In his youth he was an athlete, a musician and a fighter. His friends have told me many stories about his exploits, the most notable being the time he leveled an ex-bodyguard of the gangster Mickey Cohen with one punch. He always dismissed these stories about his pugilism and tried to insist that the man of peace will fare better than a man of war and that "you must try to kill 'em with kindness." It was good advice—which I, of course, rejected.

His marriage to my mother, Clara Hartley, was unconventional if not controversial.

My mother is an Irish Protestant—erect, blond, blue-eyed, beautiful, aloof and protective. She has simple and fundamental religious beliefs. Though he would deny it, my father is a shade this side of agnosticism. He has his doubts about the existence of a Supreme Intelligence, but he's not taking any chances. He leads a hard but good life—doesn't smoke or swear (at least in my company) and only in the past few years has succumbed to having a beer or two at lunch while discussing politics at a local restaurant with friends who love to bait him.

My father wanted me to be brought up "Jewish," even though we continued to celebrate most of the Christian holidays. He wanted me to be Bar Mitzvahed, so at the age of seven I was enrolled in Hebrew school to prepare myself for that special day that would mark my step into manhood.

In addition to wanting me to be raised in the Jewish faith, my father wanted me to be an athlete.

On Friday or Saturday evenings, he would take me to whatever athletic contests were in town—usually boxing or basketball. In fact, the local high school games were so packed at tournament time that he couldn't get a ticket for me. When I was five years old he would wrap me inside his overcoat and sneak me past the admission gate with the pushing crowd and sit me on his lap to watch the games. It was an incredible experience, hidden inside the cocoon of his coat, electrified by the fear that someone might notice a pair of extra legs emerging from the bottom of his coat and evict us from the game. It made a deep impression on me, and I loved my father for his daring and for caring enough to want to take me with him.

I also loved the smell of hot dogs and popcorn, the roar of the crowd, the passion, the combat and contact between the contestants.

So I decided at a very early age that I would be an athlete. I joined the YMCA when I was eight.

This created problems for me at Hebrew school. On Saturdays, the "Y" was open for gym classes and contests. Saturday is also the Jewish Sabbath, and we were required to attend services either at the school or at one of the synagogues.

Initially, I made a pact with my parents: one Saturday at the "Y," three at Hebrew school. I had to revise the agreement shortly thereafter to two and two; then three at the "Y"—and finally I just stopped going to Saturday services.

My split heritage of having an Irish mother and a Jewish father precluded me from ever being considered or accepted as a Jew, so I rationalized away the need to attend Saturday services. My absence upset some of my classmates, because it spoiled any chance for a perfect class attendance record and the prize that went with it. But I felt no urge to satisfy my peers and simply ignored their complaints, which always came to me secondhand.

Had my mother converted to Judaism perhaps things would have turned out differently for me, but she remained a woman of fierce independence and iron will against all the social pressures for conformity. She was Irish, Protestant and proud. She remains that way today.

I found it difficult to carry the name of Cohen and the label of Jew during the time when bigotry was rather rampant in rural Maine. I can still recall a sign posted on a private beach: "No dogs or Jews allowed."

One of my more vivid recollections is the time I was pitching in a Little League game in a small town. While I was standing on the mound, an angry red-faced man hurled a beer can at me, yelling "Send the Jew boy home!" (It was ironic that twenty-six years later, I received rocks in the mail during the impeachment investigation with letters expressing the same ethnic hatred.) I was only twelve at the time, and I can remember thinking, But you don't understand: I'm not . . . But my jaws stayed locked, and I continued to pitch. Later in the game, I hit a home run over the center-field fence and smashed the windshield of one of the cars parked beyond the fence. My heart was racing as I went around the bases. I was hoping it was the car of the man who had been yelling at me.

I had no need to resolve the confusion that existed in my mind at that time, but I could not drift forever in a fuzzy world of religious nonalignment. When it came time for me to be Bar Mitzvahed and celebrate my admission into the ranks of responsibility, I discovered that I first would have to participate in a special religious-conversion ceremony. I ran to my father with tears in my eyes. "Dad, I'm not going to do it." He responded quietly, "Billy, you don't have to."

I knew that my mother had talked to him. She had always remained indifferent to the social pressure that called for her to change her views or conduct in order to please others. Any measure of independence that I have today, I attribute to her example of self-esteem and self-confidence.

While I was relieved by my parents' decision not to ask me to participate in the religious-conversion ceremony, I was also angry. I had spent six years preparing for a special day only to learn that the long hours of study were in vain. I tore off the medal that I wore around my neck (given me for scholastic excellence at Hebrew school) and threw it into the polluted Penobscot River, which runs parallel to my father's bakery.

It was a lesson that has stayed with me for a lifetime. The Jewish community could not carve out an exception to its faith and laws just to accommodate me. I chose exclusion from the Jewish faith rather than accept the terms of confirmation. Snapping the bonds of conformity carried with it a price tag. I no longer had to struggle to be on the inside of any social or religious circle. Exclusion meant freedom from conformity, but it also meant a lack of security and identity that any group gives its membership. It meant that I could not expect to take refuge behind a common wall of numbers against the inevitable insults and assaults of future years. . . .

From that point on, I turned to playing basketball almost constantly. The "Y" became my first home. I merely slept at my parents' home. When the "Y" was closed on Sundays, I would practice outside—even in winter with snow on the ground. I would go inside only when my hands and ears ached from the cold so that I couldn't hold the ball any longer. I achieved my childhood dreams of playing before five to six thousand fans on Friday evenings and thrilling them with a high-arching two-handed head shot from thirty feet out, just like the ones my father used to shoot. It was an anachronism even then, and I think that is just exactly why I perfected it. The ball took a long time to come down, and when it did, it would cut through the net like a knife. . . .

My mother and father used to follow me all over the state to watch me play. Once I scored 43 points in a game, and on the way to the dressing room to take a shower, I asked my father what he thought of my performance. With a completely serious tone, he said, "If you hadn't missed those two foul shots, you could have scored forty-five."

Each afternoon while he was on his delivery route, he would stop by our practice sessions to urge me on—and yell when I made a mistake.

One day, the other players asked me to tell him not to come to the practices. I wasn't sure how to break the news to him that evening, but I tried.

"Dad, the other players don't have their fathers come to our practice sessions, and it makes it a little difficult for me when you stop by."

He was hurt by my awkwardly worded request and simply pretended it was of no interest to him, that he stopped by only because the gym was on his route. I held my head down when I spoke. I didn't want to see the pain in his eyes as he tried to dismiss my anxiety with indifference.

He didn't come by the gymnasium for several weeks. One day during a bad snowstorm, I was dribbling down the court when I felt someone's eyes watching me. It was dark outside, but the lights from the gym picked up a silhouette in a window. I looked out and saw my father's face peering through a window with his hands cupped around his temples. He had a hat on that was covered with snow. He had been standing on a railing outside the gym watching the entire practice session. The baker man, covered with flour, covered with snow, standing in the cold. I felt a sharp pain of guilt for having asked him not to come to the practice sessions. I also felt a deep sense of pride that he came anyway and watched in dark silence. I never told him that I saw him that afternoon and all those that followed. But I played each day knowing he was there and tried just a little harder for that face in the window. . . .

But that was a long time ago. Today, I wanted my father to witness a different kind of competition that I had chosen.

I arrived at the office by 7:30 A.M. I wanted to get my office organized early before I went to the Organizational Meeting of the Republicans that began at 9.

During the Caucus, everyone was friendly. Senator Strom Thurmond of South Carolina made a special effort to welcome each one of the new members. So did Barry Goldwater. Someone asked Goldwater about his hip, and he responded, "Hip's all right; it's my knees. They're shot to hell."

Senator Charles "Mac" Mathias of Maryland asked me how cold it was in Maine. "Seventeen below zero. But I've been in China."

"See what happens?" he retorted. "The first week in the Senate and he's off to China."

John Heinz approached me. "Bill, the vote is close. I won't press you any more. I need your help."

He was locked in a tough battle with Orrin Hatch of Utah for chairman of the Republican Senatorial Campaign Committee—the person in charge of raising the money to help finance the campaigns of Senators up for re-election or candidates seeking the office for the first time. The position not only is important from a party perspective—helping to elect more Republicans to achieve the goal of a majority party—but has a direct political benefit to the chairman. It will bring him into contact with wealthy businessmen and organized political-action groups across the country. It thus provides a solid base for wide exposure among community leaders and opinion makers and a green-backed base of support should the chairman decide his talent and ambition exceed his senatorial seat.

I wasn't comfortable with the decision that I would have to make. I thought about an article that had appeared in one of the Washington papers while I was on the China trip.

> The most astonishing hold-out has been William S. Cohen, usually aligned with the progressive element of the Republican Party. Cohen is indebted to Hatch for keeping the right wing off his back. . . . The question is whether ideology will win out or what have you done for me lately.

I was not pleased with my eventual decision to back Heinz, because I thought that on the merits, Orrin was as qualified as John. But it was like so many decisions that fall into the gray area of doubt where the respective merits of competing candidates or causes seem equally compelling. Ultimately, it is some small, even irrelevant factor, some intuitive impulse or bias, some convenient rationalization that brushes away the web of indecision.

On the floor, my temporary seat was next to that of Mark Hatfield of Oregon.

We chatted quietly as several Senators came by to say hello, including Joe Biden of Delaware and Don Riegle of Michigan. I hadn't seen Don for over a year since I'd asked him to help a young man find a job. He congratulated me and said it was an important day in my life and to be sure to take good notes. I said that I would and thought of the irony involved.

I had known Don in the House, where he had served for five terms. He is highly intelligent, intense and articulate. He also is regarded as a maverick and switched from the Republican to the Democratic Party in 1973. He issued a long statement outlining the reasons that compelled him to change his allegiance. The Republicans in the House never forgave him for his apostasy. The Democrats did not universally embrace him. I remember Democratic Congressman Wayne Hays of Ohio making a particularly scathing personal attack on Don the day he took his seat on the side of the Chamber traditionally reserved for Democrats.

It was not that Democrats did not welcome every defection from the Republican Party. Hays was expressing a contempt that a number of people shared for Don because of his book, *O Congress,* which contained an account of how things do or don't happen in the House of Representatives, the emotional turmoil he experienced in his personal and political life, and his judgment on a number of his colleagues. To my mind, it was an honest book. Perhaps it was not an entirely fair or accurate representation of the institution, but it was not far off the mark.

Whatever contribution the book made to literature or to the public's perception of its Congress, it placed the mark of Cain on Don with many of the people he had to deal with during the remainder of his career in the House.

Paul Sarbanes of Maryland also came by. We had served on the House Judiciary Committee together. He is a bright, articulate, academic type who is regarded as having one of the most analytical minds in the Senate. "Well, you didn't realize what you were getting yourself into," he said. "I tried to find out, but you wouldn't tell me," I shot back.

We were being administered the oath of office in teams of four. The senior Senator from each state would escort his new colleague down to the rostrum, where Vice President Mondale would administer the oath. Ed Muskie was my escort for this occasion.

Herman Talmadge of Georgia walked rather awkwardly down the aisle with Sam Nunn. "Look at poor Herman," one Senator said; "it looks like Sam is escorting him. What a toll has been taken on that man. First his divorce and now the Ethics Committee. . . ."*

I noticed how Talmadge was weaving as he left the Chamber, pausing to shake hands with Barry Goldwater and other members as he walked up the aisle. Just as he got to the rear of the Chamber and walked out the door, he staggered badly and nearly fell. All the correspondents in the Press Gallery, which was filled to capacity, were watching intently. They turned and whispered to each other. I suspected—and hoped—they wouldn't write about what had happened the next day. They would probably save it for an anecdote at the Press Club or at an informal gathering;

---

* The Senate Ethics Committee was investigating charges that Talmadge had filed false financial statements, had failed to report gifts from constituents, and had set up an illegal bank account.

but if Talmadge ever toppled from office or died, they would recount today's event as one of the visible indicators that the man was in trouble.

I waited until 1:25 and took my family to the Senate Dining Room for lunch. Henry "Scoop" Jackson of Washington was at his special table in the far right corner entertaining his guests of the day. The Senate Dining Room is smaller, more intimate and slightly more elegant than its counterpart in the House. While there is a greater variety in the Senate menu, the quality of the food is not distinctively superior.

A waiter whom I remembered from the House Dining Room gave us service to which I had not been accustomed during my time there. He really hustled. In the House, waiters don't move nearly so fast and aren't nearly so solicitous. My father, who insisted on paying for the meal, was so impressed that he tipped him 25 percent.

I gave everyone the Cook's Tour of the Capitol—the Senate and then the House side. We had pictures taken out front and then wended our way back to my office. I was failing rapidly, since I had had only four hours' sleep the night before.

Several members of the Maine press were in the office. I tried to put them off until the next day. I was just not up for a long interview. They did a brief one with Dad. He was remarkably restrained—for him. I called him the Mike Mansfield of Bangor. He has learned not to say too much to the press—at least, not in my presence. My father and nephew left for Maine shortly afterward.

My first official day concluded when one of my staff came rushing into my office and said, "Senator Strom Thurmond is outside and he wants to see you. Probably wants to welcome you to the Armed Services Committee or lobby you for the Judiciary." Diane, Kevin and Chris cleared out. Senator Thurmond came in while his administrative assistant and I waited with a certain amount of anticipation.

"I just want to welcome you to the Senate and to say how happy I am to see you and so many young men here," he drawled in Southern fashion. And then he handed me a big bag of pecan nuts with his senatorial card on top. In bold handwriting next to the official seal, it said:

Welcome to the Senate.
Strom

He turned around and left. I cracked up. I told Diane that tomorrow I was going to drop by and give him a hundred-pound bag of Maine potatoes.

January 17, 1979

I joined several of my new Republican colleagues on the Washington Mall to have a photograph taken for *Life* Magazine. We were supposed to be dressed in jogging outfits to give evidence of a new dynamism in the Republican Party. It was cold and sleeting. We posed for about twenty minutes jogging in place and then for a grand finale dashed toward the photographer with whatever vigor could be summoned. Click. "Got it. Wonderful shot. Good action." Several days later we were told that the film was destroyed during the process of reproduction for the magazine. The "scene" would have to be re-enacted. I decided that I could forgo "take two."

Upon arriving at my office (and changing from running shorts to pinstripes), I prepared for an interview with a Washington television outfit that was "stringing" for a station in Maine. It was a "soft news" story, reflections about my first day on the job.

I attended a Republican Caucus that was in the process of debating a change in the rules pertaining to the assignment of members to committees. The meeting was chaired by John Tower of Texas. Tower was nattily dressed in a dark three-piece suit, stiff-collared white shirt, and gray tie, with a white handkerchief tucked neatly in the chest pocket of his jacket. He wore reading glasses that sat precariously on the edge of a slightly upturned nose.

At 12:30, I attended my first meeting of the Senate Wednesday Group (I had been a member of the Wednesday Group in the House for six years), an informal gathering of Republican Senators who generally fall into the category of moderate or liberal. Actually, there are as many conservatives who are members, but they are not part of the more ideologically rigid so-called "New Right." Each week, a member hosts a luncheon in his office, where the others gather to give brief reviews of what action is occurring in their committees or, indeed, in their states. Advocacy for legislation is prohibited. The meetings are designed to be informal, informative and social in nature. It is one of the few times during the course of a busy week when members take the time to relax and enjoy one another's company. Similar meetings are held by the Republican Steering Committee, which is composed of the more conservative members. A joint Wednesday Group–Steering Committee luncheon is usually held once a month.

Following the luncheon, I left to attend a meeting at the State Department with Secretary Cyrus Vance. Sam Nunn and members of the senatorial staff who had made the China trip were present, as were Dick Holbrooke, Assistant Secretary for East Asian and Pacific Affairs, and Bob Oakley, also of the State Department.

Vance said he had read the State Department cables and thought our trip was fascinating. He particularly wanted Nunn's impressions of the Chinese and whether their expressions of peace appeared to be genuine. He also wanted an update of the situation in Korea.

It was my first meeting with Vance. He exuded a sincerity which dismissed any preconceived notions that he was just going through the motions of meeting with yet another group of Senators telling him how to conduct foreign policy. He jotted down key words and phrases as we spoke, noting the major points of our interests.

The meeting lasted nearly an hour. As I started to leave, Dick Holbrooke asked me to be sure to obtain a copy of Vance's most recent speech.

"Dick," I said, "I would really like to read it. But could I also have a copy of Brzezinski's? I want to see if there really is only one foreign policy in this Administration."

I was teasing Holbrooke, whom I had met several years earlier. I had just read an item in *The Washington Post* that quoted presidential Press Secretary Jody Powell as saying there was no difference between the Vance and Brzezinski statements in spite of news reports to the contrary.

"Cohen, don't start being a troublemaker," Holbrooke responded.

"Dick, it's been the story of my life."

JANUARY 18, 1979

A REPUBLICAN CONFERENCE WAS scheduled for 10:30 A.M. The purpose of the meeting was to select our committee assignments. We followed the seniority system. Our names were called according to numerical rank. The vacancies on Appropriations and Foreign Relations were filled immediately by the senior members. I picked Governmental Affairs as my first choice. When my name was called the second time, there were two vacancies left on Armed Services, and I took one of them.

Later in the afternoon, I went to the Senate Recording Studio—a room in the basement of the Capitol building where television and radio interviews can be conducted, taped and mailed to television and radio stations back in our states. It had been my practice in the House to do a weekly five-minute radio interview on current issues that would be of interest to my constituents. I prefer to have someone ask me questions on an interview basis.

After the interview I returned to my office, and had started to have a sandwich when I heard two loud bells ring. In the House, that would mean that a vote on a bill was taking place in the House chamber. I was unsure of the significance of two bells in the Senate and asked my staff to check with the Republican cloakroom (a room just off the Senate chamber staffed with employees who keep us abreast of the legislative proceedings). I was told that seven and a half minutes remained on a quorum call. I dropped my sandwich, ran down the corridor of the Dirksen Office Building, took the subway to the Senate floor, only to discover—to my considerable embarrassment—that it is generally unnecessary to respond to a quorum call in the Senate, as it is simply a delaying device to give the leadership time to decide what to do next.

At 4:15, I went to Minority Leader Baker's office, which is located in the Capitol. I briefed him on what had occurred during the trip and my observations about the situation with Korea. It was my judgment that President Carter could not continue his policy of pulling American troops out of Korea—not against the unanimous advice of three key Democrats (Nunn, Hart and Glenn) whose support he would need throughout this congressional session and particularly on SALT II.

At 5, the Republican members of the Armed Services Committee met in John Tower's office to consider subcommittee assignments. Tower's office was similar to many that I had seen on the Hill. His walls were lined with photographs of him with past Presidents and various national figures—John Connally, Ronald Reagan, Gerald Ford and Richard Nixon among them. There were cartoons and caricatures of John in oversized cowboy boots and a ten-gallon hat. Several walls were covered with maps of Texas.

Tower made it clear that he wanted each of us to have a ranking position on a subcommittee. He recommended that we hire professional people at top salaries to make certain that we obtained the best available personnel. He then spoke of our deteriorating military posture throughout the world and the need to increase President Carter's budget request to reflect real growth above that of inflation. There was nearly unanimous agreement on that point. I shared the belief that we had to strengthen our defense, but I knew there would be programs or policies that I would not agree to be of fundamental necessity and that I would vote against. There is a natural tendency within any minority group to seek unanimity of thought and action. I wanted to shed the shell of "maverick," but not lose, in the process, my own independence.

I left Tower's office and drove over to the Rayburn House Office Building on the other side of the Capitol. The Food Marketing Institute was holding a reception in one of the banquet rooms (where there is at least one reception by some national group every night). Two men from Maine were attending the reception, and so I felt obliged to stop by and say hello.

I arrived home at approximately 7:30 and shared what remained of dinner with Diane and the boys.

JANUARY 23, 1979

AT 9:30 A.M., the first official meeting of the Armed Services Committee was held in Room 212 of the Russell Senate Office Building. It is a relatively small room, with a minimal number of seats for the general public. I learned that there is little need for seating space, as most of our meetings are closed to the general public and conducted in executive session.

The normal raised semicircular dais was missing. Instead, dark mahogany tables with leather top inlays were placed together to form a sort of trapezoid shape on each side of the room. Overhead hung three chandeliers. Behind the Chairman's chair was a large mirror that extended to the ceiling. To me, the entire seating arrangement seemed calculated to reduce confrontation with witnesses or with each other. It resembled less a committee hearing room than a corporate boardroom where the board members flipped through projective budgets, financial statements and portfolios and reached an agreement as to a report to be issued to the shareholders.

Senator Harry Byrd of Virginia came over and welcomed me to the committee. Chairman John Stennis of Mississippi did the same just before the meeting began. Stennis opened the meeting for the purpose of receiving a report by Sam Nunn of the Pacific Ad Hoc Study Group. The Chairman advised each of us to be brief, because our official meeting began at 10, with Admiral Stansfield Turner, Director of the CIA, scheduled to testify.

Nunn summarized the findings of the Ad Hoc Study Group in less than five minutes. Gary Hart added a few words. I took the opportunity to praise Nunn for his intelligence and quiet diplomacy, which I believe brought great credit to the Senate and the Armed Services Committee. In addition, I made note of his complete fairness to me as a new member of the Senate and as the only Republican on the trip.

"Mr. Chairman, there is a debate that will continue to rage as to whether the Senate works harder than the House. It is too soon for me to make such a judgment. I can say it was the hardest-working and most productive trip that I have ever been on. The staff did a magnificent job in briefing us, and they deserve special credit."

In order to save time, I asked permission to put my additional views on the trip in the form of a letter to the other members of the full Committee.

Each of the Committee members was then allowed to ask questions. Most involved the reported troop buildup by the North Koreans and what the reaction was of our allies in the Pacific to the recognition of China.

The regular meeting began with Stansfield Turner giving a general overview of events in Iran, Afghanistan, and Africa and the role of the Soviet Union in the current turmoil. He then presented a comparison of Soviet defense spending and our own and the international implications of permitting the Soviets to establish a wide gap in actual or perceived military power. During his presentation, I had received a note stating that President Carter wanted me to join Senators Nunn, Hart, and Glenn for lunch at the White House to participate in the review of our trip.

At 11:45, Gary Hart and I jumped into my car, parked outside the Russell Building, and we drove to the White House. We met in the Cabinet Room. Defense Secretary Harold Brown, Zbigniew Brzezinski, Dick Holbrooke and Frank Moore (Assistant to the President for Congressional Liaison) were already present.

President Carter entered the room shortly after noon. He was dressed in a gray wool pin-striped suit, brown tie and blue shirt. He looked drawn and tired. He made no attempt at preliminary small talk, backslapping, or presidential stroking on family or personal matters. A meeting with Jimmy Carter was strictly business.

As he entered the Cabinet Room, he shook hands with each of us. "Gentlemen," he said, "why don't we go right to work during lunch? First, let's bow our heads in prayer."

During the lunch, Sam Nunn gave a summary of the report that the Pacific Ad Hoc Study Committee had filed with the Armed Services Committee earlier that morning. While we reported on the nature of the discussions that we had had with Teng Hsiao-ping and lesser Chinese officials, one of the major points of the report was that it was imperative that we suspend any further withdrawal of American troops from South Korea. During our trip, we had been cautioned that we would have to approach the President very delicately on the subject of troop withdrawal from that country. Carter had a strong stubborn streak, we were told, and if he took the Committee's report as an assault or criticism of his judgment, he would balk and just dig in his heels.

The President has great respect for Sam Nunn on military affairs, and he would need his support on the SALT II agreement. He listened intently as Sam related the concern on the part of our allies over their perception of the United States as being in a state of withdrawal, of growing isolationism. Our CIA had released reports indicating that a substantial buildup of North Korean troops had taken place above the DMZ. A further withdrawal of troops would be an invitation for North Korea to attack the South.

Carter did not give any commitment that he would change his policy. "We are now reviewing that situation. We have always said that the decision to withdraw was subject to change if circumstances warranted it."

He gave the distinct impression, however, that he was not persuaded by statements from allies about our perceived isolationism.

"Other countries will always say that when you seek to have them bear more responsibility for their own defense."

When it came my turn to speak, I said, "Well, I was asked to speak to Teng Hsiao-ping about China's support of Cambodia and its policy on human rights. It was the shortest conversation of the trip."

"That's the fate of junior members," the President retorted with a smile.

"Well, Mr. President, when the Vice Premier visits you here, be sure to have a large spittoon available without any microphones or amplifiers nearby."

Carter laughed, having already heard about Teng's expectorative habits. He responded that contact with certain Georgia politicians had prepared him well.

Before we left, Carter thanked each of us profusely for the contribution we had made. He said he wanted, welcomed, and needed our counsel and criticism.

On the way back to the Hill, Hart asked me what I thought of Carter.

"He's at his best with a small group like that. Comes across as being very humble and sincere. Although I think he has a tendency to overdo it. You know, telling you how much he appreciates your advice, counsel and criticism, while he is probably thinking that we should stick it in the *Congressional Record*."

"No," Hart countered, "he was probably thinking, How in hell did my staff get me locked into this lunch?"

We both laughed. All too frequently we get locked into similar positions.

At 2:30 I attended, at Sam Nunn's invitation, a press conference held by the members of the Pacific Ad Hoc Study Committee. Because I was not a member of the Committee, I kept my remarks as brief as possible.

"In my judgment, the President's policy is expensive, unwise and unnecessary. It is a policy of limited benefits with very significant risks and costs. Pending an analysis of the North Korean troop buildup and our new relationship with China, we should suspend any further withdrawal."

Later in the day, I called John Tower and advised him that I would not be able to join him for a ten-day visit to the NATO countries to discuss our military needs with their defense officials. I was flattered that Tower had wanted me to accompany him, and I wanted to go, but I was concerned that it would look to my constituents as if I had newly become a "globe-trotter." I had just returned from a major trip, and important as the NATO visit might be, I felt it was more important to return to Maine during the Lincoln Day recess period in mid-February. I did tell John, however, that I would like to join him for the two-day conference in Munich, West Germany, where defense officials gathered annually to express their opinions on a completely off-the-record basis.

At 6:30, I left my office and headed for the Capitol to join a number of my colleagues for dinner with Ronald Reagan—the heir of Barry Goldwater, and the conscience of the conservatives—who is dedicated to alerting the American people to the evils of a growing federal bureaucracy, of the trend toward a collectivist-minded society that seeks institutional help for every personal inconvenience, without realizing that the institution is turning the key in the lock on our individual freedoms. In

1976, he challenged Gerald Ford in a primary fight for the Republican nomination for President. He ran as an uncompromising conservative. The great irony was that Gerald Ford as President was much more conservative than Ronald Reagan was as Governor of California, and yet Ford was perceived as having compromised his conservative credentials and slipped into that amorphous world of presidential pragmatism. The delegates at the convention in Kansas City that year were clearly sympathetic to Reagan's candidacy. They were reluctant, however, to turn an incumbent—albeit unelected—President out of office. Reagan, who had promised to raise the bright and bold colors of conservatism high up the flagpole, made their decision somewhat easier by selecting as his running mate Senator Richard Schweiker of Pennsylvania, whose colors as a conservative were, to most of Reagan's supporters, rather checkered. Reagan was desperate for delegates; but honor, to his legions, was more important than victory.

Tonight, Ronald Reagan was courting support from Republican Senators—many of whom he had campaigned for regardless of their places in the ideological spectrum.

As I walked into S-138, the Arthur Vandenberg Room, a television film crew turned its blinding lights on Charles Percy of Illinois and me. Dan Rather's book *The Camera Never Blinks* came to mind: There is just no way to escape that one-eyed monster which politicians both love and loathe.

Senator Paul Laxalt of Nevada (Reagan's chairman for his 1980 campaign) was at the door extending greetings. He is a warm and personable man, soft-spoken and sincere, conservative but not strident. "Thoughtful" is a word associated with his name.

There was a good philosophical cross-section of Senators present: John Heinz of Pennsylvania, Orrin Hatch of Utah, Mark Hatfield of Oregon, Dave Durenberger of Minnesota, Charles Mathias of Maryland, Bob Packwood of Oregon and Richard Lugar of Indiana.

Nancy Reagan also attended the cocktail hour. When Nancy left, she and Reagan engaged in a warm embrace. They whispered to each other like newlyweds and parted with a light kiss. She appeared to be enjoying the campaign trail every bit as much as the candidate.

Laxalt gave a low-key twenty-minute introduction as to why we were gathered together for the evening. He talked of Reagan's moderation, his willingness to embrace all Republicans, as evidenced by the fact that he had campaigned for many in the room even though he was being denounced by extremist publications for doing so.

Reagan is a man of great personal charm. When he speaks, there is a slight swagger to his shoulders that signals a certain shyness rather than bravado. He looked tanned and vigorous. The lines in his face did not seem as deeply etched as political reporters kept insisting. He said that he had come not only to tell us of his plans (they were not a national secret) but to listen to our views on crucial issues, so that as an outsider he might have the benefit of those inside. He kept his remarks brief and then invited questions. Senators are not known for their reticence. The questions came cascading out:

"Whom would you place in your Cabinet?"

"How do you intend to deal with the extremist perception that many people have of you?"

"What programs or prospects do you intend to offer to the laboring people of this country?"

"What is your position on a woman's having the right to an abortion?"

Finally, I decided to ask how he would go about picking a running mate.

"Governor Reagan, two years ago, you enraged some of your strongest supporters by picking a running mate whose colors as a conservative were not bold enough. Senator Laxalt has indicated tonight that you are currently being criticized by some of the more extremist magazines for having campaigned for moderates or liberals in the Party. How do you intend to pick a running mate this time?"

I had heard that Reagan was thinking of running with someone as a team in the primaries. I was surprised to learn that he was thinking of allowing the Republican Convention a role in selecting his running mate.

"But if you do that, won't you run a substantial risk of having a vice-presidential candidate even more conservative than yourself? It is a generally accepted fact that Republican conventions tend to be dominated by delegates who are more conservative than Republicans generally—and we constitute only about 20 percent of the registered vote—just as delegates at Democratic conventions tend to be more liberal than the average Democrat. I assume that you are going to want to give some consideration to regional balance as well as philosophical balance. If you leave the decision to the convention, and you are given a running mate who gives ideological purity but no balance—how are you going to get back to the middle for the general election, where all the votes are?"

He was not prepared for the question, which struck some as being impertinent and a little insulting. But I wanted him to think about the problem, and not find himself boxed in by some public statement that was soothing to the democratic sensibilities of convention delegates but might prove disastrous to his chances for success.

Shortly after the dinner concluded, we gathered on the Senate floor and prepared to walk down the long corridor through Statuary Hall and the Rotunda into the chamber of the House of Representatives. Tonight a joint session of Congress was being held to hear President Carter give the State of the Union message.

We proceeded in a long double column. I walked beside Gary Hart. As we passed through the Rotunda, I said, "Gary, you can't appreciate how many times during these joint sessions we used to watch the Senators come through the House doors and say, 'Here come those bastards.' "

"Did you really say that?"

"Yup."

"How do you feel now?" he asked.

"Well, you're witnessing the transmogrification of a Representative," I laughed. "But it's true. There's a whole lot more bowing and bootlicking on the Senate side—in the committee hearings, receptions, and even travel abroad and the gym."

"You mean Representatives don't receive the same treatment?"

"It's not the same."

As we walked through the doors into the House chamber, the Sergeant at Arms barked out, "Mistah Speakah—the members of the United States Senate."

According to custom, the House members stood and applauded as we walked down the center aisle. I took the occasion to reach over and shake as many hands of my former colleagues as I could. It was the first time that I had seen most of them since the election. They seemed to be genuinely happy with my success.

As soon as we were seated, the Sergeant at Arms announced the arrival of the ambassadorial delegations of foreign governments to the chamber. We all stood and applauded as they proceeded down the center aisle. The galleries were jammed with wives, family members and friends. The television lights began to grow brighter as we approached the hour of 9 P.M.

When Rosalynn Carter and other members of the President's family were escorted to their seats in the galleries, a long ovation broke out—a tradition of respect for the First Family. The cameras whirred and clicked away at Mrs. Carter and Amy. Then the arrival of the President's Cabinet, followed by that of the Supreme Court, was announced by the Sergeant at Arms.

Finally, President Carter walked into the chamber escorted by a bipartisan delegation of Senate and House members. Everyone stood and applauded. Then Speaker Thomas P. "Tip" O'Neill rose and said, "It is my great honor and privilege to present to you the President of the United States."

Again the chamber erupted into a sustained ovation. It was the last expression of enthusiasm of the evening. President Carter's speech lasted slightly longer than a half hour, and it was interrupted twenty-five or thirty times by congressional handclapping—but it was applause that was polite in nature rather than spirited.

Speechmaking could not be said to be one of Jimmy Carter's strong points. His tone was halting, lilting, uneven. His voice rose on the wrong syllables. He smiled even as he said something stern. The tilt of his head and shift of his feet gave the impression of a minister or pastor preaching to his parishioners—not that of a leader exhorting and galvanizing the spirits of his countrymen.

At 9:40 P.M. the Speaker announced that the joint session of Congress was dissolved, whereupon we headed back toward the Senate chamber and to our offices.

Usually, there is a bevy of reporters waiting in the Rotunda to secure reactions from Senators on the President's speech. Senator Frank Church of Idaho was walking directly in front of me. A reporter approached him with his pen poised over the ever-present spiral-ringed notebook.

"Senator, what did you think of the President's speech?"

"No comment."

"On a scale of one to ten, how would you rate it?" he persisted.

"No comment," Church answered.

There is little to be gained in succumbing to the importunings of the press for an instant analysis or reaction to a presidential statement. Whether you agree with the President or not, you ordinarily feel obliged to find something kind—or at the least, innocuous—to say about his effort. A standard reply might be "It was a forceful presentation and certainly a step in the right direction. However, he placed too much emphasis on fiscal issues [or social programs or weapons systems]. I'll want to wait until I see more specifics before endorsing [or opposing] his programs."

Church just avoided going through the charade. But at the time, it seemed to me that a "no comment" coming from the new Chairman of the Foreign Relations Committee would be more quotable than the comments of any partisan critic.

I returned to the office, signed mail for an hour, arrived home by 11 and read until 1 A.M.

JANUARY 24, 1979

I HAD lunch with Arthur O. Sulzberger, Jr., of *The New York Times* in the Capitol Hill dining room. We discussed our respective thoughts about the new relationship with China and our current foreign policy in general.

Early in the afternoon, I stopped by a room in the Capitol where a senior citizens' group was holding a meeting. A constituent from Maine was present whom I wanted to welcome to Washington. I was called upon to give an impromptu speech to the gathering. As I left the room and headed for the Russell Building to attend a committee hearing, I was accosted by a young man who had just heard my speech.

"Senator Cohen, that was just a fine speech you gave. It really meant a lot to those people. You sounded very sincere."

I was flattered by his comments, but began to realize that he had something more on his mind.

"Do you mind if I walk along with you?" he asked.

"No, go right ahead," I said.

"Senator Cohen, I could tell just by the way you talked that you've been saved. I mean I could really tell. Do you mind if I ask you a personal question?"

"No."

"Have you ever had a personal experience with Jesus?"

"No. You see, I'm Jewish, and. . . ." I thought that might terminate the conversation more easily than if I said I was a Unitarian.

"Oh, you are. That's just great. I think the Jews are just fantastic people. They're deeply religious, and of course, they have a lot in common with Christians. . . ."

"Excuse me, but I've got to attend a committee hearing now. I've enjoyed our conversation."

January 25, 1979

I ATTENDED a breakfast meeting where a presentation on SALT II was conducted by Dr. Fred Ikle, Cy Weiss and John Lehman—all of whom had been extensively involved in the negotiations of SALT I. They made a comparison of our relative strategic position with the Soviet Union prior to SALT I and our current status. They were unanimous that we were hanging on the rim of inferiority.

At 10, an Armed Services Committee meeting began. The meeting was held in the Dirksen Senate Office Building, in a room with a traditional raised dais that separated the witnesses from the Senators. It was an open meeting and was extensively covered by the press. The room was filled to capacity. Chairman John Stennis deferred to John Tower for a brief opening statement and then yielded to Scoop Jackson. Stennis was courtly to the core, almost to the point of caricature. He strung out his remarks in a lyrical Southern fashion that ranged from the serious to the light. At one point Tower asked Stennis to yield, and the Chairman hesitated and seemed annoyed at the interruption.

"I just wanted to praise the distinguished Chairman's efforts in reducing this budget to a lean and trim one," Tower said.

Stennis' face broke wide with a smile. "Well, now, I'm glad I yielded to yah, Senator Tower."

The room erupted with laughter.

Secretary of Defense Harold Brown made an opening statement and gave a summary of our overall defense posture. He was allowed to speak for thirty minutes without interruption for questions.

I had to leave shortly after he began his testimony. The Governmental Affairs Committee was having its organizational meeting, and it was important for me to be present, particularly since we were to receive officially our subcommittee assignments.

That meeting was also in the Dirksen Building. I entered a room with an entirely different atmosphere from the one I had just left. No members of the press were present. No television klieg lights illuminated the room. The only people who were in the general audience appeared to be staff members or professional lobbyists.

Charles Percy came in and took Dave Durenberger and me to speak with the Chairman of the Committee, Abraham Ribicoff of Connecticut. Ribicoff was wearing an elegantly cut suit. His large, round horn-rimmed glasses give him a sagacious and pleasantly sophisticated appearance. He is a man of gentle manner and strong self-command.

Ribicoff opened the meeting by welcoming the new members and noted how many Senators had sought membership on the Committee—a testament to the quality of the Committee's work. He noted that in 1978, 280 days of hearings were held and 52 bills were passed into law. He and Percy spent the next ten minutes praising the nonpartisan spirit that has prevailed on the Committee in the past and expressing their hope that it would continue in the future. Ribicoff praised Percy's contribution to the success of the Committee's work. Percy reciprocated with glowing flatteries of Ribicoff. The assuaging and stroking of senatorial egos was becoming a familiar liturgical exercise.

Scoop Jackson offered the observation that the United States had become paralyzed with indecision.

"In 1929, it took one year to build the Empire State Building. Today, it would take five years. If oil shipments are cut off, we'll have to turn to coal and nuclear. But we can't even get a decision on an energy policy."

After the members had had a chance to comment on the Committee's budget, it was approved without dissent. I returned to the Armed Services Committee in time to ask Secretary Brown a series of questions.

One of the most difficult tasks for any new legislator is the penetration of the language barrier that looms like a ten-foot-high roll of rusted barbed wire.

I knew that the Armed Services Committee would be different from any previous experience, but I was wholly unprepared for the strange environment I had chosen to enter. Almost immediately I felt as if I had just parachuted into a swamp filled with unusual-looking and -sounding beasts. MIRVs, AWACs, ALCMs, SLBMs, SLCMs and GLCMs . . . the acronyms slithered and slid around in the dense fog, terrifying the innocent and unarmed. Of course, I didn't want to appear ignorant of the code words (after all, Senator, you are presumed to be knowledgeable or you shouldn't be there), and so I started, somewhat tentatively, calling the beasts by name as if they were familiar friends or old enemies. Within a few weeks, and after intense study, I started to hack away with my

newfound verbal machete and suddenly knew the joy of proclaiming that
I intended to wage a fight against the creatures.

"Mr. Secretary [said with great indignation], why did the DOD defer
funding of the AV-8B Harrier aircraft? [Never mind that I had no idea
what the AV-8B aircraft was.] Didn't the Commandant recommend that
it be funded?"

"It is my understanding that the F-18 would not be any more cost-
effective than the purchase of a combination of the advanced Harrier and
the re-engined A-7, and I am told that the flyaway costs of the F-18 are
likely to exceed that of the AV-8B and even approach that of the F-14."

"What is the role of the Marine Corps? You retained their O&M
funds at the '79 level. You have rejected the AV-8B. You have cut out
the LSD-41; and you say the Corps will have an even greater role in the
future?"

I was stalling for time like a fighter against an unknown opponent—
just snapping a few jabs in the first two or three rounds until I became
confident of his weaknesses.

It became clear within a few short weeks that mastery of the technical language is simply the equivalent to a knowledge of the rules—it has
little to do with the merits or the substance of the subject matter, which
involves political, economic and practical decisions.

The Strategic Arms Limitation Agreement (SALT II) that was scheduled to be brought before the Senate for ratification involved the principles of chess as much as those of science. The question that I would have
to confront and resolve was whether the United States would be placed
in a strategically inferior position to the Soviet Union or be *perceived* by
our allies or adversaries as having been placed in an inferior position. In
this regard, it would be important to consider what had happened following our agreement to arms limitation in 1972 (SALT I).

The record was not encouraging. In simple terms, the American people were lulled into thinking we could drop our guard, reduce expenditures on strategic weapons, because we thought arms limitation was to be
interpreted literally and followed spiritually. The Soviets, by contrast,
had expanded their war-making capacity to the limits of, and perhaps
even beyond, the letter of the treaty.

We cancelled production of systems that we thought were either too
expensive (B-1 bomber) or immoral (neutronic weapons). The Soviets
proceeded with the production of a Backfire Bomber which can be used
to attack our European allies or the United States itself. They maintain it

is not their intention to use the bomber for this purpose and expect us to rely upon their declaration. By contrast, we developed a cruise missile on which the Soviets want to place launching restrictions because they do not trust our intentions.

We were told that the Soviets would soon have the capacity to destroy 90 percent of our missiles in a surprise attack and that we would have to take immediate action to ensure the survivability of our land-based ICBMs. The President contends that even if they should destroy 100 percent of our land-based missiles, we could, theoretically, fire our SLBMs (submarine-launched ballistic missiles) into their civilian population centers. A comforting thought. The question becomes, would any President do so—knowing that a third strike would be launched by the Soviets at our major cities, thereby destroying most of our population?

Once the language is mastered, it is clear that the decisions involved for Senators are not scientific. Calculus is not required. The principles of chess become more obvious. Numerical equivalence is not controlling. Strength is determined by mobility and position. Cruise missiles are pawns. Bombers are knights. Intercontinental ballistic missiles are kings. If the Soviets have so positioned themselves that they can checkmate our king without moving against us militarily, the game is over.

If through laxity, self-deception or blundering stupidity, we have allowed ourselves to slip into a position of actual or perceived inferiority, we will never run the risk of countering a first strike at our military sites with a second one aimed at their population—particularly if they have the reserve capacity to destroy all of our major cities. The war is over without a shot being fired. And this is really what the SALT II debate involves. Not scientific calculations, although they are indispensable in producing bombs and their precision delivery, but political and diplomatic decisions involving the willingness to comply with the goal of reducing tensions; the ability to monitor compliance; the perception of the existence of power between the adversaries and their respective allies. Ultimately, it is a combination of poker and chess. The movement of fire-breathing, life-annihilating pawns on a global board of a spinning planet and the hidden intentions behind a blank stare and noncommittal face. I raise you one thousand MIRVs and call. Check. Checkmate.

I returned to my office to meet with some municipal officials from Maine. They were interested in securing a federal grant for the construction of a project that would benefit our local industry. The difficulty of harmonizing the loud drumbeat for a balanced federal budget with the pressure and entreaties to help people whom I had been elected to represent in Washington began to pulsate into a harsh and cacophonous reality. Everyone, it seemed, professed to be a fiscal conservative—"We have got to cut back on federal spending"—and yet everyone reached into the federal pocketbook to pay for local projects. Ideological conservatives and liberal practitioners. It is a schizophrenia that is easily diagnosed and perhaps impossible to treat.

Local officials are interested primarily in promoting growth and new development without adding to their property-tax burden. They develop the fine art of "grantsmanship" to secure federal grants and a "fairer" share of the federal pie. The red ink flows, inflation climbs, but the quest for more federal dollars for worthy projects goes on. It is, perhaps, a Pavlovian condition that has been infused into our psyche since the New Deal days. It is also a prescription for financial disaster.

JANUARY 26, 1979

OUR YOUNGER SON, Chris, missed his bus to school. I drove him and then stopped at my office to pick up my airplane ticket to Maine.

A reporter from the *Washington Star* called just as I left the office and wanted to discuss John Connally's candidacy for the presidency. Three years ago, I managed to get myself deeply embroiled in a controversy with President Ford over the selection of his running mate. My comments managed to enrage Connally and his supporters in Congress. I had neither the time nor the inclination to return the reporter's call. I was determined not to serve as a dull blade to open an old wound if I could possibly avoid it.

My silence proved no haven from the Connally controversy or candidacy. The reporter simply noted that Congressman Railsback and I had cautioned President Ford against choosing Connally as his running mate because of potentially damaging conversations that had been tape-recorded by Richard Nixon. The story was accurate as reported, but it implied a certain contemporaneity to my past statements that I knew would evoke the question of what I had against John Connally. . . .

At 12:30 I arrived at Logan Airport in Boston and prepared to switch to a small commuter airline, Air New England. I was notified that the flight to Augusta had been cancelled because of bad weather. I boarded another flight to Waterville and then had to deplane. I went back to Delta Airlines and managed to secure a seat on its 4 P.M. flight to Portland.

I finally arrived in Portland at 5:30, changed clothes and was driven to Augusta by David Ault, a State Senator, who works for me on a part-time basis in my field office in Lewiston.

There was a crowd of five hundred people in attendance at the Civic Center. They were all enthusiastic supporters of Representative Olympia Snowe and me. Following the banquet, I gave an obligatory fifteen-minute speech, describing my trip to China and my impressions of our stature in the Far East, and thanked them for their loyal support. The next hour and a half I spent speaking individually with nearly everyone in attendance.

I arrived back at the hotel in Portland by midnight.

JANUARY 27, 1979

AT 7:30 A.M. I was standing in line to purchase a ticket back to Washington. I looked over the shoulder of a man in front of me and read the headline of the morning paper. ROCKEFELLER DEAD AT 70. I was surprised at the news, but not struck with grief. Rockefeller had led a full life, one that was always in high gear. He had incredible wealth at his disposal, but he put it to good use—for public purposes and for political ends. He was tough, smart and feisty. "Rocky" fitted his spirit and his voice—a bed of gravel and rough, sharp-edged stone, sliding down a metal chute. He was denied the ultimate position of power: the presidency—the one he wanted most. But he never sank into smallness or meanness in spirit when he reached for and missed it.

I thought of Robert T. Ingersoll, who said, "Let us suck this orange of life dry, so that when death does come, we can politely say to him, 'You are welcome to the peelings. What little there was, we have enjoyed.' "

I felt sorrow only in the sense that a large star had blinked out; a dynamic and forceful personality had slipped into darkness.

I have a photograph of Nelson Rockefeller on the wall of my den. He is returning an obscene gesture to a heckler. There is a glee on his face that says he had been waiting a lifetime to return just one of the insults, verbal abuses, and indignities that every politician endures as part of the purchase price of public office.

One time, I had to present him with a painting by Bill Moise, one of Maine's outstanding artists. While we were posing for photographs that could be sent to Moise and the local papers, I asked him to sign a copy of the photograph I had obtained of him. He did not indulge in the usual "Best Wishes" or "To a Good Guy" squibs. He just looked at me, winked and signed it "Rocky!"

JANUARY 29, 1979

AT 8 P.M. I left for the Kennedy Center to attend the formal reception for Teng Hsiao-ping, who was visiting the United States for one week. Diane was starting to come down with the flu and decided to stay home.

When I arrived at the Kennedy Center, I walked through the glare of the television klieg lights with Congressman G. V. "Sonny" Montgomery of Mississippi. I was looking to see if there was someone I recognized so that I might give him or her my extra ticket. A journalist I knew said, "Why don't you just walk out into the crowd and give your extra ticket away at random and show what a Senator of the people you really are?"

He was kidding, of course. There had been an incident earlier in the day when two people with press credentials had disrupted the official exchange of salutations between Teng and Carter at the White House. It would have posed a security risk for me to have given away Diane's ticket to a stranger.

I spotted a former secretary of mine who worked part time at the Kennedy Center and asked her to arrange for someone to use the ticket.

The President was nearly a half hour late in arriving. As I sat there, I scanned the magnificent three-tiered room, with red satin walls, posh red carpeting and soft seats, a ceiling dramatically set off with a cluster of lights that resembled a sunburst or the brilliant explosion of a July Fourth rocket. The people present were Washington's and New York's elite. The men were dressed in tuxedos. The women were elegant in long dresses, their necks draped with jewels. The room was pervaded by a sense of power and wealth. The president of Time Inc., the president of RCA, the chairwoman of NBC, members of the Cabinet . . .

Just three weeks ago, I was sitting in a small, sparse room in China watching the Peking Opera. The men and women were not members of any elite class. They were all workers, dressed exactly alike in heavy layers of clothes—the same ones they wore during the day. The "Opera

House'' there reminded me of an old, run-down movie house with hard chairs, their wooden backs chipped away with use.

The performance finally started at 9:30. The program had been designed to provide a historical and cultural cross-section of the performing arts in America. The artists included jazz pianist Eubie Blake, classical pianist Rudolf Serkin, folksinger John Denver, the Robert Joffrey Ballet Company and the Harlem Globetrotters.

The highlight of the evening occurred when Carter and Teng came to the center of the stage with the performers during the grand finale. The four-foot eleven-inch Teng stood next to the center of the Harlem Globetrotters, who towered nearly two feet above him. Teng's jaw hung open in amazement as he leaned back and gazed at the human skyscraper. Teng proved to be the biggest crowd pleaser of the evening.

I stopped by a reception that was held after the performance. Just as I was leaving, I ran into author Theodore White, who was talking with Ed Muskie. White was in a lighthearted mood and tossed us a bouquet.

"Maine has the most outstanding delegation in the Senate," he said. Then with a smile, he added, "Well, New York, with Javits and Moynihan, is pretty outstanding too. Seriously, Ed, I'm quite impressed with the talent in the Senate—these young bastards are really good."

"Can I quote you on that?" I asked.

"All I heard him say was 'young bastards,' " Muskie bantered.

Then White turned somewhat pensive. He noted that a lot of important men were dying in the month of January each year—Chou En-lai among them.

Muskie nodded in agreement. "Yes, Phil Hart [former Senator from Michigan], Hubert Humphrey and now Nelson Rockefeller."

There was a momentary silence and sadness between two friends who knew that other members of their generation would soon be moving inexorably into the obituary columns of the national newspapers.

JANUARY 30, 1979

AT NOON, a luncheon was held in the Senate Caucus Room in honor of Teng Hsiao-ping. It was for Senators only and closed to the press. The floor, however, was thrown open to questions.

Claiborne Pell of Rhode Island asked a question concerning the use of force by China against Taiwan. Another Senator in the rear of the room shouted out to Frank Church, who was chairing the meeting, to "repeat the question in English" (a Chinese interpreter was translating the questions for Teng). No double entendre was intended, but the request provoked a snicker among a number of Senators who thought he was mocking Claiborne's distinctive accent.

Teng fielded the questions with a directness that most American politicians might envy—and avoid.

George McGovern: "The United States made a tragic mistake in Vietnam. Will China intervene in Vietnam?"

Teng: "We do not approve of interference in affairs of another country—but we are opposed to hegemony.

"The Vietnamese, supported by the Soviet Union, are provoking China and escalating tensions. We intend to protect ourselves—safeguard our security and our boundaries. China needs to act appropriately.

"If we allow hegemonists to run rampant without scruple, that will not be beneficial. In interests of world peace and stability, we sometimes may be forced to do something we don't wish to do.

"Chinese are a patient people. We will not just react this way or that. . . ."

Robert Dole: "Are you prepared to stop nuclear testing in the atmosphere in exchange for trade preference?"

Teng: "This was discussed with President Carter. There is no reason for China not to undertake further tests. United States and Soviets have had many atmospheric tests; ours have been small.

"In the future, we will try our very best not to carry out such tests, but can't commit ourselves to it."

Jesse Helms: "Will you renounce force or boycott against Taiwan?"

Teng: "I have answered the question."

Edward Kennedy: "Give your appraisal of the Korean situation."

Teng: "China supports North Korea and a peaceful reunification of Korea. We hope that you will help to bring about a direct dialogue between the North and South.

"Such worries of North Korea launching war are needless. . . ."

I returned to an Armed Services Committee meeting to express my interest to the witnesses about the need to preserve Loring Air Force Base in northern Maine at its present strength.

Later, I attended a Republican Policy Committee meeting that had been called for the purpose of setting an agenda for policy initiatives to be taken in the Ninety-sixth Congress. Everyone looked tired. It was another meeting in a long day, and yet the members sustained a certain dogged drive to get our party organized and moving on issues.

At 6, a reception was being held in the Caucus Room of the Cannon House Office Building by the National Association of Chain Drug Stores. Several constituents from Maine were there, so I stopped by.

JANUARY 31, 1979

SENATOR TED STEVENS of Alaska invited me to attend an "Off the Record Club" dinner being held at the International Club in downtown Washington. The Club consisted of the members of the Washington press corps. Stevens wanted to give the new members of the Senate as much exposure as possible to the reporters who would be analyzing, commenting on or criticizing our daily deliberations.

Each of us in attendance was called upon to give a two-minute speech and then was asked questions on current issues by the reporters. What do you propose to do to combat inflation? Are Republicans unfairly exploiting single-issue constituencies? Do you support a constitutional amendment requiring a balanced federal budget? Who will be the Republican nominee for President? Who is your choice? . . .

Although the Club titles itself "Off the Record," I discovered that our comments are "on the record" unless we specified otherwise.

CHAPTER 5

FEBRUARY 1, 1979

My FIRST ACT of business today was a matter of high priority: I had to take my car to a garage near Capitol Hill. I own a 1969 Porsche that, when washed and polished, looks as bright and beautiful as a daffodil blossom. It happens, unfortunately, to suffer some congenital deficiencies that require it to be hospitalized every third week of the month. I have a mechanic friend named Clarence Davis. He specializes in the repair of German automobiles and qualifies as a genius. I call him "Dr. D." Equal to his skill is his honor: He doesn't charge unless he fixes the problem. In Washington, sooner will a camel pass through the eye of a needle than an auto mechanic charge a fair fee for his service and guarantee his work. According to one investigative reporter, "Dr. D." is the only person who calls my office and doesn't get put on hold.

I arrived at the Russell Senate Office Building to listen to testimony concerning a report on our nuclear forces. The Undersecretary of Defense for Research and Development, William J. Perry, was the principal witness. He is an impressive man—knowledgeable, direct and straight-forward in his answers.

For the first time I began to feel comfortable with the military jargon, the aircraft, the acronyms and arcane complexities of our national defense system. A good deal of time was devoted to SALT, first- and second-strike capabilities, launch on warning, launch under attack, SLBMs, ALCMs, ALBM, MX, hard silos, soft targets . . .

I had tried to develop a line of questions independent of the ones that had been prepared by the Committee staff. It was important to gain their respect on my own merits and not simply parrot their questions. When you do independent thinking on a committee, the staff cannot afford to take you for granted. It serves to keep them on their toes. It also gives them incentive to dig a little deeper in their research to make sure that you are fully briefed. It becomes a mutually reinforcing and beneficial relationship. I want to continue to expand my knowledge, and the committee staff members want to see that my appetite is well fed with their considerable expertise.

At noon, a group from the Reverend Sun Myung Moon's church gathered in my office to protest Senator Bob Dole's investigation into the activities of religious cults. The murder of Congressman Leo Ryan and the massacre at Jonestown had produced a public outcry for something to be done about the fanaticism practiced by some of the extreme sects.

The outcry was not loud or long enough. Church groups across the country denounced the Senate hearings as a witch-hunt and warned that if the government could investigate the Moonies or the Hare Krishnas, Methodists might be next on the list.

So the fringe groups had wrapped themselves up in the First Amendment and joined hands with the established conventional religious organizations and cried that the Senate would burn them all at the stake.

Dole's hearings were squelched almost immediately. Jonestown would form a large bloodstain on our history books and nothing would be done to prevent other madmen from stealing the property and souls of their dispossessed followers.

The words flashed across our television screens: "Members of the American Agricultural Movement are heading for Washington on tractors and in trucks. They will camp on the outskirts of Washington and then head for the nation's capital on Monday morning to voice their complaints to Congress and renew their demand for 100% parity. Motorists should plan to leave for work early."

It sounded as if we were about to suffer an attack from alien forces. They were U.S. citizens who feed us and a large part of the world, but tomorrow they were coming as enemies of order and civility.

Washington is a city for demonstrations. In the Sixties, there were massive civil rights marches, waves of black and white people filling the Mall in a swaying, singing mass of humanity right up to the steps of the

Lincoln Memorial. In the Seventies, the anti–Vietnam war protesters came—long-haired, T-shirted, bearded, beaded, angry, and morally outraged. There was much of middle-class America out there demonstrating and marching, too. The parents of sons who had died, college professors, senior citizens. But the mind's eye is not good at retaining detail. General images remain, somewhat blurred and out of focus.

In 1978, the farmers took to the streets to demonstrate their anger. They stayed for weeks, walking in groups of ten or fifteen into Congressmen's offices, demanding meetings, answers and commitments. They left in early spring with little to show for their anger or their efforts. Inflation was killing their farms with the deadly deliberateness of a locust storm. There was no spray or insecticide available for this plague. They were "buying retail, selling wholesale," and nothing was available to bring their crops back or their profits up.

In 1979, they came back to plead their case again—only this time they were more militant, angry, arrogant, and spoiling for a confrontation. They were dressed in blue jeans, jackets, and baseball caps—not their working caps, but new and crisp ones that they saved for dress occasions. Some were wearing high-heeled boots, carrying cameras. Others wore cowboy hats. They were leather-faced and ruddy, burly and wiry. Their wives were dressed in slacks or jeans and wool-lined jackets.

The problem was that they had miscalculated the mood of the country and the Congress. There was little sympathy for their affliction. Inflation was hitting everyone: oil and gas prices were rising daily; a moderately priced pair of shoes cost $20 to $30. The prices of food in the supermarkets (most consumers do not sort out how the distribution of that price increase never reaches the farmer's pocketbook) were producing a counterforce of anger. Boycotts of produce were threatened and carried out. The farmers were demanding parity—the same purchasing power they had had in the years from 1910 to 1914. Everyone wanted that kind of parity. The only realistic way to achieve an increase in purchasing power was to increase the value of the dollar by reducing inflation. The problem is that so many of the farmers are so hard-pressed that they cannot survive the time period or the economic policies that we need to squeeze inflation out of our economy.

It was bad timing and bad strategy on their part. But from the farmers' perspective, they had little to lose. They could not plant or harvest. It was a slow time on the farm, and they needed to ventilate their frustration.

I left early that morning to beat the traffic. I was not entirely successful, as the tractors were already rumbling down the George Washington
Parkway and other major routes into Washington. At one point, I saw a
giant fifteen-foot-high tractor turn suddenly and cross over a cement di-
viding strip and head straight for me as I sat stalled in the traffic. My first
thought was, My God, he must have spotted my green license plate [bear-
ing a U.S. Senate identification]. I've got to get rid of those plates. My
paranoia was unfounded. The driver was evidently getting impatient with
the congestion that his brethren were inflicting up ahead and simply decided he wasn't going to wait in line any longer.

As he whipped by me, I relaxed and decided my plates could stay—
at least for the time being.

I should note parenthetically that the benefits of having one's vehicle
identified as that of a Congressman are dubious. Congressional plates
may provide easy access to the parking lots at the airport or reduce the
risk of being towed away in downtown Washington, but they also serve
as a red flag to citizens who happen to be in a bullish frame of mind.

On one occasion, I returned to the airport to find someone had broken into my car and turned on my headlights, draining the battery.

On another occasion, I returned from a long weekend in Maine to
discover that some creative soul had thought my yellow sports car needed
a splash of red and had taken a can of spray paint to it with the zest of an
Abstract Expressionist.

Then there was the occasion one morning, while I was driving into
the office, when I had apparently cut in front of a lady and exceeded the
speed limit. Several days later, I found a four-page letter on my desk
accusing me of forsaking the ideals of the nation, destroying the trust and
admiration I had gained from some people during the impeachment proceedings before the House Judiciary Committee, and generally contributing to the cynicism that was spreading across the country.

Recently, I was stopped at a red light on Connecticut Avenue in the
heart of Washington when a taxi came up and bumped me from behind. I
turned around and blurted out some expletive and then turned to watch
for the changing light. The driver proceeded to put his bumper onto the
rear of my car and push me through the intersection. I stepped on the
accelerator and roared around the corner and jumped out of the car to see
who this madman was. I was prepared to commit mayhem!

I saw an old man wearing a soiled T-shirt slouched over the steering
wheel of his cab. He raised his fist in an angry gesture and pulled out

around me and sped off. My blood was gurgling. I was angry with the cabdriver—but obviously not as angry as he was with me as a symbol of the government. The green license plate turned red as it was refracted through the lens of his eye. At one time (I am told) the government used to be seen as a friend of the people, dedicated to solving human problems and reducing poverty and blight. The people responded during World War II and worked in a spirit of partnership right through the administrations of Truman, Eisenhower and Kennedy. But something has snapped. The blood vessels and connective tissue of mutual respect have ruptured, and no clotting agents appear to be available or at work. The government is now seen as an enemy of the people whose taxes support it—bloated, turgid, wasteful, insensitive, and contemptuous of those it is supposed to serve.

Official Washington, it seems, has developed a reciprocal kind of contempt. It likes to compile statistical information: wholesale prices, discount rates, inflation trends, housing starts, investment and productive capacities—all seasonally adjusted, of course. Figures can be extrapolated with the latest mini-computers so as to forecast a future that will produce a euphoric or ominous mood for the month. What Washington does not like to do is deal with people in the flesh. Once those who pay the taxes to support official Washington shuck their statistical shells, they are seen as an inconvenience and as a nuisance. Such was the mood and attitude that greeted the members of the farm community when they arrived in Washington.

The farmers caused havoc that day, blocking traffic for miles, confronting motorists and riot-outfitted policemen. Several fights broke out. A number of them were arrested.

That evening they parked hundreds of their vehicles on the grounds of the Mall, which faces the West Front of the Capitol. In the morning, they were taken by surprise. The police had surrounded their tractors with buses and police cars, and prevented any vehicles from being moved. The farmers were furious, but foiled. So they directed verbal anger at the police and stormed up the Hill to see their representatives.

The reception they received varied, depending upon what states they were from and how many members were in the ranks. One Senator, seeing a horde gathering on the horizon, drove a tractor himself that morning. Those from farming states (or those who had presidential aspirations) had signs on their doors: FARMERS WELCOME HERE.

It reminded me of the signs I had seen in stores in certain parts of

Maine: WE ACCEPT CANADIAN MONEY. The farmers were foreigners in their own land.

FEBRUARY 7, 1979

TODAY, with several other Republican Senators, I was scheduled to meet with President Carter for breakfast at the White House. I was not excited about the meeting and was troubled by my own indifference. I went out of a sense of obligation rather than with enthusiasm at the prospect of breaking bread with the President of the United States and exchanging views on domestic and global problems. I feared that I was becoming jaded or irreverent.

Three Presidents had occupied the White House during my three terms in the House: Richard Nixon, Gerald Ford and Jimmy Carter. I had not been on close terms with any of them.

My only intimate contact with Richard Nixon had occurred shortly after the "fire storm" had erupted and impeachment resolutions had been filed against him. A young lady from Maine had won the title of Miss Teenage America, and her sponsor had prevailed upon me to arrange for her to meet President Nixon personally.

I was surprised when the President's appointments secretary granted the request.

He was dressed in a dark suit with a stiff-collared white shirt, and had a high polish on his black shoes. He seemed uncomfortable, almost awkward, in his conversation with the young lady. I am not exactly a Dale Carnegie graduate in social diplomacy and contributed to the tension by remaining silent most of the time.

Finally, he asked, "Well, young lady, what exactly do you get to do with the title that you have won? Will you be traveling?"

"Yes, Mr. President. Well, I was supposed to go to the Mideast, but because of the trouble there, my parents don't think it would be safe for me. So I guess I won't be going there."

President Nixon stiffened visibly. For the first time, he expressed a genuine interest in the meeting. He got up from behind his large mahogany desk in the Oval Office and said, "Oh, come, now. Don't worry— there's no danger in the Mideast. Your parents don't have to worry about your safety."

I wondered if I was being given a scoop on some new peace agreement that was about to be signed. The excitement of the thought quickly evaporated.

"Besides," the President continued in a melancholic and more measured tone which prompted me to look directly at him, "even if it is dangerous, that doesn't mean you shouldn't go. After all, sometimes it's necessary to look into the face of danger, meet it head on. It builds character. . . ."

Nixon was no longer looking at the young lady or at me. He was staring out the window, slipping into a soliloquy as if he were completely alone. It was a long, eerie moment. Then, suddenly, he turned back to us, as if he had heard a finger snap in his mind, made some small talk, reached into a drawer and gave the girl some presidential gifts.

We had spent about twenty-five minutes alone with the President. The young lady was elated with the experience. I was shaken by it.

Several weeks later, one of the weekly newsmagazines ran a story suggesting that Nixon was starting to crack under the pressure of Watergate, that he had been seen having two or three martinis at a state function and was starting to slur his words, and that he had been observed having difficulty replacing the cap on his pen.

After the story ran, a reporter from the magazine asked me if I had seen anything unusual in Nixon's actions recently. I ducked the question.

"I don't know him well enough to know what is usual or unusual. But I think I would probably slur *my* words after two martinis. And what is so strange about fumbling to put a cap on a pen? You know, the press has a capacity to generate enough external pressure to produce the very signs of inner emotional instability, a verbal slip or a physical lapse, and then turn and write about it, thereby fulfilling its own prophecies."

As a member of the House Judiciary Committee, I was going to have to pass judgment on Richard Nixon's conduct in office. I didn't want to have to pass judgment on his inner turmoil as well.

Other than for social functions, I went to the White House on only two occasions when Gerald Ford was President: once to ask him to allow a Maine company to compete for a government contract on equal terms with the Belgian government; the other time, when Ford wanted me to change a vote that I had cast against one of his energy proposals.

While President Ford was always openly friendly to me, I knew that

I was not on good terms with him. He liked team players, loyal soldiers, and I clearly did not conform to the mold.

My first breach of the rules came when Gerald Ford appeared before the House Judiciary Committee during confirmation proceedings for Vice President under the Twenty-fifth Amendment. I thought that the Republican members were taking the proceedings too lightly. They knew Ford from his long years in the House and as the Minority Leader. They liked him and trusted him and had no desire to press him on any serious issues beyond his age, citizenship, education and law practice. Several Democratic members were pursuing his ill-conceived attempt to impeach Justice William O. Douglas and his personal finances, but their attacks smacked of political partisanship and carried very little weight.

When my turn came to ask the nominee questions, I inquired as to what he thought about the reports that the Nixon Administration had offered the FBI directorship to Judge Matthew Byrne while he was still presiding over the Daniel Ellsberg trial. He dismissed that as a case of bad judgment and then added, "Actually, it was not a promotion, but a demotion."

It was a good throwaway line and provoked general laughter throughout the hearing room. We were operating under a five-minute rule for each member of the Committee, and I was unable to follow up on the answer, since I had several other questions to which I wanted responses.

The next day, I proceeded to give a lecture on the subject of ethics.

"In 1968, at a Lincoln Day speech, you [Ford] made a statement that 'Without truth in government'—this was in reference to the Johnson Administration at that time—'without truth in government, there can be no confidence in government. Without confidence in government, the nation finds itself in great peril.'

"I believe that statement is as relevant today as it was in 1968, and I raise it because yesterday when I inquired about the ethical and legal ramifications of inviting the presiding judge of the Ellsberg trial out to San Clemente, you indicated that at the very least there was a lack of discretion and perhaps poor judgment. . . . I appreciate the note of levity that you injected in considering the FBI directorship as a demotion rather than a promotion, but I refer to that incident because I would like to express my own reaction to this: that it is one of the most singularly destructive acts of the judicial process that I can think of, because I think it was calculated to influence the impartiality and neutrality of the presiding judge in one of the most historic cases of the decade. I think it is important to state that the Administration officials who secretly met with a judge to find out if he was interested in joining a law-enforcement team while that team was prosecuting a case before that very judge violated our fundamental notions of due process. I think it would have been reversed on due process alone, and I think you share that view. It brought to my mind yesterday another question.

"Several years ago, John Mitchell stated, 'Watch what we do and not what we say.'

"Taking it at face value, many of us accepted that statement as a paraphrase of the quote 'Deeds often speak louder than words.' But over the years it has come to be viewed by many as a rather cynical expression of calculated duplicity, that our deeds are going to be, indeed, different from our words, and I think this is perhaps the frustration that I feel, that many people in Congress feel, and I know many millions of American people feel, that there seems to be a great disparity between what we profess and what we practice.

"I just want to say that one of the strongest consolations I have is that we have in you a man who does believe in the rule of law, and I am satisfied from my experience with you and what I have heard today and yesterday, and reading over your records, that these activities will never take place with you as Vice President or as President of the United States."

My colleagues were aghast. "Who in hell does he think he is?" "What's he trying to prove?" In retrospect, I think they were justifiably outraged with me. It was not so much what I said, but the manner in which I said it. I was too strident, too self-righteous, too eager to lecture the leader of our party, the next Vice President of the United States, possibly the next President. I was flaunting my disrespect for the rules of the game and team membership.

I didn't consider myself a maverick, but that's the label with which I was quickly smacked. Reputations are made quickly in politics and are not easily erased. . . .

When President Carter came into the Cabinet Room, I had every intention of just listening to him or possibly offering a few comments if called upon. He had been to Maine on two occasions in the previous year to campaign for my opponent and had sent nearly every member of his family and his Cabinet to help as well. I wanted to demonstrate that there was no personal animosity on my part. It didn't work out that way.

As he entered, I noticed now much smaller he is than he appears on television. He walks with his head and shoulders flexed slightly forward, which gives him an even smaller appearance. Television is a deceptive medium. Those tight zoom-in close-ups of the President's face give him the appearance of having a much larger frame. I suffer from a similar misperception. I am a sliver under six feet and weigh 170 pounds, and yet when meeting people for the first time, I am greeted in a somewhat re-proachful fashion: "Gee, I didn't realize you were so short. You look much bigger on television."

Carter sat down almost directly across from me. He is a no-nonsense man and dispenses with small talk quickly. "Thad [Cochran of Missis-sippi], would you please give the blessing."

The President then immediately launched into a discussion as we were eating breakfast. He focused initially upon his domestic programs that were designed to provide some measure of restraint to the exponen-tial growth of government: a mandatory cost-containment program for hospitals; a revision of the Social Security Disability Act, the costs of which were threatening to bankrupt the so-called Social Security Trust Fund; then a wage-insurance program to protect those workers who agreed not to exceed a 7 percent guideline in their wage demands.*

On the international front, SALT was the pre-eminent issue. He said it was beneficial to the United States, that a rejection would be disastrous for us and our allies, and that it would give the Soviet Union a tactical advantage in public relations: "Here's a country that ostensibly is com-mitted to a reduction of tensions and reduction in the risk of nuclear holocaust and yet the Soviet Union has approved a SALT treaty and the United States has rejected it."

The President went on to say that the breakfast meeting was an open invitation for us to call on him personally at any time by phone or through a memo and he would guarantee that he would get back to us in no more than twenty-four hours certainly, and usually within the hour.

Vice President Mondale injected at this point that as Senators we have access to the top levels of the Cabinet. "For example, if you have a problem with foreign policy, call Vance. Or a question about defense, call Brown. You should make use of this opportunity which you probably didn't have as Representatives." Mondale also recommended that we

* This proposal never gained the support of Congress. The potential liability to the federal treasury in the event inflation soared above 7 percent for any sustained period was simply too great. Congressional skepticism proved well founded as the inflation rate soared near 20 percent in 1980.

travel as much as possible so that we would have a better appreciation of the nature of the problems involved in our policy debates on the Senate floor. "You should take advantage of going to the United Nations, not just to sit as a tourist, but as an actual participant in various debates that are going on, even as an aide to Andrew Young. Go to Geneva to take part in the dialogue and negotiations going on with SALT."

Carter then picked up the theme and said that we should contact Charles Schultze on economic matters. "He might not have been available to House members unless you were part of the leadership, but he is available to you as Senators."

Carter went on to say, "You should not think that your party affiliation is any matter of concern to me. . . . You are the principal avenues to my constituents in Mississippi, Minnesota, Maine, Wyoming. . . . You'll find less partisanship in the Senate than you did in the House. . . ."

At the conclusion of his remarks, Nancy Kassebaum raised the subject of farmers—saying that in the farm belt the overwhelming majority of the farmers feel the Administration has been insensitive to their problems. The President responded that the facts simply did not warrant that kind of conclusion and then went on to cite farm income, production capabilities over past years.

Al Simpson of Wyoming asked a question concerning Carter's veto of the beef-import bill and wanted to know whether, if prices went up, the President would open the door to imported red meat. Carter said he had vetoed the bill not because he was opposed to the substance of it, but because it contained some provisions which reduced his flexibility as President; that if the measure were introduced again and eliminated those provisions, he would probably comply with it and sign it.

And so it went, with each member raising issues of personal interest. Finally, John Warner of Virginia inquired about SALT II. The President repeated the point that a rejection of the treaty would be of great damage to the United States, especially with our own allies.

"If you view the past ten or fifteen years, the United States has done rather well as far as foreign policy is concerned. With respect to India, the People's Republic of China, and Japan, we have better relations today than do the Soviets. The ASEAN nations are strongly supportive of the United States; the North Koreans are looking to China rather than to the Soviet Union. In Australia and New Zealand we have allies. The Philippines have recently signed a new base agreement. In Indonesia we have made great progress, and India is now coming toward us. Egypt is now aligned with the United States, and even Syria and Iraq seem to be more sensitive to the need to have greater relations with the United States. Angola and Mozambique now want relations with us.

"The Soviets are an atheistic and racist country, and they may secure temporary advantages through military means. But United States can compete economically and ideologically. . . ."

I was dismayed at how bright the President had painted his foreign-policy initiatives and accomplishments.

"Mr. President," I said, "the perception of power is just as important as the possession of power. As has been suggested here this morning, I have been doing some traveling, and I recently came back from a trip to the Far East. I found that many of those countries look upon the United States as a helpless giant that is caught up in the strings of indecision and intellectual paralysis. They see the dollar in decline, no consensus on how to curb inflation or reduce our dependence on oil imports, and believe that we are sliding into military inferiority. We are now in the position of having a President possibly faced with a decision of whether or not to retaliate against a first strike by targeting our missiles at civilian populations in the Soviet Union knowing that two-thirds of the Soviet missile capability could then be fired upon our major population areas.* In essence, this means that the war would be over without a shot having been fired because we have allowed ourselves to fall into a position of inferiority. This inferiority was brought about by SALT I, because we were lulled into believing that we could reduce our defense spending when in fact the Soviets were increasing theirs even beyond the spirit of the treaty. And there is a danger now that under SALT II, people would be very reluctant to support appropriations for further funding of our strategic forces, which will be indispensable with or without a SALT II treaty. So the danger is that we will be unable to fund, for example, the MX missile system, which will cost in the neighborhood of $30 to 40 billion."

The President responded very emotionally to my statements and then went on to a long recitation of how the United States would benefit from a SALT II treaty, that this would curb the number of missiles that the Soviets had. I hesitated momentarily, but finally decided to interrupt him

* On July 25, 1980, President Carter signed Presidential Directive #59, clarifying the evolution of our strategic targeting policy. This policy provides the President with a greater range of targeting options (including military targets) in response to a Soviet nuclear attack on the United States.

to point out that there would be no restriction upon the number of missiles developed by the Soviets—only upon their actual deployment, not upon their production. I regretted that I had chosen to interrupt and correct the President. It was bad manners and poor judgment on my part. He stumbled briefly and then acknowledged that no limitation would be placed upon the number of missiles that could be produced. Then, in a weak, almost forlorn, voice he expressed his concern that Republicans might try to politicize the SALT debate.

"My God," the President said. "There are times to be partisan, but this is not one of them. The security of our country is at stake."

The meeting ended moments later. On the way out, one member turned to me and said, "Man, you really scissored his trousers. He just doesn't have his facts straight on SALT."

The very thing I had wanted to avoid had in fact occurred—the appearance of a confrontation. Obviously, I hadn't been concerned enough, or else I would have remained silent.

Several days later, I received a call from syndicated columnist Robert Novak. He is known in journalists' circles as the "Prince of Darkness"—because of his dark mien and the cloud of foreboding that always seems to hang over his head. At a political roast held in his honor, one of his friends stated, half-jokingly, to a reporter, "You scratch the surface of evil and what you find underneath is . . . evil."

"Senator Cohen, my sources tell me that you really gave the President a tough time recently."

"No," I answered. "I think your sources are wrong. We had a frank exchange of views. . . ."

I was teasing Novak. I have always been on good terms with him. But when he is on a story, he doesn't tolerate playfulness or sidestepping.

"Well, I talked to some of your colleagues, and as I understand it, President Carter was stung by some of the things you said. In fact, he was visibly angry. Are you saying that this information is incorrect?"

I decided to relate my account of what had taken place and tried to water down the impression of any confrontation with the President.

The story ran a few days later in *The Washington Post*.

"It was first-term Republican senators fresh from taking their oath of office who, over breakfast at the White House last week, dared tell Jimmy Carter that the emperor has no clothes. . . ."

FEBRUARY 8, 1979

I ATTENDED a breakfast meeting with Henry Kissinger at the Capitol. Kissinger was dressed in a dark gray three-piece suit. He wore a stiffly starched white shirt and a red striped tie. He looked trimmer than I had seen him in the past.

He tried initially to be lighthearted in greeting a number of Senators. But it was apparent that the weight of Nelson Rockefeller's death hung heavy on his spirits.

Following breakfast, he outlined the geopolitical considerations that he believed should be taken into account as we pondered the SALT II treaty. He noted that the Carter Administration had spent two and a half years negotiating a position that was worse than the one it had inherited.

"I cannot accept the proposition that SALT II is a significant improvement in our position," Kissinger said. "I cannot accept the statement that SALT II is a move toward peace under the current circumstances. . . ."

Kissinger was generally sullen and foreboding in his comments. He gave a gloomy prediction of the inevitability of future conflict and crisis and of the inability of the United States to measure up to prevent the kind of instability that he foresees taking place. It was one of the most forceful and dynamic presentations that I had seen Kissinger deliver. His message seemed to strike Henry Bellmon of Oklahoma the hardest. Bellmon requested another meeting as soon as Kissinger returned from Acapulco, where he was going for the next month to work on his book. A tentative date was set for March 8.

We adjourned by 9:30, and I left to attend a Governmental Affairs Committee hearing in order to question Administration witnesses on their proposal to create a separate Department of Education.

At 1:30, a group of presidential classroom scholars came to my office for a photo-taking session. At 2 I recorded my weekly radio show; then I returned to my office to meet with an architect from Maine who was outlining a development project for the downtown renewal of a city which would, of course, require federal funding.

I returned calls to members of the press who wanted my comments on the possibility of gas rationing by June, and my position on SALT II. I finished signing my mail for the day and arrived home by 7:30.

CHAPTER 6

THE SENATE CHAMBER IS routinely filled with formal flatteries which ring rather hollow through overuse. Almost every sentence is punctuated with an unctuous "my able colleague from Massachusetts," "my good friend from Florida," "the distinguished gentlelady from Kansas". . .

But Congress has never been a place of quiet gentility. In the early years of our Republic, unbridled passions erupted into deadly violence. I am reminded that in 1839, Representative Jonathan Cilley of Maine was shot and killed in a duel by William Graves of Kentucky. Congress, its wisdom coming quickly on the wings of hindsight, adopted an antidueling measure.

In 1856, Senator Charles Sumner of Massachusetts was attacked by Representative Preston Brooks of South Carolina, who came into the Senate Chamber after debate had concluded for the day and beat him over the head with a heavy cane. It took Sumner more than three years to recover from the assault. The Massachusetts Senator was known for his acid tongue, once having referred to a colleague as a "noisome, squat and nameless animal, who, switching his tail, filled the Senate with an offensive odor." Little wonder that he was capable of inciting rage.

In 1938, Tennessee Senator Kenneth McKellar charged at Royal Copeland of New York with a Bowie knife. Copeland apparently was as fleet of foot as he was of tongue and avoided a premature termination of his career as a Senator.

Once at the turn of the century, there was a brawl on the Senate floor between John McLaurin and "Pitchfork Ben" Tillman (Tillman had only his nickname in hand at the time), both of whom were from South Carolina.

And of course, many still remember the time in 1964 when vigorous Strom Thurmond of South Carolina and Ralph Yarborough of Texas grappled outside a Senate committee room as their bitter differences over civil rights boiled over into fisticuffs.

Such outbursts appear to be a thing of the past, consigned to folklore and fantasy of the rougher and rawer times of our history. But if physical confrontation has been subdued by a superior sense of civility, it does not follow that senatorial tempers or political stakes are any less intense, for politics is essentially concerned with power—who holds it, who uses it and who benefits from its use. It can be held by the large- or small-minded, and used in magnanimous or mean-spirited ways. Much depends upon the personality of the person possessing it. The stakes usually determine how it will be exercised. Sometimes it falls with the heavy thud of the guillotine blade. On other occasions, you can detect only the faint whip and whisper of the sword as it is about to slice into flesh. It takes longer in the latter case to know that a fatal wound has been inflicted.

On February 5, 1979, I received a call from the Minority Leader's office. "How would you like to do us a favor?"

"If I can I will," I replied. I had been well treated by the Republican leadership. I had received good committee assignments and had been selected to make the trip to China. I certainly was prepared to reciprocate.

"Would you be willing to serve on the Select Committee for Indian Affairs?"

"Of course—but why?" I really did not want an extra committee assignment. I was a member of the Armed Services Committee, and the SALT deliberation would be extremely time-consuming. I was named the ranking member of a new Subcommittee on Governmental Affairs which would have wide latitude in investigating areas of government regulation. I was intent on making the Aging Committee a very active focal point of national concern. There were not enough hours now. . . .

"It seems that the Democratic leadership is upset with us for interfering with their intraparty affairs. Our two members have pledged to support a junior member of the Indian Affairs Committee over the current senior ranking member.* If we do this, it will cost us positions on the Aging and Intelligence Committees which we want very much."

* Ordinarily, the members of the Republican minority do not cast votes for the selection of the chairmen of the individual committees.

"So if I agree to serve on the committee to replace another Republican member, you just want me to stay out of Democratic politics and leave them to their own devices?"

"Right."

"Okay, I accept. But can I get off after it's all over?"

"Sure, if you want to."

I hung up the phone and didn't give the conversation much more thought until later that evening when the dimensions of the problem became much clearer to me. I had learned that certain Indian advocates and spokesmen had been working behind the scenes to encourage a Senator from the West who represented a significant Indian population to challenge the Senator who was next in line for the chairmanship. He had quietly secured pledges from two Republicans who did not really care who was chairman and who were persuaded by his interest in the subject matter and the size of his Indian constituency.

When word of the subversion of the seniority system finally reached the Senate Majority Leader's ears, he responded by threatening to cut out two positions that the Republican leadership wanted to fill with key people on our side. We had unwittingly shot ourselves in the foot and had to come up with a tourniquet to stanch the flow of our self-interest. I was to be the tourniquet.

While it did not occur to me initially, my acceptance of the position suited a special interest of my own. Not only would I become the ranking minority member of the Committee, and thereby acquire the additional staff that goes with the position, but I also would be in a position to help Maine, which had been confronted with a major lawsuit by two Indian tribes. While a settlement was being negotiated, congressional action would be necessary to implement the settlement and appropriate the dollars. The case would be setting a very significant precedent for the others that were likely to be filed.

Thus, I would be in a unique position to initiate a review of the entire question surrounding one of the most perplexing and emotional areas of the law—the rights of Indian tribes against the states and federal government.

It took nearly twenty-four hours before the Senator who aspired to the chairmanship realized what had happened.

I spoke with him on the Senate floor the next day.

"Bill, how are you going to vote on the chairmanship?" he asked.

"I'm not. I think that is a matter for the Democratic majority to decide. I don't think Republicans should interfere."

"So, if a vote is taken, what will you do?"

"Abstain."

He accepted my words and his defeat graciously. I was impressed with his restraint and almost smiling acknowledgement that his plans had been undone, that it was sometimes inevitable in his chosen career.

As he sauntered off the Senate floor, I thought of the old expression of making sure not to turn your head too quickly in politics, lest you find your head in your lap.

I served as a neutral instrument in this particular skirmish. But somewhere in the future, I knew I was bound to hear the whisper of the blade and know the sting of steel on flesh.

CHAPTER 7

FEBRUARY 11, 1979

SIXTEEN YEARS AGO, our elder son was born. Diane and I were living on Beacon Hill in Boston at the time. The apartment was little more than a hovel, and yet more than we could really afford. The bathroom was across the hall from our kitchen door. The toilet had a long chain hanging from an overhead tank. We were living on a budget of $8 a week for food.

Diane's labor pains started coming on the evening of February 10. I hooked up a string to a naked light bulb located in the center of the bedroom so that I would keep checking the clock to find out when the pains were three minutes apart.

At 4:30 A.M. I had to wake neighbors in order to use their phone to call a cab. There was a light snow falling. The flakes fell in silence and covered the grime in the streets with white crystals. The cab drove slowly, and the snow gave way in a soft, crunching sound. As about-to-be parents, we took it as an anointment, a blessing of our first child. . . .

We spent the day preparing for an evening party to celebrate Kevin's birthday. It is almost impossible to grasp what has happened during the flick of a cosmic eyelash. He has sprung from seed to a young man—long, muscular, handsome. His shadow stretches beyond mine in the afternoon sun. He is on the rim of manhood. Two more years and off to college—or possibly to war.

There is serious talk now of reviving the draft in some form to replenish our reserve and Guard units. It sounds so mechanical and harmless. We use language that treats people as fungible units—like grain, wheat, or feed stocks, as if we were simply filling up a storage bin to an acceptable level with exchangeable goods.

Testimony was being presented to the Armed Services Committee which indicated that it might be necessary to return to some sort of lottery or draft. The Joint Chiefs of Staff had stated that at a minimum we should reinstitute peacetime registration and possibly classification of our young men.

As we prepared for the evening celebration, I pondered a question that had recently been nibbling away in a dark corner of my thoughts. I wanted both our sons to serve their country in time of war; but I wondered, What if I should vote to reinstitute registration or eventually the draft and a war broke out in some foreign nation and either one or both of my sons were killed or disabled in fighting a war that we no longer seemed committed to winning—the kind of war we fought in Vietnam, defensive, a holding action, with demilitarized zones that served as a one-way road to eternity for so many of our young men?

At one time, it was much easier to perceive the reasons for conflict, the values that we were pursuing, the necessity to preserve those values through war. The good guys and the bad guys were readily identifiable in our minds and scheme of things. But future shock has exploded old rules. Our foreign policy (if one could call it a policy) was adjusting daily to shifting international realities and realignments.

The China that had fought us in Korea was now considered to be indispensable to establishing stability in the Far East. The Soviets were backing the Vietnamese in their conquest of Cambodia and warning China not to interfere. Vietnam was seeking diplomatic recognition by the United States. Iran, one of the last bulwarks against Soviet Communism, was in a state of chaos. Saudi Arabia was looking nervously at its vulnerability and America's uncertainty and international paralysis. . . .

There was the prevalent assumption that we were at peace with the world, and thoughts of a conscription in peacetime were unconscionable. But wars were going on, and a poison was seeping deep into the soil of nations and the souls of men around the world.

I pushed these thoughts back into their dark corner and helped prepare our house for an invasion of twenty-three teen-agers. But later that night, after the opening of the presents, the eating of cake, the toasting with champagne, the dancing to disco, after the bubbling voices of the young had faded and the house had grown still in the coolness of a winter night, I watched the shadows of the naked trees shift across the ceiling of our bedroom and wondered whether I would have the blood of my sons on my hands in a cause that could not be identified—or if identified, one that would not be revised out of our history with the stroke of a diplomatic pen.

The loneliness I felt that night was darker and colder than the distance to the nearest star.

CHAPTER 8

IT IS very cold in northern Maine's Aroostook County—the temperature can drop to 30 or 40 degrees below zero, and the average winter snowfall is 162 inches. People are hardy, independent and proud. In Maine, it is known as "The County." I wanted to appear officially there first because it is the most remote part of my state and one of the most supportive. I wanted to assure the people that now that I was a Senator who represented the "South" as well as the "North" I had not forgotten them.

That evening I spoke about my trip to the Orient, what I had observed and said while there, and most importantly, what I believed the people of those countries thought about us. I did not paint a bright picture. I spoke about Iran, Mexico, Saudi Arabia, not to display a rising interest in foreign affairs, but to show how helpless we were becoming in determining our own future and a coherent and comprehensive foreign policy—and what this spelled for our domestic difficulties: inflation, unemployment and rising costs for fuel. I repeated the phrase "This country cannot be led by a question mark. We can no longer afford the luxury of indulging in the comic routine. Who's on first, What's on second, and I dunno is on third. . . ."

A question-and-answer period followed. A very bright and successful businessman in the area asked me to explain why I had called for a suspension of the withdrawal of troops in South Korea. "Exactly what is our purpose and policy in being in Korea? What is our national interest?"

The question did not lend itself to an easy answer.

"I assume that we committed ourselves to defend South Korea," I began, "at a time when we wanted to prevent people in foreign countries from being run over by force and against their will. That policy has changed. The problem now is how to withdraw from Korea—whose economy we have made one of the most dynamic in the world—at a time when the North Koreans are engaged in a massive buildup; when the Soviets are supporting the Vietnamese who are taking over Cambodia; when the Cubans are running throughout Africa without restraint; when we have just terminated our official recognition of Taiwan—without adding to the already deep impression that we are withdrawing from world affairs, that we are a superpower in retreat, that having had our nose bloodied and our soul scarred in Vietnam, we no longer have the will to support those people who are friendly to the United States and dependent upon us."

He was not satisfied with my response. "Yes, but that's a negative. I want a positive explanation as to why we are there."

"Perhaps there is no positive explanation. The domino theory that was so denigrated during the late Sixties and early Seventies is proving to be valid. The dominoes are falling, and we can let the dynamics of unrestrained revolution and force continue its course or we can try to stop the collapse. I agree with the statement that 'We cannot be the world's policeman.' But neither can we allow ourselves to become the prisoner of world events. . . ."

Someone spared the audience further dialogue on this subject. My relief was short-lived. "Will you support a constitutional amendment on the right to life if a majority of the people in this country want it?"

"No," I answered, "constitutional amendments should not be decided by majority sentiment at any given time. That would not influence my judgment."

"Will you support the amendment?"

"No."

"Do you think President Carter will compromise on the illegal-alien question in return for Mexican oil?"

The questions continued for forty-five minutes. I could feel my voice start to crack. I had never fully recovered from the attack of laryngitis during the final days of the campaign. I had kept talking and debating right up to election day, even though I was described by one rapier-witted reporter as sounding like "Fa, the Talking Dolphin."

The dinner terminated, mercifully, at 9:30 P.M.

I stayed that evening in the home of friends in the neighboring city of Caribou.

At 6:15 the next morning, I got up to do a little reading and preparation for two press conferences later that morning. After breakfast, I discovered that my Avis rental car did not try hard enough. The sub-zero temperatures killed the battery. I arrived at the airport through the kind services and warmhearted automobile of my host. The plane was late.

At 9:35 A.M. I arrived in Bangor. Winter was escalating its war on man's artifices. The battery of my car in the parking lot had died during the night.

I hailed a cab to my office at the Federal Building. I was running late. I had an appointment with a local rabbi whom I had disappointed while he was in Washington two weeks before by failing to attend a meeting that was important to him. I had been attending the first day of my committee hearings, trying to establish a reputation for diligence and hard work. Through a lack of communication on my part, I had totally ignored a constituent, who was irate with the treatment he had received. I had scheduled a ten-minute meeting with him to try to make amends.

My mother was waiting in my office to say hello. I kissed her and, almost in the same breath, asked her if she could wait until I spoke with my constituent. That is one of the saddest aspects of politics: in the pressure-cooker pace of trying to stay on a tyrannical schedule, wife, children, and parents always take a back seat to constituents. It is a terrible confusion of priorities. You rail against it in the privacy of your thoughts—and openly to your staff. But the battle is always lost—until the day you decide that you've had enough of politics or your constituents decide they've had enough of you. Then a peace comes to the waters that roil inside. A calm that permits you to see the absurdity of what you regarded as so critical to your self-importance. . . .

At 10 A.M., the press conference began.

"Will gas stations close on Sundays?"

"Do you see gas going to a dollar a gallon? When?"

"How will your position on the Indian Affairs Committee help the State of Maine?"

"Do you think the federal government should maintain a guardian–ward relationship with Indian tribes?"

"What will it take to get your support for a SALT II treaty?"

The questions tumbled out for forty minutes. At the conclusion of the conference, I was handed a note that Delta Airlines had just notified the Civil Aeronautics Board that it intended to terminate service to Presque Isle in accordance with the Airline Deregulation Act of 1978. I notified the press of this latest development (and most recent addition to a long list of bad news for Aroostook County) and said that I wanted to check out the matter before commenting publicly.

One of the members of the press in attendance at the conference was J. Russell Wiggins, a former editor of *The Washington Post*, former Ambassador to the United Nations and current editor and publisher of the *Ellsworth American*—a biweekly newspaper that wins a national award each year for its excellence.

Mr. Wiggins is a man of giant intellect. He is seventy-six years old, robust, vigorous, and possessor of an unbridled energy that consumes you. We correspond periodically on world and domestic affairs. Once I had dinner at his saltwater farm in Brooklin. We concluded the evening by reading poetry from Dylan Thomas and T. S. Eliot to the other dinner guests.

He rode to the airport with me.

"Senator, I agree with what you said about America's failure of will and the danger of allowing the Soviets to develop a devastating first-strike capability. But we are losing sight of the barbarism of nuclear weapons, the immorality of the very notion that we have the capacity to destroy all life on this planet. Somebody has got to take the case to the people all over the world.

"The Soviet society does not allow debate to percolate through to the people. But somehow the message has to get through. Maybe we should build some model cities in the deserts of Africa or in selected spots around the world and set off just one of those bombs. Then take the evidence to people all over the world and ask them if this is what they want. My God, Hiroshima and Nagasaki were mere popguns."

As the plane lifted off and headed for Portland (and another press conference), I thought about Ambassador Wiggins' statement. He was right, of course.

What was missing from the dialogue was the question of the immorality of all nuclear weapons. We had become so mesmerized by science and the siren song of technology that in the name of love of peace, we were embracing the most disease-ridden, destructive lepers in the history of all mankind. We have locked arms with a thermonuclear monster that will blow a cloud of radiation across the world. We have seen that the pollution or smog in Los Angeles or New York or New Jersey or Washington

does not confine its poison to the place of its emanation—it fills the skies
of Montana, Colorado, and Maine. Think if our cloud banks were filled
with radioactive particles that would rain their blistering fire on the wheat
fields of Kansas, the bluegrass of Kentucky, and the cornfields of Nebraska. London would know a different kind of fog. . . .

As the signal was given to fasten our seat belts for landing at Portland, I thought of some notes I had written a few years before and stuffed
into a yellow folder:

Suppose the line clicked dead
and no voices screaming
"Stop, it's a mistake!"
could be fed to foreign ears?

Suppose the heavens
opened up and a rain
of missiles fell on earth
and strung a chain of neutrons
into the horror of every war
and the roar was louder
than the cries of every man
that ever died with a bullet
or bayonet in his throat,

And all the blood that
had ever spilled and stained
the earth was boiled
in one atomic vat?

Suppose the earth
became a ball of sun
and flamed until it
cindered into dust,

And laughter cracked
across the universe
as evil did rejoice?

Would God conclude
that His mistake
was giving man the choice?

CHAPTER 9

FEBRUARY 14, 1979

I TURNED on the television set at 7 A.M. to catch the morning news.

"The American Embassy in Iran has been stormed by Iranian leftists. The Ambassador and seventy Americans were taken into custody. Two Marines were wounded. Latest reports indicate that the Americans have been released and are now safe.*

"The American Ambassador to Afghanistan was murdered last night by unidentified terrorists. . . ."

The full cup of frenzy was being passed to parched lips around the world. The broth was producing a blind malevolence that was curdling the minds of men. The United States, once seen as a powerful ally of Iran, was suddenly the object of intense hatred. The American Ambassador to Iran, William Sullivan, and our embassy personnel were being taken in handcuffed submission as hostages of the revolutionary forces. Our power to react was confined to diplomatic channels. Confrontation was not an option available to us. The image of wild-eyed Iranians storming the gates of the American Embassy in their fury would not be erased easily from the mind's eye of the world. There is no way that we can quantify or assess the impact of a single photograph reprinted on the pages of the world's newspapers and magazines. But the sight of an American helicopter lifting off our soldiers from the rooftop of our em-

---

* Nine months later, Iranian militants overran the American Embassy and took more than sixty Americans as hostages.

bassy in Saigon in 1973 remains a vivid reminder of the loss and limits of
our power in foreign affairs.

"President Carter was awakened during the night and apprised of the
situation in Iran. He is still planning to leave for Mexico. A White House
source says the President can act from Air Force One as well as he can
from the Oval Office. . . ." *

There was not an inflection of irony in the broadcaster's voice as he
read the last statement. None was needed.

The news the following day did not improve. We had issued a strong
protest to the Soviets for their role in the death of Ambassador Adolph
Dubs.

Reports indicated that we were unable to take any action to rescue
the Americans in Iran. We were left to rely upon the Ayatollah Khomeini
to protect their lives.

President Carter received a lukewarm reception in Mexico and some
sharp words from President José López Portillo. President Carter absorbed the public rebuke and tried to inject levity into the meeting by
joking about an incident of Montezuma's Revenge. The levity soured in
the stern public judgment of its inappropriateness.

The Soviet press reported that Americans had inspired and plotted
the takeover of the embassy in Iran so that we would have an excuse to
send troops into Iran. They continue to add insult to outrage.

FEBRUARY 16, 1979

A CAR from the Pentagon arrived at our house at 6:15 A.M. to take me to
Andrews Air Force Base. As I started to put my luggage into the trunk, I
heard a strange hissing noise coming from somewhere under the carport.
It was too dark to see anything. I discovered the source of the noise when
my shoes suddenly became soaked with water. An outside water pipe had
snapped under winter's frigid squeeze. The entire carport was flooded
with water. It was not an auspicious beginning for my trip to Munich,

---

* One year later, President Carter adopted a different strategy against his challenger,
Senator Edward Kennedy. He refused to campaign or leave the White House until the
Americans being held hostage by the Iranians were released.

where I had agreed to meet John Tower for two days of closed-door discussions with defense officials from the NATO (North Atlantic Treaty Organization) nations.

At 7:52, a presidential support plane carrying Stanley R. Resor, Undersecretary of Defense for Policy, and me lifted off. Four hours later, I received word through a member of the flight crew that Ed Muskie had called my Washington office and wanted to speak with me. I returned Muskie's call while I was somewhere over the Atlantic. The voice quality was faint and poor, but I was able to determine that Ed was about to announce to the Maine press a new judicial-selection system for the purpose of picking a new federal judge for Maine. I agreed with the general procedure and said he had my complete support. As a matter of principle, Muskie was absolutely right in his selection system. As a matter of practical fact, I had absolutely no choice in the matter anyway.

At 10 P.M. we arrived at the Hotel Bayerischer Hof in Munich. It was the beginning of Fasching—the German equivalent of our Mardi Gras. The hotel was mobbed with happy people, who filled the restaurants and cocktail lounges. The high cost of living in Munich (or the low value of our dollar) hit our group immediately. Cocktails were $4.50 each.

FEBRUARY 17, 1979

THE MEETING BEGAN at 10 A.M. It was held in a room where three long tables with men sitting on both sides ran perpendicular to the head table. There were opening greetings extended. Each member wore headphones through which the statements could be translated into the appropriate language. There were television cameras from several stations and a balcony behind us where the translators were headquartered.

The purpose of the meeting was to gather together defense-oriented people to meet without pressure or partisanship and to discuss issues in a private and "off the record" manner that enhanced candor—after the television cameras were cleared from the room.

The conferees had their heads bowed over their notes. With their headphones, they looked like somber Martians tilting their antennas periodically.

The opening speaker gave a wandering, sprawling dissertation about the balance of power, SALT II, and so-called "gray area" weapons systems. Each participant had the opportunity to comment. Some present

made speeches; a few made trenchant observations. During the course of
the morning, heads started to nod, attention spans faded.

The faces of the Germans were fascinating. Some were dark, somber-
looking. Others were blond and Nordic. All of them conveyed strength
and confidence. Arrogance is too harsh a word, and coldness stirs the
ashes of accumulated prejudice.

We broke for lunch at 12:15, and then returned to the afternoon
meeting. Congressman Robin Beard of Tennessee picked things up
around 4:30 with a blistering attack on SALT and its weaknesses.

That evening the Deputy Mayor of Munich hosted a dinner in honor
of our delegation.

FEBRUARY 18, 1979

AT 9:45, I arrived at the meeting shortly after Sir John Killeck of Great
Britain started his major presentation. He is a character out of a novel. In
looks, he resembles an Irish wolfhound—tall, angular, strong, high-
browed, prominent nose, white-gray hair and mustache. He is articulate
as only the British can be. A composer, an artist with the English language. Words sing like birds, whole paragraphs take flight and fly in
perfect formation. Thought achieves a perfect clarity of expression. His
art leaves you intimidated and hesitant to step forward.

Shortly before noon, the only member of the American delegation
who had not spoken, I decided to offer a few comments.

"Senator Tower invited me to this meeting because he said this is
where our friends let their hair down and say privately what they cannot
say publicly. . . . Let me venture a few thoughts.

"The United States is not faced with a technological or strategic
problem, but rather a psychological problem. The possession of power is
an important factor in the chess game we call geopolitical strategy. The
perception of power is as important, if not more important, as a factor in
deterring aggression.

"In my judgment, neither the United States nor NATO is currently
perceived as being as powerful as the Soviet Union and its Warsaw Pact
countries. What is most troublesome is that the Administration and our
military officials in their public statements are now citing and stressing
our economic power. But our economic power is fragile and only as
strong as a stable supply of energy. James Schlesinger in a recent article
for *The Washington Star* quoted Bismarck as saying that 'of all the events

that influence history, only one does not change—geography.' The Persian Gulf is our jugular vein, which is becoming increasingly vulnerable, and so with it is our economic power. . . .

"I say this as a preface to the problem of what we say publicly and what we think privately—that is, that the free world is in trouble—not because of a lack of strength but because of a lack of will, a lack of clear-cut policy or one that is at least consistent in application, one that does not cancel weapons systems unilaterally, or order an aircraft carrier to Iran and then cancel it before it ever arrives.

"I say this as a preface to the discussion of SALT because I believe that SALT cannot be considered as an abstract exercise in the pursuit of peace with blinders on, blocking our vision to what is happening around the globe. . . .

"Sir John Killeck said that there is not a quantitative difference between nuclear wars and conventional wars; perhaps even fewer men will be killed than through a war of attrition. But there definitely is a qualitative difference. The possession of nuclear weapons may reduce the possibility of a large-scale non-nuclear war. But a large-scale nuclear war would reduce the likelihood of having a conventional anything that survives.

"We are now talking about building a civil-defense system to match that of the Soviets. What absurdity to think that we can hide in the earth and emerge once the fireballs have burned out! Would we bring our cattle, our hens, our sheep, our fish into these tunnels, these underground arks of cement? Shall we bring two of each kind? And if we did, would we emerge into an atmosphere that was habitable, productive, sustainable? Would the layers of ozone have perished in the holocaust? Surely, if hair spray can destroy our protection against the sun, the clap of atoms splitting into a fire storm would be no more comforting.

"We are embarked upon a course that is predictable, inevitable and irreversible in its consequences: this planet of beauty and plenty being shattered into cinders.

"We are conscience-stricken when we see films or photographs of napalmed babies or the disfigured faces of the survivors of Nagasaki. Then where is the moral outrage now when catastrophe is hiding in a silo less than thirty minutes away, waiting for its fiery birth and our incineration?

"The alternatives offered are not attractive. If we continue to make unilateral gestures and concessions, we will slide into a strategically inferior position and thereby invite a threat of nuclear blackmail. Rather than risk the extinction of human life, we would sacrifice our commitment to freedom. If we continue to climb the ladder of science in the stratosphere of what is technologically possible, achievable, then we will lose the capacity to control our destiny and survivability. Science is not constrained by concepts of morality. No value judgments spin around neutrons and protons—$E = MC^2$. Laser beams can be used to defeat man's diseases, or disintegrate mankind itself. The monster becomes our master. . . ."

My speech was received enthusiastically. Members slapped the conference table with their hands in approval. It prompted a sharp counter by a representative from the Defense Department: "Let's have the politicians start supplying money instead of a lot of rhetoric. . . ."

At 4, we lifted off and headed for Shannon, Ireland, where we were to refuel. As the plane took flight, I carried with me some deeper impressions of Germany. I had visited Bonn in 1977, and this two-day visit reinforced the picture that had developed in my mind. Germany's streets are impeccable. Their buildings are solid, heavy and permanent-appearing. Efficiency is a hallmark that is advertised by the quiet hum of the Mercedes-Benzes and BMWs that zing by like silver bees. There is a pervasive sense of opulence, noticed immediately in the quality of goods in the store windows (and their price tags) and the high fashions worn by the women.

There is deep in the German character, in the centuries of genes, an immutable sense of strength and confidence. A large-boned toughness and timbre that is at once admirable and intimidating.

The value of the meeting that I had just attended was not so much in what was said but in the people whom I had met—people I could call upon for information and honest judgments of political situations in their respective countries. It also served to force me to expand my interests in the social, economic and military problems that are facing our allies.

Michael Hastings, a member of my staff, was along on the trip. He was struck by the treatment we received as Senators.

"It's incredible," he said. "Everything is done for you. When you arrive at the foreign airports, there is no hassle with long lines at Customs. Buses and cars are waiting to whisk you directly to the hotel. The rooms are waiting without the necessity of checking in. Everything is organized to achieve maximum convenience. . . .''

It's true; we are spared all the inconvenience that would confront the average citizen traveling abroad. Practically no detail is overlooked. It is one of the many perquisites that go with the office. It also serves to pick the scab of our constituents' wounded sense of fairness—that elected officials are treated as an elite class, higher, different and better than those who work to pay the bills.

It is a strange paradox. Most people would think it's silly for elected officials on missions of diplomacy to waste precious time standing in long Customs lines or waiting for transportation. And yet, it is the very notion that public officials are insulated from the inconveniences that ordinary mortals must endure which builds such anger.

I have found that trying to reduce this sense of anger can even prove embarrassing.

For example, on a trip I had taken to Presque Isle, Maine, earlier in the week, an airline ticket agent at the Boston airport had tried to give me a ticket for my return in the first-class section. I had stopped him gently, saying, "No, I think I'm booked in coach."

I did so with as little notice as possible, so that he would not be embarrassed in front of the other people who might take note that he had tried to give me an extra perquisite. I could have just accepted the ticket and then sat in the coach section. I did that once—and it proved to be a disaster!

It was an early Sunday morning flight from Bangor to Boston. There weren't more than four or five people on board. I accepted a first-class ticket and went to the coach section. One of the stewardesses came back and insisted I sit up front because I had paid for the first-class ticket. At that point, I was faced with a dilemma: If I said that I hadn't paid for the first-class ticket, I might cause the man at the ticket counter a problem. So I simply said, "I realize that, but I prefer to sit back here."

She then went around to the other stewardesses and pilots explaining that some nut was on board who had bought a first-class ticket and then insisted on riding coach. The ride to Boston (twenty-nine minutes) was the longest I had ever experienced, as I sat slouched in the rear of the plane, next to the window, my face hidden behind a newspaper. . . .

We arrived at Andrews Air Force Base at 9:15 P.M.—in the middle of one of the most severe snowstorms ever to strike Washington.

February 19, 1979

At 7:30 a.m. we woke to the cries of excitement from our younger son, Chris. "Mom! Dad! Look. Outside. Look!"

Joy was leaping in his wide eyes. He was wearing the green cap with yellow tassel that I had purchased for him in Shannon, along with his pajamas. Never has he looked more like an Irish leprechaun.

Washington had become a winter wonderland. More than two feet of snow had fallen during the night. The roofs of houses looked like those of ski chalets in Switzerland. The snow gave everything the softness of a watercolor painting.

Later in the morning, we went out and wrestled in the snow, which was over our hips, and engaged in a snowball fight.

The snow had paralyzed the city. It had fallen like layers of gauze and imposed a veil of silence everywhere. There were no commuters. No buses. No rail service. No movement. Tons of white crystals had forced us to turn in toward ourselves, our families, and accept, however briefly, this miracle of nature.

The shrieks of neighborhood children pierced the silence. Then came the cries of the birds. The snow had buried their source of food. Then the radio news that hospitals were in need of doctors and nurses. Anyone with a four-wheel-drive vehicle was asked to provide transportation. The farmers who were still in Washington manned a command center at a local hotel and ordered their tractors into emergency service. They became saviors instead of scourges. A week earlier, they had tried to cause mass inconvenience. Now they were relieving it.

The beauty of the moment was slipping. The danger of prolonged human paralysis became obvious. Looters were on a rampage in Baltimore.

We started the long process of digging out, plowing back, reconstructing our networks of travel and commerce—like ants who have had their hill buried under someone's indifferent foot.

CHAPTER 10

FEBRUARY 22, 1979

THE SENATE CONSIDERS itself the "world's greatest deliberative body." Perhaps this self-inflation was long ago inspired by Alexis de Tocqueville's observation, found in *Democracy in America,* that the Senate ". . . is composed of eloquent advocates, distinguished generals, wise magistrates, and statesmen of note whose language would, at all times, do honor to the most remarkable parliamentary debates in Europe." Of course, one would have been hard-pressed to dispute the description in the days of John Calhoun, Daniel Webster and Henry Clay.

But the fact is that the words "greatest" and "deliberative" are open to qualitative challenge. Perhaps "longest-debating" or "-delaying" legislative body is a more accurate assessment. The Senate, in its procedural rules, permits unlimited debate, delay and filibuster by a heavy-lunged few, until cloture (termination of debate) is invoked by 60 members. The role of delay in our legislative process is not to be denigrated. Indeed, it can be indispensable in generating enough attention to an issue to bring the public's interest into the legislative process. While respect for tradition, and the rights of the minority party, must run deep, the workings of the legislative process should not be held hostage by the vocal cords of a few. As the sun must set to close the day, the voices of dissent must at some point be stilled if the majority will is ever to prevail.

Although the Senate has been reluctant to silence the voice of any Senator by invoking cloture, it had assumed that once cloture was invoked, a vote on the pending legislation would follow.

During 1977, the Senate discovered that it labored under a misapprehension of its own rules and underestimated the determination of two of its members.

Senators James Abourezk (of South Dakota, and now out of office) and Howard Metzenbaum, furious over President Carter's deregulation-of-natural-gas legislation, conducted a filibuster lasting two weeks by introducing several hundred amendments and calling them up even after cloture.

Today, after four weeks of uninspiring debate and behind-the-scenes caucusing, maneuvering and compromising, the Senate agreed to limit the right of its members to debate after cloture has been invoked to one hundred hours.

Senator Lowell Weicker was trailed throughout the day by four burly young men—which could mean one of two things. I concluded he either had been threatened or was about to announce his candidacy for the Presidency.

At the end of the day, Gary Hart came over and sat next to me and asked me how I was enjoying the Senate. I smiled and responded, "Gary, I think the House has misunderstood *us* all these years."

FEBRUARY 26, 1979

AT 9 A.M., I drove my car to "Dr. D." for more repair work. After a meeting with Tom Daffron to review the general operation of the office, I started to write an article on the SALT II treaty which I hoped to submit to *The New York Times* or *The Washington Post*.

At noon, I went to the Senate floor to serve as Assistant Whip for two hours. I sat at Alaska Senator Ted Stevens' desk and listened to the debate. My primary duties were to keep other members apprised of the status of the debate and the nature of a vote if one happened to be under way—and to make sure that the interests of the minority were protected from any skullduggery by the majority.

For the first time, I took notice of the difference in the decor of the Senate from that of the House.

The carpet is a soft blue wool with gold flecks, and the walls are painted a dark mustard color. The dais is dark marble with white streaks, and the desks are a deep, rich mahogany color. Each is equipped with a microphone that can be hooked onto the lapel of the speaker's suit so that both hands can be used—to turn pages of speeches or for waving, as Majority Leader Byrd is accustomed to doing. He is histrionic and seems to revel in flailing his arms to make a dramatic point.

The upper level of the Chamber is covered with gold wallpaper. There are twenty enclaves where busts of past Vice Presidents are situated, marble judges sitting as eyeless and impassive reminders of a rich and eloquent history.

It is quiet and more dignified in the Senate Chamber than in the House. Senators who want to talk go to the cloakroom or to lunch. I noticed also that Senators take much longer to make a point. They ramble and repeat the same themes. The lack of the time constraints that we had in the House does not produce any more enlightenment, simply more words.

Robert Byrd enjoys showing what a master he is of the arcana of Senate procedure. When Senator Dale Bumpers of Arkansas asked to speak for five minutes, Byrd immediately asked him to withdraw the request, assuring him that he would be protected and not lose his right to the floor. Bumpers agreed, and then Byrd addressed the Chair and said, "Mr. President, I ask unanimous consent that the morning hour be extended for ten minutes and that each member be allowed to speak, but not to exceed five minutes." The President Pro Tempore of the Senate then recognized Bumpers and he proceeded for five minutes. Byrd had made the point that he was in control of shaping the Senate procedure to feather it into an art form.

I had lunch at 2 in the private dining room for Senators. This is located directly opposite the public Senate Dining Room to which we take guests, constituents or staff members. There is a buffet table in the first of two small rooms and a large dining table in each of the rooms. I ordered haddock and started to go into the back room to sit with Russell Long and Bill Bradley. The waiter for that room said that he would take my order. I indicated that I had already placed it with another waiter. He turned his large frame to me and said, "No, sir, this is my dining room."

Rather than cause a scene, I got up and went to the first table and ate alone. I didn't want to get the first waiter in trouble (he was much smaller and appeared to be intimidated by the other fellow, who moved like an old rhino in high gear).

After lunch I sat at the second table and talked to Senator Long about a proposed value-added tax similar to that used in European countries. Jesse Helms came in and sat at the table; in his case, the waiter from the first room was able to serve him. Seniority counts—even in the dining room.

I had a meeting at 3:30 with the Vice President of the Chamber of Commerce, but had to interrupt it to go to the floor to vote on the Leonard Woodcock nomination for Ambassador to China. While I was on the floor, a number of the members were chiding John Tower over an article that had appeared in the *Washington Post* style section. The paper contained a photograph of Tower in a Superman costume. Tower took the ribbing gracefully and said, "Wouldn't you know it: I make some substantive statement about SALT or some other domestic or foreign-policy initiative and get absolutely no coverage. I go to my home state [Texas] to take part in a festivity for the local people and *The Washington Post* sends a journalist to cover it."

I returned at 3:45 to the meeting with the representative from the Chamber of Commerce. At 4, fifteen members of the Federal Credit Union inundated my office. They were disappointed with the smallness of my new quarters and didn't hesitate to let me know.

The size and location of a Senator's office is one of the status symbols and signs of seniority. Each time a Senator retires or is defeated (one-third of the Senators' terms expire every two years), his office becomes the prime object of the survivors. Its desirability will depend upon its size and location. Members send out a legion of assistants as scouts armed with clipboards, rulers and tape measures. After the initial territorial search mission is completed, the Senator will usually make an on-site inspection to satisfy himself that the quarters adequately accommodate his needs and new status.

Most senior members prefer the Russell Office Building. The ceilings are high, the rooms large—and there is a mustiness about them that is somehow becoming, a light haze of history that is compatible with the member's longevity or growing prestige.

But the process of moving resembles an evacuation of a tortoise breeding ground. For freshman members, the delay and inconvenience reinforce his vulnerability within the system. If the senior members have not completed their selections and moves prior to January 3, the new member will be assigned to the office of his or her predecessor. He or she will unload and unpack the desks, drawers, cartons and files, only to be moved to a permanent location two or three months later.

Rather than wait and hope that I might obtain an office in the Russell Building and go through this maddening process, I requested to locate in the office of New Mexico Senator Harrison "Jack" Schmitt (who was moving to the Russell Building), provided I would not have to move again. It had just enough space to accommodate my desk, a couch and two chairs. Three people in the room might not set off the fire inspector's alarm, but they would have to turn very slowly if they were to avoid putting their elbows into their neighbor's ear. The office, I concluded, had probably seemed palatial to Jack, a former astronaut. Anyone whose meals were once contained in a packet the size of a Hershey bar could find luxury in a tiger cage.

The saving grace of the office was that it was on the first floor, giving me easy access to the street. Because it was located at the end of a long corridor, I would not have to deal with the crush of tourists or vacationers who flood through the front doors daily in search of directions to their Senator or sight-seeing attractions.

I had anticipated the reaction of my constituents. They found it too small, undramatic, and inconsistent with the prestige that a Senator is supposed to have.

"Bill, your office in the House was much nicer than this. Maybe you should have stayed there. . . ."

"Well," I countered, "it's much more important that the staff have adequate space in which to work. Don't forget that on the House side, ten of them were crammed into one room. Besides, I don't spend much time in the office, so I don't need a lot of wasted space. By the way, that wall will be coming out in a week or two, adding almost a third more floor space. . . ."

It didn't matter how much I rationalized. The room did not measure up their expectations of the trappings of power that loom so large from a distance. A daily headline in the hometown paper might read "SENATOR COHEN BLASTS CARTER." The image that flickers on the wall of the mind is one of "By God, our boy is taking on the White House itself in a major assault!" But the reality of seeing the office from which the war of words is being launched shattered that image and reduced ''our boy'' to a lonely guerrilla lobbing cherry bombs from a bunker against an advancing nuclear-resistant tank. Its size and lack of anticipated splendor only served to reinforce my junior status on the seniority ladder—which is why the evacuation and rebilleting process is conducted every two years.

FEBRUARY 28, 1979

THE SENATE WAS not in session today. At 10, I attended a joint meeting of the Governmental Affairs and Banking committees. Only Senators Ribicoff and Proxmire (of Wisconsin) were in attendance when I arrived. Both were supporting the abolition of the three existing agencies that regulate the banking community: the Federal Deposit Insurance Corporation (FDIC), the Federal Reserve and the Comptroller. The Administration was testifying in opposition to the measure. It was too complex an area for such drastic amputation and surgery.

Banking is one of the most arcane and complex subject matters to master. It is also one of the most tedious, particularly if you are not an ex-banker, accountant or currency expert.

It was interesting to note that Senator Ribicoff praised Proxmire as one of the most knowledgeable men in the entire Congress on the subject of banking, and yet Proxmire's counsel was whispering to him throughout the entire hearing, feeding him statements, observations and responses like a ventriloquist. It is not that Proxmire is not knowledgeable; it is simply the fact that the staff member was more knowledgeable and probably had spent months drafting the provisions of the bill.

To anyone in the audience it must seem conspiratorial to have somebody whispering in the ear of Senators. Conspiratorial or confounding. After all, the Senator is supposed to be familiar with the subject. He serves on the Committee.

Once again, the answer is obvious to those on the inside only. Senators are spread too thin to be truly knowledgeable in any one field, much less in all of them. Policies are comprehended. Objectives are understood. The fine print contained in Sec. 8 *(b)* *(2)* (i) of Article III of a given bill is beyond the scope of attention or interest of most, if not all, Senators. There are too many hearings in too many committees on too many different subjects. Thus the staff takes on the role of expert.

At 12:30, I went to the Wednesday Group. My colleagues were deeply concerned about the state of the nation, and I had never seen them so agitated.

"This is the most dangerous period that we have ever passed through," one said. "The President is not exercising any leadership. I believe the country is ready for sacrifice. Whether it's Minnesota or New York, the people realize we cannot consume gasoline at the current rate. The President ought to get on the phone and tell Sadat, 'Listen, get yourself over here now. I got you the jets necessary for self-defense. I helped get the Camp David agreement. Don't you tell me that you're too busy to be bothered with minor details.''

Another Senator said, "At the meeting we had the day before, the President seemed to have lost confidence in himself. He doesn't understand the nature of the problem in the Mideast. These are not minor or insignificant matters—they are vital to Israel."

I left the meeting even more depressed than when I had heard Kissinger and Haig speak about SALT. I jumped into my car and headed for Dickinson College in Carlisle, Pennsylvania, where I was scheduled to address the student body on the relationship between liberal arts, poetry and public service.

Once I got about thirty miles outside of Washington on my way to Carlisle, the gloom lifted. The sun was shining. It was warm. The suburban sprawl had thinned out. The rolling hills and old farmhouses came from a different age than the marbled halls of Washington.

Living in Washington, one quickly becomes a news addict. But out in the country, near the mountains, the pressure eases, the veins filled with adrenaline slacken, and you can see a little clearer, think a little freer, without the telephone yelling. . . .

March 1, 1979

As I LISTENED to the radio this morning on my way back to Washington, I thought about the fickle nature of politics. Chicago was about to get a new mayor (Jane Byrne) because the incumbent (Michael Bilandic) couldn't do anything—or enough—about removing all the snow that had fallen and paralyzed that city.

I saw something that symbolized the contradictions of our times along the highway. A blue sign read, POLICE HEADQUARTERS UP AHEAD.

Right beside this sign was a large billboard advertising FUZZ BUSTER. BEATING THE RADAR TRAP.

I arrived as the Senate was going into session to consider the nomination of George M. Seignious to be director of the U.S. Arms Control and Disarmament Agency.

Following lunch with a friend in the Senate Dining Room, I returned to the office for a photograph with the presidential classroom students. Then I went to the recording studio to tape two five-minute radio programs on issues.

After being in session for a month and a half, we had voted on only two issues—cloture and Leonard Woodcock.

At this time in each session there is usually very little business. This year there was unusually little, reflecting the mood of the country, which does not want any more legislation.

The hustle from the White House has begun. Late yesterday afternoon, I received a call inquiring if I would like to sit in the President's box at the Kennedy Center to watch the ballet.

Today, Defense Secretary Brown's office called and asked if I would go to dinner and the Kennedy Center with Brown.

I declined both invitations.

MARCH 2, 1979

THE SENATE WAS not in session today.

I took my administrative assistant, Tom Daffron, to lunch. As we boarded the subway, somebody said, "Hey, don't sit in the front seat."

"Why not?" I asked.

"Because a Senator is coming, that's why."

"Well, there's one already here," I snapped.

I should have anticipated the challenge. Instead of a dark pin-striped suit, I was wearing a tan Lee sports coat that would have been more appropriate for my older son. I hadn't thought to wear my little Senate pin that sends forth secret signals to all the employees that a Senator is behind the insignia!

What was most disturbing was the tone in which I was asked—and admonished—to stay off the front car. It was not polite. I was a mere citizen, and that spot was reserved for somebody important.

When the Senate is in session, Senators should be given priority passage to the Capitol in order to catch votes. But when a vote is not in progress, and most particularly when the Senate is not in session, Senators should not enjoy special privileges on the cars. The signs standing near the subway cars call the distinction to the attention of the public, but the operators routinely ignore the sign and ask tourists to wait for the next car.

It is a minor matter, but one that only serves to aggravate an already serious problem of constituent contempt for our government.

While I was at lunch, I had received a call from an irate constituent. She wouldn't talk to anyone else. "He promised to be available to the people. I have a problem and I want to know if he's going to keep his promise."

I placed the return call personally. Her husband had just lost his job. She knew that I could not get his job back or find him a new one. She only wanted to describe the circumstances that had led to his unemployment and express her hope that I could do something to stop the economy from deteriorating so badly.

MARCH 5, 1979

THE SENATE CONVENED at noon. At 1, I attended an Indian Affairs Committee meeting to consider the Bureau of Indian Affairs budget, goals and objectives on current Indian issues.

A meeting with a VFW delegation was held in a Senate committee hearing room at 3:15. The veterans were coming to make their case for more money to be allocated for veterans' programs. Initially, they were concerned about appropriation of the necessary money for the removal of bodies buried in the Panama Canal area which was being turned over to the Panamanians. Secondly, they wanted additional money to maintain Togus, the veterans' hospital in Maine, at its current level of service. They were also against cutbacks in the commissary privileges in the Bangor area. Finally, they wanted to know why the money for the Veterans Administration was being withheld.

Senator Muskie and I went directly from that session to a meeting with Israel's Prime Minister Menachem Begin.

As we entered the Senate Caucus Room, the meeting was already in progress. Senators Javits, Byrd, and Baker were all sitting at the head table with Prime Minister Begin. Begin was in the middle of a presentation. He looked tired. His thick lenses resembled large magnifying glasses, which distorted the size of his eyes. He spoke with a heavy accent, dropping words for emphasis and drama, but losing most of his audience in the process. The acoustics in the Caucus Room are horrible, and most of the Senate members who were in attendance that afternoon could barely understand what was being said.

On some issues, however, there was no mistaking his position. "Israel cannot be pressured into signing a sham document that creates the illusion of peace. How can we call it peace when Egypt can join at will other Arab nations at war with Israel?"

In concluding, Begin warned about the plans of the Soviets for expanding their control. It now included six countries by proxy. "They scheme to take over more countries in Africa, Asia, and now Iran," he said. "Where are we going? There are 151 nations in the world—and only 35 democracies are left. Israel is the only country in the Middle East that has an inherent stable democracy. We live in difficult times, a perilous period. I beg you to support an effort to keep democracy alive."

That evening, Elliot Richardson called me concerning an article on SALT II that I had written which was published by *The Washington Post*.

Elliot is a man of considerable intellect, a skilled administrator who has held four Cabinet positions during his public-service career. He is now serving as the chief negotiator of the Law of the Sea Conference being held in Geneva and New York.

He is a handsome man, with a square jaw and a chiseled face. His horn-rimmed glasses add distinction to, rather than detract from, his appearance. There is, however, an impenetrable quality to his character; for some, a formidable one. There is something geometric about Elliot: complete, squared, harmonious. His doodles have become, justifiably, collector's items. They begin with seemingly random but bold strokes that sweep around curves and corners until, suddenly, they achieve a design so intricate yet proportioned that it is easy to imagine them as patterned after a lost Leonardo drawing Elliot had kept pressed since childhood beneath the sweat-soiled "secret" flap of a worn leather wallet. His conversation is no different. He does not talk; he parses. Sentences emerge from him full-grown, and he pauses between them, as if to enable listeners to see for themselves that each of the several semicolons is properly placed and that no participle had dared dangle. But his pauses brook no intrusions; not, at least, before it is clear that he is ready to listen himself, that he has not simply been squaring, planing, and sanding his next thought into maximum syntactic proportion. Interrupt the process and he will take no visible notice, but leave you with the sinking feeling of one caught trespassing on private ground.

He was interested in exploring my current thinking on the SALT agreement, my assessment of where ratification stood. We exchanged thoughts on the decline of U.S. prestige throughout the world and what could be done to reverse it.

Throughout the conversation, I sensed in Elliot's voice a certain melancholy—that of power and ambition permanently frustrated or relegated to a secondary level of influence.

He had the talent and desire to hold high office, and yet he had no base from which to operate. With his resignation as Attorney General in 1973, he had jettisoned the support of the hard-line reflexive conservatives—those who tend to dominate Republican Party conventions.

The press consistently questioned whether his manner was too aristocratic and aloof to appeal to the man with the lunch bucket under his arm. His absence from the center stage of public debate had pushed him further into the shadows of the "formerly" category of political leadership. There was a good possibility that he could have run for and won Massachusetts Senator Edward Brooke's seat in 1978, but Brooke would not concede the depth of his political difficulties and Richardson would not—in fact, could not—have challenged Brooke in a primary without earning the charge of climbing on the back of a wounded friend.

So, he remains at the helm of a critically important post, one that will earn him credit or blame within the narrow confines of international negotiators.

He is an example of the adage that "life is not fair." Elliot is far more talented than some of those now in the Senate. But his talent cannot be squared with the times, and there does not appear any way that he can reconcile a political future with the current trends. Then again, who can say? Perhaps there is a snowstorm in his future.

MARCH 8, 1979

AT 8:30, I attended a breakfast meeting with Henry Kissinger and other Senators.

The meeting was running over the 9:30 time when the Senate was to go into session. I left the meeting and went directly to an Armed Services Committee meeting realizing that there were two people waiting to talk to me in my office. I called over and had them brought to the meeting, during which a confidential briefing was being presented by the Assistant Secretary of the Army and various personnel from the Pentagon on our combat aircraft.

I was annoyed that I had to break away from the Armed Services Committee meeting to discuss the programs and policies that a "rural center" had to offer. But the meeting had been set up and there was no way that I could avoid it without generating some hard feelings.

When I returned to the Armed Services Committee hearing after twenty minutes, I felt as if I were sinking in the quicksand of military arcana and jargon.

As the debate before the Armed Services Committee was taking place, a vote was in progress on the Senate floor. The problem was, it was a voice vote, and none of us had really been alerted to the implications of what had been done. The Senate, with only one or two members on the floor, had revoked the $8,625 limitation that we had placed two years earlier on outside income.* Under the amendment offered by Ted Stevens of Alaska, the ceiling would be elevated to $25,000 for the next four years, ostensibly to protect those members who came into the Senate with the knowledge that that was the limitation and not the $8,625 that was voted at a later time.

Almost as soon as the vote was over, the phone in my office had started to ring with calls coming from the Maine press to explain where I had been and how I would have voted had I been present on the floor. No one could comprehend why I had not been on the floor when the vote occurred.

---

* On March 1, 1977, Congress voted to increase its salary from $44,600 to $57,500. At the time of the pay raise, Congress also voted to restrict outside earned income to 15 percent of its salary, or $8,625. By virtue of the Senate vote on March 8, the 15 percent restriction was removed and replaced with a maximum $25,000 restriction on outside income.

MARCH 9, 1979

THERE WAS no session today. At 10:30, there was a briefing on the strategy for the MX amendment that would be offered by Senator Tower next Thursday. The strategy was consistent with the notion I had advanced in the article for *The Washington Post:* namely, to force the Administration to make a decision on the MX and its basing mode prior to the SALT debate.

Around noon, I went to the carry-out to get a sandwich. On my way back, a young "elevator watcher" (the elevators are automatic) saw me carrying my sandwich, yogurt and coffee toward the elevator door—and stopped me. "Sir, these elevators are reserved for Senators."

I didn't bother to explain. I simply said, "I know," and got on.

I returned a call to UPI. The reporter wanted to know about the Senate action on increasing the outside limit on earnings, the XM-1 tank difficulties reported in *The New York Times* earlier, and the wood-fuel tax credit.

I also received word that Maine potatoes were in for tough going once again. A federal agency charged that they hadn't been meeting their quality grade upon arrival at their destination. The Commodity Futures Trading Commission (CFTC) was cancelling the April and May contract dates in order to avoid the possibility of defaults at a later time. The press was calling, demanding answers.

The last item of business for the day was also discouraging. The managing editor of one of Maine's daily newspapers thought that my profile had been too low in the state and wanted a reporter to find out why. It was really a no-win situation. I have tried to strike a balance between rushing back to Maine and increasing my substantive knowledge by using weekends to study as many articles and position papers as possible. The problem is that I had set a very high standard as a Representative by returning to the state on virtually every weekend. Those whose nature or profession it is to be critical interpret my less frequent trips to be a sign of diminished interest in the state.

On the other hand, if I should return *every* weekend, apart from the stress on Diane and the boys, who have seen little of me in the past six years, my knowledge on issues would be more superficial, thereby laying the foundation for a charge that I have failed to establish a national reputation as a substantive Senator. Damned if you do . . .

MARCH 12, 1979

I SPENT the entire morning in the office clearing out an avalanche of paperwork. At noon, I had lunch with Representative Jack Kemp of New York to discuss his political plans. There is an intensity about Jack which separates him from most of the people on the Hill. He reminds me of the quarterback he used to be—reading a blitz from the Pittsburgh Steelers' linebackers line and about to call a change of plays. He is ambitious, but realizes that his kinetic energy needs some direction. I was pleased he had called me for advice.

The Senate spent most of the day debating the disposition of the real estate owned by the Friends of Taiwan.

During the debate, I suggested to Ed Muskie that we take some action on the potato-futures problem and ask for an investigation of possible criminal activity which had led to the Commodities Futures Trading Commission's decision to cancel the April and May contracts. Ed agreed, and we had our staffs prepare a jointly signed letter to the Commission.

I met with a representative of an English firm that wants to put a new starch plant in northern Maine. The company is seeking federal assistance. I also received word through some Defense Department sources that a final decision to reduce the operation at Loring Air Force Base had been made, which meant that Maine was in for some more bad news. The loss of Loring could produce a general depression in the northern part of the state.

I called Muskie to alert him to this most recent development and then called General Charles Blanton, who serves as an Air Force liaison officer, to inquire as to the truth of the report.

Blanton said that the Air Force was behind in its work and that no final decision had been made.

"Senator Cohen, I appreciate the fact that you don't want to get blind-sided on this matter."

"My interests go well beyond that," I assured him. "I want to be in a position to pursue some alternatives—and there are some at my disposal."

"I can tell you that the decision has not been made, but we expect one soon. Mrs. Chayes [Assistant Secretary of the Air Force for Manpower, Reserve Affairs and Installations] and Secretary Duncan are well aware of your interest and that of Senator Muskie."

But I received another call almost immediately thereafter from another source saying that the decision had been made and that we should lean as heavily as possible on the Defense Department before it goes public.

MARCH 13, 1979

AT NOON, I attended the Republican Policy luncheon. It was announced by the chairman of the Policy Committee that the weekly luncheons would be going up to $5 per meal. There were groans, moans, and low whistles from the members.

Only Barry Goldwater spoke up. "Damn it, I'm not going to pay $5 for a lunch unless the quality of the food in this place goes up with it. I'll brown-bag it first!"

He was saying exactly what all the rest of us were thinking as well, but didn't have the courage to say for fear that we would be considered cheap. Goldwater doesn't have to worry about the cost of any meal. It was the principle that outraged him—greater cost for less quality!

The other members started to cheer and clap when Barry sat down. His candor cost him an election years ago, but it continues to win him the admiration of his colleagues.

Everyone knew he wouldn't carry out his threat of boycott.

I spent the remainder of the day at an Armed Services Committee hearing listening to the Joint Chiefs of Staff testify in favor of reinstituting draft registration in some limited form.

Around 6 P.M. I went back to my office to sign mail and received notice for the first time that the Nuclear Regulatory Commission had just ordered the Maine Yankee Atomic Plant in Wiscasset, Maine, to close. Apparently a computer error in the design of the secondary cooling pipes had been made some years ago and the Commission concluded that they would not withstand the shock of a major earthquake.

I arrived home around 7 P.M. and during dinner decided to discuss the question of the draft with the boys.

Kevin was the most pessimistic. "Dad, if I'm drafted and have to go to war, I know that I won't be coming back."

"Kevin," I replied, "come on, now. Aren't you being a little over-dramatic? What if everyone took that attitude? You might not fight any wars, but you wouldn't have a country to fight for. Don't you think you have a responsibility to give something to a country that has given you so much opportunity?''

I was preparing to make a speech when Chris cut me off: "Dad, I don't want to fight in any army and get killed. . . .''

Chris is the rebel of the family, the free spirit who shuns material acquisitions; wears outrageous (but colorful) combinations of clothes, bandanas, safari hats; cooks blueberry pancakes on Sunday mornings for the entire family, and longs for the day when he can drive a Jeep and live in the rolling hills of Buckfield, Maine.

Diane joined in and saved us from what might have been an abrasive and unproductive confrontation. She helped to lower the rising volume of our voices. She reminded them of our friend Colonel Pete Dawkins.

"Look at Pete, boys. He served in Vietnam two or three tours and he's still alive. We need good people. Besides, registration doesn't mean that you would automatically be drafted. . . .''

I was surprised at what she said. I had expected her to be sympathetic to the boys, because she is such a peace-loving person. She knew that I was truly divided on what the right course of action was on the registration issue, and I think she just sensed that I had had a long day at the office and wanted to give me some moral support—at least for the time being.

I can remember only one other night at the dinner table when I sensed so much tension. It was on November 21, 1973. The day had been dominated by news accounts of U.S. District Court Judge John J. Sirica's disclosure that there were 18½ minutes of conversation missing from a potentially crucial tape recording of the first meeting between President Nixon and H. R. Haldeman following the Watergate break-in.

Walter Cronkite interrupted our dinner conversation. His raspy voice floated from the television set in the family room across the front hall into the dining room, where Diane and the boys had become grudgingly tolerant of *The CBS Evening News* as a staple of my daily diet. For them, Cronkite had become a regular uninvited dinner guest.

We listened, digesting it briefly, and I turned to Kevin, then ten, to ask, "What do you think?''

Flatly, without pause, he replied, "I think the President is lying.''

It shocked me. We had never discussed Watergate—I had assumed it was too complicated for him or too irrelevant to his world of Little League and multiplication tables—and I glanced quickly at Chris, then eight, who had been so much impressed by the splendor of the White House. Chris was wide-eyed, but said nothing.

We sat in silence as I tried to frame a lecture to Kevin and reassurance to Chris about the need not to prejudge, to presume honesty, to await a full explanation; but I held back. Kevin had said what I could not bring myself to say aloud that day.

Finally Kevin broke the silence. "Dad," he said with an innocence anyone might envy, "I wish we were living in the days of Washington."

Again I was surprised and mute. How nice it would have been for all of us to live in Kevin's wistful world of cherry trees and silver dollars across the Rappahannock. Instead we were reeling from the concussions detonated by the thirty-sixth man to succeed Washington as our President: The Watergate special prosecutor had been fired; the Attorney General had resigned in regret. Impeachment was being studied by the House Judiciary Committee, on which I served. The Committee was simultaneously acting on the nomination of a new Vice President to succeed the man whom Richard Nixon had twice chosen to be his heir apparent but who had instead resigned as a disgraced income-tax evader. The cinders of the latest conflict in the Middle East were still hot. An Arab oil embargo was producing economic dislocation and personal frustration. Our confidence in the ability of government to manage the economy was being sapped by unchecked inflation. It was, taken together, unimaginable. But it was history, not hyperbole. And it was not what I expected to be able to understand, much less resolve, barely a year after the sweet taste of election to Congress.

It was an acute embarrassment to have asked Kevin what he thought and to be unable to comment when he told me. This is ridiculous, I thought; I'm supposed to be intelligent, articulate, but I don't know what to say to my own ten-year-old boy.

Later I came to understand why that meal had ended in silence. At the time, I did not know what to say to myself in response to each episodic event in what Gerald Ford would call our "long national nightmare." My own muteness was in fact symbolic of the initial doubt, fear, frustration and indecision that plagued others, especially my fellow Republicans, on the House Judiciary Committee. We were being asked to pass judgment on the man who had been the dominant political figure of the last quarter-century, the man who had claimed a mandate from Middle America, a mandate from us.

We wanted desperately to believe that our President, for all his evident character flaws, would not have authorized such a petty and stupid venture as the Watergate burglary and would have had the political sense to avoid being ensnared in a cover-up. We were predisposed to blame the media and especially the Democrats for trying to steal in Congress what they had not been able to win at the polls. Yet we agonized over each development that chipped away our comfortable rationalization: Why had Elliot Richardson resigned if the President was in fact cooperating with the investigation and Archibald Cox was indeed on a partisan mission to ransack White House records? Why had two tape recordings turned out to be missing and a third have an 18½-minute buzz instead of inane Oval Office chatter? How could we satisfy Republican constituents with an explanation of the need for an impeachment investigation and at the same time assure Democrats and independents that we would treat our party's head with objectivity? Each of us, by a force of circumstances beyond our desire or control, was placed on a high wire that was strung between disloyalty to party and disloyalty to principle. . . .

Tonight, Diane, after attempting to alleviate Kevin's and Chris's apprehensions about the prospect of war, wisely shifted the conversation to another subject.

MARCH 14, 1979

TODAY WAS a classic example of the diversity of subjects that a Senator must confront. At 8 A.M., Senator Muskie, Congresswoman Olympia Snowe and I met with a group of bankers from Maine to discuss legislation of interest to them. For one and a half hours we covered the subjects of regulations, balanced budgets, and interest-rate differentials.

At 9 I met with a representative from the Maine State Teachers Association who was in Washington to lobby me to vote in favor of creating a new Department of Education. I explained to her the reasons I could not do so and invited her to the Committee markup.* I was obviously overpowering in the articulation of my arguments against creating a new Department of Education. The vote was 14 to 1 in favor of the new department.

During the markup of the bill, I learned that Senator John Glenn was holding hearings on nuclear-waste disposal. He invited me to join his

---

* After all the hearings on a proposed piece of legislation have been completed, the committee that has jurisdiction over the subject matter will conduct a line-by-line analysis of the bill and give consideration to the adoption of any amendments to it. At the conclusion of the "markup," a final vote is taken to either report the bill to the full Senate or to reject it.

subcommittee. For fifteen minutes I questioned the chairman of the Nuclear Regulatory Commission on the decision to close Maine Yankee.

Then I left to attend a Wednesday Group discussion about budget rescissions*, coming to the floor later in the day. I rushed back to the office to meet the new director of the General Services Administration (GSA) and then to the floor to serve as Assistant Whip for the afternoon. I signed mail while listening to the debate.

Senator Edward Kennedy was leading an effort to block $33.6 million of budget rescissions made by President Carter in the health field. The Administration did not want to allow the floodgates of higher federal spending to be opened—particularly not by the heavy hands of the Senator from Massachusetts.

Kennedy engaged in a fiery, fist-pounding, desktop-thumping speech that encouraged members to storm the gates of capitation-grant containment for medical, veterinary and nursing schools. He argued that the proposed rescissions constituted a breach of contract, a breach of faith by the federal government.

Ed Muskie rose to speak and said that he agreed with the Senator from Massachusetts 95 percent of the time. But today was part of the 5 percent when he must disagree with Kennedy. This did not come as a surprise. Muskie could hardly have supported Kennedy's effort to restore the proposed rescission in this matter and then call for stern budget-cutting measures when the Budget Resolutions were to come before the Senate in several weeks.

What was surprising was the coalition of conservative Republicans who joined Kennedy in his effort. Senators Hayakawa of California, Helms of North Carolina, Jepsen of Iowa and Thurmond of South Carolina. Orrin Hatch of Utah said that he disagreed with Kennedy 95 percent of the time, but this was the 5 percent when he agreed that the President's action constituted a breach of agreement.

Kennedy huffed and puffed, but could not blow down the Administration's walls. He lost 55 to 42. The Administration lobbyists expressed great satisfaction that the budget-cutting mood of the country had prevailed over the pressures generated by the medical schools and that Kennedy had received something of a setback in the process.

---

* A budget rescission is enacted legislation cancelling budget authority previously provided by the Congress.

But they could take little comfort in a 13-vote margin at this stage of the political season.

After the vote, I returned to my office to meet with a group of county commissioners. They wanted assurances that their favorite programs would continue to receive federal funding.

MARCH 15, 1979

AT 8 A.M. the Research and Development Subcommittee of Armed Services met to listen to a presentation by Pentagon officials of research programs now under way to produce futuristic weapons systems. The inventory included ray guns, laser beams, particle beams, infrared goggles and gun scopes. *Star Wars* is not some imaginative figment or fantasy —only a prologue of what is currently on its way from draftsmen's drawing boards to death-dealing destruction.

At 10, the full Armed Services Committee met. The first clash among Senators John Culver of Iowa, Jackson and Tower occurred. Culver is impressive in his knowledge of military weapons and strategy, and articulate in an effective way. He has a bullhorn voice, looks as if he belongs behind a Mack truck and runs over you as if he were driving one. He has a disarming way of suddenly reducing the volume of his voice, smiling and then furrowing his brow as if declaring peace and asking you to simply reason with him. But Culver's mood and manner shift mercurially, and you can see that he is capable of backing you into an intellectual corner quickly if you make the slightest concession.

I arrived late for a meeting in Senator Domenici's office scheduled for 2. A group of Republicans uncommitted on SALT were trying to map out a strategy that would provide them with the questions they should be asking and the direction they should be taking in analyzing the treaty.

During the radio taping at the recording studio, I gave a response to the charge that I had deliberately missed the vote on outside-income restriction.

Finally, late in the afternoon, I worked on an article on the Department of Education for the *Washington Star* which appeared on March 18. If I could not persuade my colleagues on the Committee, perhaps I should vent my reasoning to the general public.

There is a strong current of opinion running across the country that Congress must take action to reduce the dramatic growth of government and its bureaucracy. The public roar in the heartland, however, has been reduced to a murmur in Washington. Marble has its acoustical advantages.

In the name of management efficiency and the need for a federal eye over the pyramid of education, Congress appears ready to take the "E" out of HEW and create a new agency, a new head, a new house, and, yes, a new foundation.

Earlier this week the Senate Governmental Affairs Committee voted overwhelmingly for a bill to create a new Department of Education. Congress, of course, has a responsibility to rest its judgment on something firmer than the shifting sands of public opinion—particularly when its action is calculated to add a new and permanent star to the growing federal constellation of heavy and heavenly bodies. Past experience, common sense, and the rules of probability must be considered as well as the "felt necessities of the times."

As one who is opposed to a separate Department of Education, however, I respectfully suggest that the imminent congressional action contravenes not only common sentiment, but sound public policy as well.

There can be no dispute that many education programs are entangled in the present organizational briar patch of HEW. Name a health or welfare program that is spared this agony. But there has been no persuasive evidence indicating that the problems plaguing the federal education programs—duplicative and conflicting regulations, burdensome and unnecessary paperwork, and unclear lines of authority—would be significantly reduced were a separate Department of Education created.

To the contrary, a case can be made that were the spirit willing, a reorganization plan could be fleshed out to produce consolidations and efficiencies within the existing HEW structure.

One of the major reasons advanced by advocates of a separate Department of Education is that greater efficiency would result from the consolidation of education programs now scattered throughout the federal bureaucracy in departments as diverse as Justice and Interior.

The proposed legislation, however, does very little to promote consolidation. Many federal education programs, including school lunch, Indian, and veterans' education programs, would not be transferred to the new department. Each is too deeply rooted in the subsoil of its political constituency.

While it may be advisable to place all federal education programs under one roof, this legislation does not accomplish that goal. Perhaps proponents of the new department hope that if Congress creates a shell now, the President could use his reorganization authority in future years to transfer additional programs with only minimal congressional review or political opposition.

Since this legislation neither consolidates existing education pro-

grams nor offers any reasonable assurances that the current administrative problems would be alleviated, we must consider what a more
centralized focus would imply for educational policy in this country.

It is argued that a Department of Education would increase the
status and visibility of education in the federal government and would
recognize it as a fundamental national activity. Indeed, it would, but
the question is whether we want to increase the federal role of education.

The diversity in our present education system is one of its
strengths. This attribute stems at least in part from our strong tradition of citizen involvement in determining education policy at the
state and local levels. Unlike other countries, we do not have a national "ministry of education," which establishes and controls education for all of the nation's schools. Instead, we have local school
boards comprised of the community's elected representatives who
make educational decisions for public schools. The federal government's role has been a limited one, particularly in determining policies.

The distinguished Senate sponsors of the Department of Education have gone to great lengths to try to satisfy the serious concerns
that many have concerning the possibility of federal encroachment on
the rights of state and local governments to control education. But a
Cabinet level office, is, by its very nature, a policymaking office and
it is short-sighted to think that we can have greater federal focus,
visibility, coordination, appropriations, and still retain local control
over policies, standards or curricula.

Indeed, if the past is merely prologue, then the future for this
new agency, and the taxpayers who must support it, is not promis-
ing. . . .

President Carter once pledged to hack through the organizational
thicket of 1900 agencies that encumber the federal triangle and give
us a government as slim and efficient as we deserve. We cannot hope
to curb the growth of bureaucracy by indulging its appetite and calling
it reorganization. We deserve better.

MARCH 18, 1979

I STOPPED OFF in Boston on my return from a weekend in Maine. I visited
with Tom and Elizabeth Lambert in their apartment overlooking the
Charles River. Tom is the editor-in-chief of the *Journal of the American
Trial Lawyers Association* and a professor at Suffolk University Law
School.

He had been a Rhodes Scholar, the Dean of Stetson Law School in Florida at the age of twenty-seven, a top prosecutor at the Nuremberg War Trials under Justice Robert Jackson, a professor at the Boston University Law School, and he is regarded in legal circles as the finest public speaker in America.

Following law school, I had had the great privilege of working for him, and with the exception of my father, no man has had a more profound impact on my life.

For fifteen months we exchanged novels and philosophy and poetry books while we worked to produce a monthly newsletter and annual journal for trial lawyers across the country. In the evenings, after work, I would be invited to join him for martinis mixed by Elizabeth. We watched the sun set over the Charles River while sailboats leaned like white wings in the blue water and then turned red in the glow of the sun. It was always a time for long thoughts, for polishing words and ideas.

During the impeachment hearings held by the House Judiciary Committee in 1974, I often called Tom, late at night or early in the morning. I needed his support and reassurance. He never advised me on what to do. He would just quote from his favorite philosophers.

Even now, when I call him, he reminds me gently, "Bill, it's better to be a second-rate poet than a first-rate Senator."

He doesn't want me to become so preoccupied with the power struggle of politics that I fail to listen for the "echo of the infinite."

MARCH 21, 1979

I ARRIVED at the office at approximately 9 after working out in the House gymnasium. An editorial page was coming in on the telecopier. It contained a cartoon of a figure with a distinct resemblance to me walking around a corner with two bags of money—$57,500 and $25,000—and a cat in the corner offering a comment to "stop—er—uh, the thief."

I thought it was unfair, but there was absolutely nothing that I could do about it. Complaints would only generate more attention, controversy and criticism. Explanation of what the Senate had done would produce little understanding and no sympathy. Inflation was stretching everyone on a cruel rack. How could we urge a 7 percent wage-increase guideline for the salaried wage-earning people and relax the standard on outside income for ourselves? The fact that we were technically moonlighting and not violating the inflation-fighting guidelines was not important. We appeared to be violating the spirit of the guidelines.

On the Senate floor between the hours of 10 A.M. and noon, only 5 Senators are present. The visitors' galleries are jammed. The people seemed perplexed. No doubt they came expecting to see 100 Senators sitting diligently at their desks listening to the oratorical flights on matters of high political drama. Instead they saw a virtually empty chamber with few members uttering some strange, passionless procedural catechism: "Mr. President, I ask unanimous consent that I be allowed to . . ." The Senator presiding over the chamber (the Vice President, Walter Mondale, who is technically President of the Senate, occupies the chair on only a handful of occasions during the course of a legislative session) responds in a monotone: "Without objection, it is so ordered."

Then Majority Leader Byrd says, "Mr. President, I suggest the absence of a quorum." The President Pro Tempore orders, "The Clerk will call the roll." Whereupon the Clerk, who sits behind the marbled first tier, starts to call the name of each Senator, pausing nearly twenty seconds between names. A bell rings twice in every office and room throughout the Senate, apprising Senators that a quorum call is under way. No one ever responds to two bells, because it is not a real, or "live," quorum —only a stalling device used by the Senate leadership to suspend the proceedings to work out some conflict in the calling up of legislation or to allow a Senator time to come to the floor to make a speech or participate in the debate.

After a minute or two, Byrd will say, "Mr. President, I ask unanimous consent that further call of the roll be suspended." "Without objection, it is so ordered."

The litany is repeated throughout much of the morning. The visitors are ushered out after ten or fifteen minutes to make room for the next flock of constituents. As they shuffle out, many look back at the chamber. Disappointment is stamped on their faces. Singer Peggy Lee's sad refrain comes to mind: "Is That All There Is?"

Bill Armstrong of Colorado was preparing to offer an amendment to the Debt Ceiling Limit Bill that was on the floor today. He was sitting at his desk in the back row, near the door, studying material for the debate. At this point we were the only two members on the floor, and it was obvious that the majority was simply going to call a series of quorums until well into the afternoon in order to allow Russell Long to return to Washington and control the debate. I asked Armstrong if he would assume my duties as Assistant Whip so that I could return to the office and sign mail.

I arrived at the office to do some reading. My thoughts were constantly punctuated by the buzzer that is wired into the clock in my office. Two long, annoying rings every few minutes. I turned on the "squawk box" that sits on my desk. This permits each Senator to listen to the debate on the floor. The Clerk, in his low monotone, is calling the roll again. "Mr. Byrd of Virginia. . . ."

At noon, I attended a Wednesday Group luncheon. Jacob Javits of New York is pessimistic about the economic choices facing the country, our lack of military readiness, and the absence of a clearly defined foreign policy. John Danforth launched into a powerful speech about getting back to basics. John is a lanky, hard-boned former Attorney General of Missouri who has a distinctive swath of white hair on the right side of his head. It looks as if a devilish boy had run a two-inch paintbrush through his dark hair. As an heir to the Ralston-Purina family fortune, he is considered one of the wealthiest men in the Senate. He is also regarded as one of the brightest and nicest members.

"We fritter away our lives hustling between committee hearings, filing bills to keep our names in the paper. We have some fundamental choices to make: Do we believe in a growth society, and if so, how do we reconcile it with environmental concerns? Are we willing to fight for anything? If so, where? Fundamental!" He slapped his hands together to drive home the urgency that he felt.

"Do we want to continue to run trade deficits? If not, are we willing to adopt the policies necessary to change the present decline? We can't be drawing pictures with the fine lines of an artist—just broad, sweeping policies that we have to be willing to commit ourselves to.

"Unless we are willing to raise these questions and do something about them, then we will witness the decline and fall of our nation."

With that I got up and left and joked about Jack's passion. I had a 1:30 meeting with Jake Henshaw of the Gannett News Service, who was interested in my views on Indian legislation. I was running twenty minutes late. I was a prisoner of that damned 3×5 schedule card that we all carry—the very point that Danforth was making so emphatically.

MARCH 22, 1979

SPRING CAME to Washington this week. The wrath of February had melted away, leaving deep potholes and crumbling pavement as the only visible scars of the blitzkrieg launched from the north. The memory of pain was short, and the ice wounds had stopped throbbing. The raw redness and swelling had sunk below the level of consciousness. Green shoots were peeking up from the soil, preparing to announce the arrival of the golden glory of daffodils. Buds were swelling with pink pregnancy on the magnolia tree outside our family room.

As I started the familiar route in to the Capitol, it was hard to be overwhelmed by the dark clouds of world events. Not even the poison of the PLO that was filling the airwaves with protests over the Egypt–Israel peace treaty, not the latest reports of the inflation rate, not the daily accounts of savagery and violence that filled the Metro section of *The Washington Post*—no, not even the bottom-line total of all the bad news could diminish the magic and mystery of spring or fail to remind me of the smallness of our contrivances, our insignificance in the face of nature's force and infinity.

During the "morning hour" (a time reserved for general speeches and nonlegislative matters) today, several Republicans including Howard Baker were going to take the opportunity to blast the Carter Administration for not appointing a special, independent prosecutor to investigate alleged irregularities of the Carter peanut business. I wanted to join in challenging not only the Administration's less-than-enthusiastic pursuit of the facts in this case, but also the press's acquiescence in what appeared to be a clear double standard.

But the Armed Services Committee was meeting at the same time to continue the markup of the fiscal 1979 Department of Defense Supplemental Military Authorization Request.

There was a spirited confrontation between Senator Culver and the rest of the Research and Development Subcommittee of which Culver is the Chairman. We had agreed tentatively to adopt language concerning the MX missile program as drafted by Culver. Once we saw the fine print, we reneged, and John was angry with our breach of agreement. Of course, we had made the error of agreeing to language without seeing it fully in writing or thinking it through and without the benefit of a record of our subcommittee's hearings. It was not a pleasant session, and the stakes involved necessarily heightened the emotions.

Later, during our deliberations, Senators Harry Byrd and John Warner offered a motion to amend the FY 79 Supplemental Budget request to include a provision that a major overhaul-and-repair contract for the *Saratoga*, a large aircraft carrier, be subjected to the "most cost-effective test" established by the General Accounting Office (GAO), a congressional watchdog agency.

On the surface, this seemed a fundamentally sound and rather innocuous request. After all, shouldn't all government contract awards be made on a sound economic basis? But the political process does not simply weigh dispensation on the scales of its economic merit. The Byrd-Warner amendment, wearing the oral garb of economic prudence, was really designed to reverse the Department of the Navy's decision to grant the overhaul contract to the Philadelphia Naval Shipyard instead of the Newport News Shipyard, located in Virginia.

A GAO study indicated that the award would cost between $80 and $100 million more if the work was done at the Philadelphia yard. It was rumored that the Navy's decision was dictated by a campaign promise made by Vice President Mondale.

The politics involved was rather fascinating. Bath Iron Works, a major private shipbuilding facility in Maine, supported leaving the work with a private yard.

The Portsmouth-Kittery Naval Shipyard in Kittery, Maine, supported the transfer to Philadelphia, another public yard, ostensibly because it was free of the labor strikes now being experienced at Newport News in Virginia. It was also concerned that if Philadelphia did not secure contracts for work on aircraft carriers, it would bid for work on nuclear submarines in direct competition with Portsmouth-Kittery.

Regional politics entered as well. The New England–Midwest Caucus (of which I am a member) was banding together to support Philadelphia, because of the dramatic drain of military bases from the so-called "Frost Belt" into the "Sun Belt" states. The attempt to keep the *Saratoga* in Virginia was seen as an effort to prevent federal dollars from flowing into a Frost Belt state.

I voted against the interests of my region because of my concern about the impact of the total budget. I knew that similar concern would not readily surface if the shoe were on the other foot. But I would have been hard-pressed to reconcile a vote to spend $100 million of the taxpayers' money out of regional concern only—particularly after the Air Force had decided to close a major base in my state on the basis that it would save $26 million annually.

I spoke with Ed Muskie late in the afternoon and apprised him of the *Saratoga* matter so he would not be caught without notice. I also mentioned that Iran had just cancelled its order for two more destroyers and that the Navy was going to purchase them at the expense of other programs in the fiscal '80 budget. That was bad news for Maine, because the Navy would simply cut out ships scheduled to be built there.

Ed was in the middle of a conference on legislation raising the debt ceiling and calling for a balanced budget. He was the principal national figure trying to prevent rash action by Congress or, indeed, by the country at a Constitutional Convention.

Here was part of the classic dilemma. I had already voted to increase the budget authority under the supplemental bill to the 1979 budget to allow for flexibility in view of the rapidly deteriorating situation in the Mideast. This would require a waiver by the Senate, which would be difficult to secure because of the country's mood to reduce spending rather than expand it. I would probably vote to add money for the purchase of the destroyers in order to protect the frigate program in Bath— recognizing that in a time of budgetary crunch, the probability of success was not clear.

Ed chuckled about our predicament. We were about to be squeezed from both ends against the middle, trying to balance our budget and save our state's jobs.

MARCH 26, 1979

A STATE DINNER IS being held tonight, but I am not on the guest list. The costs are high, the tickets are limited. President Carter has, in fact, taken to seeking corporate contributions to defray the expenses of the dinner. Although not without precedent, somehow it seems inappropriate.

Not only does it appear to be a case of arm-twisting (few corporations will think it advisable to be in a noncharitable mood on this historic occasion), but it comes at a particularly inappropriate time. The announcement last week that corporate profits achieved a 26-percent increase for the last quarter of 1978 produced loud complaints from labor boss George Meany to presidential adviser Hamilton Jordan.

President Carter has promised public name-calling for those engaged in profiteering. Any large corporation, under the circumstances, is not eager to invite such attention and may be inclined to open its treasury for a contribution of $5,000 as insurance against presidential wrath. All the promises of public disclosure of the contributions and the impartiality of the President's assessments of violations of the war against inflation turn a little sour in the sensitive stomachs of the public.

The hearings before the Arms Control Subcommittee today were being chaired by Henry "Scoop" Jackson.

Admiral Hyman G. Rickover was scheduled to testify. He is a wiry little man of eighty years whose white hair is cropped close on the sides and parted in the middle. He reminds me of photographs I've seen of Carl Sandburg. But there is no poetry in his heart. Rickover, who has persuaded Congress to waive the retirement age of sixty-two in his case, is a feisty, sharp-tongued dispenser of blunt-edged aphorisms. He dismissed critics of low-level radiation emissions for workers at nuclear facilities with the suggestion that more people die of heart attacks than die working in a nuclear facility.

Rickover then went on to say that he had read in the paper that 495 people were killed each year by lawnmowers. Thousands of people will be called to investigate why 495 people were killed by lawnmowers and the remedy will be not to have any lawns.

His hyperbole produced a laugh and a yuk among the room filled with Defense Department employees who were saying to themselves, "Listen to the old man giving them hell. He hasn't slowed down a bit. . . ."

I knew I was treading on hallowed ground, but felt compelled to point out that over 50,000 injuries are suffered each year by virtue of the negligent design of lawnmowers; that as a result of lawsuits filed against the manufacturers of these machines for negligent design and inadequate safety features, thousands of injuries have been avoided, and I thought that that was a worthwhile social purpose of the law.

Rickover did not budge or become conciliatory in any way. He suggested that all anyone has to do is yell "radiation" and there are millions of dollars spent on investigations.

I was told later by the chief counsel to the Republican minority that Rickover was not in the habit of being confronted with hostile questions in his appearances before the Armed Services Committee.

MARCH 27, 1979

SHALOM. SALAAM. PEACE

THIRTY YEARS OF WAR ENDED
BETWEEN EGYPT AND ISRAEL.

So ran the headlines in thirty-six-point type. The vision of birds of peace taking flight with olive branches in their beaks was shattered by the other lead news items.

OPEC MINISTERS MEET IN GENEVA.
VOTE TO RAISE OIL PRICES 9% ON APRIL 1st

BOMB EXPLODES IN JERUSALEM, KILLING ONE,
WOUNDING 20—PLO CLAIMS CREDIT

A reception was being held at 10 on the third floor of the Russell Senate Building for Prime Minister Begin and President Sadat. Members of Congress would line up to shake their hands, be photographed with each of them, and secure their autographs. I had planned to join the celebration, but found that the Manpower and Reserve Subcommittee of Armed Services was meeting at the same time on the subject of the all-volunteer army. I chose to go to the committee hearing instead.

Legislation to amend the national debt ceiling was on the Senate floor today. Because of congressional spending, the debt ceiling had to be raised temporarily from its permanent level to cover the bills that the United States has incurred. Each year the scenario is virtually the same. Republican conservatives who have voted against the expensive programs that are spilling the red ink on our Treasury refuse to vote to lift the ceiling.

"Let the Democratic majority that votes for the programs now vote to pay for them" is a familiar cry. It is an understandable position, because every election they are attacked for voting against popular, albeit expensive, programs.

Those whose position is not defensible are the so-called "liberals" who vote for every major piece of legislation, taking full and complete credit for their compassion and interest in the social and economic advancement of the downtrodden, and then vote against raising the debt ceiling to pay for the programs. This hypocrisy lets them stand tall in the saddle of social justice and solidly on the ground of fiscal conservatism —and only their colleagues will ever know or care!

Today, the debt-limit bill has an added complexity. There is a ground swell of public support for a balanced budget, and efforts are under way to attach an amendment calling for a balanced budget by 1981.

Gary Hart has added another dimension to the problem. He is seeking to offer an amendment to force a vote on the outside-income limit that was raised three weeks ago. I walked across the Senate floor to speak with him. He seemed exasperated.

"We are about to increase the debt of the United States to some $800 billion, and look at the press—they don't give a damn. All they want to know is how we are going to vote on our outside income. Bill, let's start a newspaper business when we get out of this place. . . ."

It was clear that the vote on Hart's amendment would not come until tomorrow, so I left and went to a Maine delegation meeting to receive some bad news about Loring Air Force Base, which is located in the northern tip of the State of Maine. The failure of three years of effort. The Defense Department has rejected our military as well as our economic justification for continuing the base in full operation. Ed Muskie had sent a long and impassioned letter to President Carter and asked if he would wait at least twenty-four hours before breaking the bad news to our constituents. He was holding out hope that perhaps Carter would make good on his word to Muskie and to the rest of us about taking into account the severity of the economic consequences of any such action.

I left Ed's "hideaway" office in the Capitol and evaded the members of the press who were waiting outside for our comments. When I arrived back in my office, I found a letter from a constituent in Maine whose desperation was scribbled out in longhand in a letter to me.

Dear Senator Cohen,

I probably shouldn't be writing this considering the mood I am in right now (and in any event doubtful your staff will pass this on to you anyway), but, Senator, I am ripped.

For the past several evenings I have been sitting in my somewhat less than elaborate living room watching with disgust the elaborate shinnangans of a few frustrated farmers screaming about how poor they are. Tho I do notice they are driving some pretty fancy equipment while I'm driving what I can afford at this point—a rather beat 1968 Ford station wagon pushing 92,000 miles, front end shot, body rusted, etc. etc. Yes, I'll admit my wife also has a car—a 1974 Dodge Monaco that's costing her $88 a month in payments. However.

In a way I do sympathize with the farmers—they probably are having a tough time making $20,000 or so a year, and I'll admit prices for their equipment are astronomical. However, I'd like to see somebody do something at the source of these high prices. I'm enclosing my grocery bill for this past week. Around here the typical prices needed to survive—

Hamburger—$1.69/lb
Bologna—$1.09 for 8 oz
Sliced cheeze—$1.45/lb
Hot Dogs—$1.09/lb
Bacon—$1.49/lb (Armour)
Boneless Ham—$2.99/lb ($7.17 for 3.13 lbs)
Milk—$1.75/gallon (thanks to the milk commission)
Rice—$1.65/for 1 lb, 12 oz.

Doesn't mean much to someone making $56,000 a year plus expenses, Senator (or in the words of your predessesor, Bill Hathaway, "My wife and I sympathize with you every time we go to the grocery store!")

Now to get to the source of these abominable prices—it all lies in the middleman—the packer, the trucker, etc.

Thanks to government interference trucking rates are a mess. Seems the fastest way to screw something up is let the government stick a finger into the pie.

Anyway, I currently bring home a paycheck of $115.77 a week. You fellers down there in Foggy heaven ought to try and live on that. Maybe then you'd begin to see our side of things. Granted I have an edge with a monthly retirement check from the Coast Guard of $429 a month—and the wife, working three days a week, does bring home $95 a week. But how about these folks around the country don't have this extra income?

While I'm putting my gripes down let's get into gas and oil prices. Seems you who supposedly represent us folks forget our problems when you cross that state line going south (and try and prove to me you don't!!) If I (as I have to) pump my own gas it's now costing me 65.9¢ or 66.9¢ per gallon. The wife filled her car the other day at 73.9¢!! Latest fuel oil price to heat the house here cost me 54.5¢. Those figures don't mean much to you, I'd imagine. Now we got a bunch of bureaucrats running around Washington screaming "Car Pool, Car Pool—saves gas!" Sure. I work 9 p.m. to 4 a.m. six days a week—and there isn't anybody I can car pool with since I work alone. Fortunately I only have to drive a round trip of 4 miles. The *wife has to drive 14 miles round trip. Car pools don't work for her since more gas would be used just driving around picking up others.*

I don't know why it has to be but it seems that a crisis situation has to arize afore you people can do anything. Seems to me you people should worry less about what is going on in the world and get this country on its feet first.

I notice, Senator, it didn't take you long to spend the tax payers money on a trip to China!! Sure wish I could afford to take my family on a little vacation trip!!

All in all it seems to me you all should get off your collective duffs and start remembering who goes to vote and give you the job you got!!! Raising the minimum wage only eliminates jobs; farm price supports only encourage inefficiency; higher prices, higher taxes can only lead to a consumer revolt—as proven in California.

Yes, I've got complaints and no solutions. But that's what we elect you people for. I'm tired of going without—tired of trying to make ends meet—tired of trying to live on a limited income. While you bureaucrats spend, spend, spend. Its time Washington reorganized and cut back.

Yours,

———

P.S. My 15 year old son just reminded me that government statistics seem to be based on a family of four—which doesn't work for everybody when incomes are figured.

And my wife says that things always look good on paper but never seem to work out in practice when the bills come due.

PPSS Pardon the handwritting—can't afford a decent typewriter or a fancy secretary or two or four or ?

A member of my staff had proposed a response which I felt was too righteous and indignant. So I absorbed the insults and the anger and dictated a letter trying to express my understanding of the predicament he found himself in and what I was doing to try to help him.

CHAPTER 11

DURING THE HEARINGS on the impeachment resolutions of Richard Nixon, the mail poured in like water into a storm sewer during a cloudburst. Some of the mail would have been more appropriate in a sewer system.

"Jew boy. Hitler was right. His only mistake was that he didn't burn all of you in his ovens. . . ."

There were long typed letters in multicolored ink with elaborate cut-outs and pastings from *Soldier of Fortune* magazines; drawings of swastikas, directional arrows, tortured faces and Nazi rantings.

Then there were the envelopes containing small rocks—so that I might cast the first stone.

I often thought of the time the man threw a beer can at me when I was pitching Little League baseball. Hate always lurks just below the surface of civility and waits for an excuse or cause to erupt.

My staff tried to shield me from the really profane and perverse mail. They also tried to cheer me up periodically by taping letters or notes to the back of my leather chair so that I would be certain to take note of their urgency or levity.

One evening after a particularly long and bitterly debated day behind closed doors in the Judiciary Committee, I returned to my office and found a short letter taped to my chair. It had a return address of Spokane, Washington:

Dear Congressman Cohen:
    May a thousand camels relieve themselves in your drinking water.

                                        Sincerely yours,
                                        _____

                                        A dedicated Republican

The image of those desert beasts of burden with dumb faces relieving themselves in choral unity of their hot, rancid waste somewhere into a reservoir of water destined for delivery to Capitol Hill, the horror of ingesting the yellow fluid of their arid existence, the agony of inflamed or perforated intestines—all this compressed into two lines of rage! The man from Spokane had a touch of the poet. It was the only letter that brought laughter during a very dark period.

Today, another short letter was taped to my chair. Brevity in the expression of discontent has the reward of being read.

Dear Senator Cohen:
    Everybody knows that base closures are political. Get off your duff and do something for Northern Maine.
                                        Sincerely yours,
                                        _____

I dictated a prompt and abrupt reply: "Dear Sir, Where have you been for the last three years?" The letter was never sent. I was angry with the suggestion that I had done nothing about preserving the base. Nothing had consumed more of my time and energy, or that of my staff, since the action was first proposed by the Air Force in 1976.

But I knew the man was swinging at me out of desperation. He and a lot of other people would probably go bankrupt as a result of the Air Force's decision.

His anger, at least, was not as intense as that of the cabdriver who tried to push me through an intersection when he saw my congressional license plate.

MARCH 28, 1979

AT 9 A.M., the first official meeting of the Select Committee on Aging was held. Lawton Chiles of Florida is the new Chairman of the Committee, replacing Frank Church of Idaho, who has become Chairman of the Foreign Relations Committee. Chiles is a quiet, competent man who seems to wear a constant sleepy-eyed grin. An irrepressible cowlick on top of his head gives him a boyish look.

The purpose of the meeting was to establish what the members wanted as priority areas for investigation or oversight. Chiles made note of the fact that the Committee is extremely fortunate to have two of our members serving on the Finance Committee as well. The clear message was that this will help secure funding for those programs the Committee feels should be adopted in behalf of our senior citizens.

When Bill Bradley came into the meeting, Chiles repeated his statement about our good fortune in having John Heinz and Bradley also serving on the Finance Committee.

Bradley demurred. "I appreciate your confidence, but just remember, six John Heinzes and twelve Bill Bradleys don't equal one Russell Long."

This expression of humility produced a light ripple of laughter. Bradley was a good student. The knowledge of one's limitations is the beginning of wisdom.

Later that afternoon, after the vote on Gary Hart's amendment to restore a stricter limit on outside income (it failed), I was told by my staff that I had cast an erroneous vote on Dennis DeConcini's amendment the day before. I had intended to vote against DeConcini (who would achieve a balanced budget by raising taxes rather than reducing expenditures) and thought I had done so. But the vote was not on the amendment itself. It was instead a motion to table the amendment. My "nay" vote meant that I actually voted in favor of the amendment.

I sought recognition from the acting President of the Senate, stated my error and asked that the permanent congressional record be changed to reflect my true intent. I learned an embarrassing lesson that the Senate does not always vote on a straight "up or down" basis on amendments. Frequently the parliamentary device of a motion to table the amendment is employed.

As soon as I corrected my error, I left to join Ed Muskie at his "hideaway." Offices such as this one are reserved for the most senior members of the Senate and located in the Capitol building itself. His office is located on the first floor. As you look out the window, you can see all the way to the Washington Monument and Lincoln Memorial.

Today we were holding another meeting of the Maine delegation.

This time members of the Maine press were invited to be told officially what they had printed yesterday on the basis of "informed sources."

The bad news was official. Maine would lose a major SAC (Strategic Air Command) base in the northern part of the state. Muskie's appeal to President Carter had failed.

As we walked to his office, I congratulated Ed on his sixty-fifth birthday and said he was living proof that mandatory retirement was wrong. He laughed and said, "I'm thinking of voluntary retirement at this point. Bill, I've never had a worse birthday present in my life than the news that we're going to lose Loring."

Ed Muskie at sixty-five reminds me of a tall, weathered axe handle —lean and durable. His face and speech tell you immediately that he is a man from Maine. He is a person of great passion and therefore has his allies and his enemies. But he has worn well during his long years of public service.

In 1976, I gave serious thought to challenging him for his Senate seat. I had commissioned several polls to determine if I had a reasonable chance of beating him. Each one indicated that I could win—provided I raised sufficient funds to run a topflight campaign; provided I was prepared to work twenty hours a day for eighteen months. Yes, I was told, I could be the young David who slew the aging Goliath and be catapulted into the national limelight for my daring and my deed.

I really don't know if I could have beaten Ed Muskie. I do know that it was not in my heart to try.

I made the decision not to run while on a skiing vacation with my family at Sugarloaf Mountain in Kingfield, Maine. The national and local press had intensified the speculation on a long-awaited confrontation. Indeed, CBS News anchorman Walter Cronkite once called to invite Diane and me to dinner with him and his wife, Betsy. He concluded the evening with a light inquiry: "Well, are you going to or not?"

"Going to what?" I asked disingenuously.

"Are you going to take on Ed Muskie?" Cronkite could not quite suppress a smile at the corners of his mouth as he probed.

"I haven't decided yet. It will depend upon a lot of things, money being one of the key factors. . . ."

I really hadn't decided what to do. The challenge was tempting—just as the odds of winning were sobering. I did not have a large campaign war chest (I was still in debt). I did not have a prominent position on an important committee. There were no coattails of a popular President that could help offset Muskie's prestige. In short, even though the opinion polls showed me running ahead of Muskie, it would take a fistful of four-leaf clovers, in addition to more than a half a million dollars, to win the election.

It was while I was at Sugarloaf one morning, reading from Robert Pirsig's *Zen and the Art of Motorcycle Maintenance,* that something clicked in my mind and locked the decision irreversibly into place.

> When you try to climb a mountain to prove how big you are, you almost never make it. And even if you do it's a hollow victory. In order to sustain the victory you have to prove yourself again and again in some other way, and again and again and again, driven fore-ever to fill a false image, haunted by the fear that the image is not true and someone will find out. That's never the way. . . .
>
> To the untrained eye ego-climbing and selfless climbing may appear identical. Both kinds of climbers place one foot in front of the other. Both breathe in and out at the same rate. Both stop when tired. Both go forward when rested. But what a difference! The ego-climber is like an instrument that's out of adjustment. He puts his foot down an instant too soon or too late. He's likely to miss a beautiful passage of sunlight through the trees. He goes on when the sloppiness of his step shows he's tired. He rests at odd times. He looks up the trail trying to see what's ahead even when he knows what's ahead because he just looked a second before. He goes too fast or too slow for the conditions and when he talks his talk is forever about somewhere else, something else. He's here but he's not here. He rejects the here, is unhappy with it, wants to be farther up the trail but when he gets there will be just as unhappy because then *it* will be "here." What he's looking for, what he wants, is all around him, but he doesn't want that because it *is* all around him. Every step's an effort, both physically and spiritually, because he imagines his goal to be external and distant.

I knew that I was in danger of letting ambition race beyond my abilities and that even if I could defeat Ed Muskie (and that was by no means clear), I could not have claimed victory for the State of Maine.

I finished the book, sat down and wrote out a long explanation of my decision not to run for the Senate that year. Shortly before a press conference that I held two days later, I called Ed to tell him of my decision. He seemed relieved. I never mentioned the role of Zen and motorcycles.

As I sat across from him this afternoon, I was even more satisfied that I had made the right decision. Ed is in that stage of his life which resembles a light bulb that glows brightly before it burns out. He is in the final bloom where, as a survivor of life's exigencies, its random joys and tragedies, he has a self-confidence and self-awareness of his place in the uncompleted puzzle of existence. It is a security that can be seen in his eyes and says that personal gains or losses don't count anymore. There are no more ladders to climb.*

I had learned from Ed's experiences some lessons about the national press. Washington is the most transient city in the world. Not all of the flotsam is in the Potomac. Even in banana republics the powerful do not rise and sink with such regularity. Politicians need publicity to survive, but one runs a serious risk in inviting close press scrutiny. One man's beauty mark is another man's wen.

The Ed Muskie whose fireside television chat on the eve of the 1970 elections turned him into a national father figure watched his character dissolve over the next two years under the intensity of the hot lights of exposure and scrutiny. His meticulousness was turned into indecision, his centrism into a lack of conviction, his capacity for moral outrage into a lack of self-control. He was puffed up into something much larger than he was and then the pin of disapproval punctured his presidential balloon and he emerged as something much less than he is. It was unfair to make him larger than life and then prick him into pygmyism—but the press is expert at that. We all know that and yet take the risk anyway.

Publicity to show we're on duty, notice to attract editorial approval, attention to prompt constituent pride in the Senator or Congressman who can gain the notice of a network interviewer—these are nearly as important to the survival of a legislator as the quality of legislation he might draft or endorse. We are moths fascinated by candlelight and forewarned of its destructive power. We flutter by thinking we will just warm our wings near the flame. Inevitably, we are consumed.

I caught an evening flight to Chicago from National Airport, and had to transfer there for a flight to Los Angeles.

Upon arriving at O'Hare Airport, I was greeted by a droning voice over the public-address system: "Call for Senator Cohen. Please call a United Airlines operator."

---

* On April 29, 1980, President Carter appointed Ed Muskie to replace Cyrus Vance as Secretary of State. Vance had resigned his office following our unsuccessful attempt to rescue the American hostages in Iran.

I picked up the receiver and was told I was to call a television station in Maine. I knew before I dialed that the reporter wanted my reaction to the base-closure decision for the 11 P.M. news.

The plane out of Chicago was delayed for more than an hour. The flight was packed—nine seats across, window to window. I felt as if I were a steerage passenger heading for Ellis Island.

During the flight, ticker tapes spread the word that was heard around the world: a nuclear accident had occurred near Harrisburg, Pennsylvania.

I arrived in Los Angeles at 3:30 in the morning. It had been a very long day.

MARCH 29, 1979

THE NEXT MORNING, I drove to Pepperdine University Law School to address the students. I didn't realize it until I saw posters taped up all over campus that I had selected an inappropriate topic of "foreign policy." I managed to work in, with some tortuous footwork, a discussion of the role of a law-school education in participatory politics!

I spent the afternoon touring the campus, which consists of a cluster of architecturally appealing white buildings with walls of glass set into the side of dramatic hills overlooking Malibu Beach.

I advised the students that they shouldn't advertise the location of the school to future employers. The clear conclusion would be that nobody could possibly study in that breathtaking environment!

The next day, I drove to Whittier College to address a class of political-science majors. The trip was paid for by the Richard Nixon Fund.

I then caught a plane to San Francisco in order to put in a campaign appearance at a rally for the Republican candidate for Congressman Leo Ryan's seat (Ryan was murdered in Guyana while on a fact-finding mission).

Finally, on Saturday, I drove down the coast to Monterey to address the Young Republicans of California, a moderate group that had survived the long assaults by right-wing conservatives.

At the conclusion of my talk about the need for diversity, one middle-aged woman challenged me with a question: "I've been told you voted for federal funding for abortions and the ERA. Is that true?" It was clear from the tone of her question that she could not accept the fact that any Republican could have voted so.

Rather than give a long, tortuous explanation which might have the effect of minimizing her hostility, I simply looked at her and said, "Yes."

The Young Republicans immediately broke into a cheer that lasted for twenty seconds. It was not so much that they agreed with my votes as it was an effort to reaffirm the right to disagree within the party and not be run out on a rail. It was exactly the kind of attitude exhibited by this lady that they had been fighting against.

An older man sitting next to her said, "You say you're a friend of Pete McCloskey [Republican Representative from California]. He's no Republican—so I can't agree with you if this is the kind of people that you are supporting."

I responded, "Pete McCloskey is my friend, John Rousselot [Republican Representative from California] is my friend and this party is big enough for both of them."

Again, the YRs broke into applause.

I left on a wave of emotion and goodwill.

It was during the drive back to San Francisco that I noticed that my left cheek was involuntarily quivering. I glanced in the mirror to see if the quiver was visible.

The muscle in my face felt like a fish hooked on a nerve line that was being jerked about under the surface of my skin. The muscle twitched spasmodically as if to free itself from the hook. Good grief! California Tic! I worried all evening that it might be permanent.

The next morning it was still jumping. I wondered if I should stay in San Francisco and seek out an acupuncture specialist. There wasn't enough time to indulge my vanity. United Airlines had gone out on strike, and I had to be at the airport by 6 A.M. to make alternative plans to return to Washington. I secured a flight that was not exactly direct: San Francisco to Dallas on Delta; change to American Airlines in Dallas and fly to Washington via Memphis.

I held my left forefinger over my twitching cheek during the flight until I realized that I looked like a preposterous imitation of *The Thinker*.

On the descent into Dallas, just as we started to touch the runway, the pilot gave the engines full throttle. I opened my eyes to see if the airstrip was near water, as I had become accustomed to this procedure in landing at Logan Airport in Boston. But Dallas was landlocked! The passengers looked at each other quizzically. The pilot broke in on the intercom.

"Ladies and gentlemen. There is nothing to worry about. There is just a little too much traffic on the runway for comfort right now. So we're just going to ease around the flight pattern one more time and we'll be landing in a few more minutes."

The words of traffic congestion brought to mind the air crash in San Diego in 1978—one of the worst aviation disasters in our history. Passengers started looking out the windows for any large or small aircraft that might tear a hole in the fuselage. We saw none. None of us knew how close tragedy was that morning. The black breath of death was somewhere down there mingling in the shimmering fumes of a jet exhaust. The calm assurances of the captain erased our apprehensions, and we eased back into the cushioned chairs and waited for the screech of the rubber tires on the hot pavement.

The flight from Dallas to Memphis was uneventful, except that just as we were about to receive refreshments we ran into severe thundershower activity. The plane was tossed about violently, first up, to the side, and then down. One of the stewardesses was knocked to her knees.

Suddenly the passengers became very quiet—like animals sensing danger. We listened to the roar of the engines, trying to detect after each lateral slide and vertical drop whether they were failing. We looked out the windows at the wings that were bouncing like trampolines. I wondered if they would crinkle like aluminum foil. Fear permeated the silvery cylinder that contained our fate. It became something of a deathwatch.

Except for Preston Pearson, Number 26 of the Dallas Cowboys. He sat directly across the aisle and slept (or appeared to) throughout the entire flight. Whenever the plane bucked against the wind drafts, his long fingers would reflexively tighten around the back of the seat in front of him as if it were a pigskin he was grabbing out of the air on a long fly pattern. But he never opened his eyes or sensed the panic that had seized the rest of the passengers.

There is something to be said for being a pass-catching halfback.

APRIL 2, 1979

Ambition is a lust that is never quenched,
but grows more inflamed and madder by
enjoyment.
                    —THOMAS OTWAY

IF YOU WERE to peel back the layers of consciousness of a group of politicians in search of their motivations, you would find a garden variety of psychological drives, impulses, altruistic aspirations, ego gratifications and reinforcements. But the diversity of the driving forces would be awash in a common chemically charged solution—ambition. It might be ambition to do something or to be something, a deep desire to accomplish deeds or the unbridled quest to achieve position or a place of power. Whether it is a noble or ignoble force, it is an all-consuming passion which refuses to acknowledge the folly of its relentless pursuit.

There is no such thing as an unambitious politician, although the flame of desire may burn with different intensities. Gerald Ford, for example, spent more than twenty years in the House of Representatives and wanted only to one day be Speaker of the House. The winds of fortune gathered him up in its arms and carried him to the highest office in the land. Indeed, many people thought he was more honest and trustworthy than most of his predecessors precisely because he had never aspired to be President.

Family needs, friendships, privacy, quiet moments for reflection, time to collect time—all are sacrificed upon the bloody and brutal altar of public service. We are transfixed by the constant beat of the power struggle, the morning newscasts, the daily papers, the machine-gun chug of the AP and UPI wire services, the evening papers and late-night news flashes—so that we can be informed, up-to-date, geared for action. As if we were in control of the whitecapped waves of world events!

We spend a lifetime rationalizing that we envy those who have a more traditional life-style, who have time to enjoy the splendors of God's bounty, or to simply be "gone fishin'." Of course, if we really wanted to enjoy a private life without press releases, we need only step off the treadmill at the next election. Until recently, few have retired voluntarily.

I struggle to maintain a larger perspective on life. I read the philosophers who admonish me about the transience and fragility of existence, the idolatry of bowing to power, the folly and incurability of the self-induced disease. But I do not always heed their words, their wisdom.

Late this morning, I received a call from Jim Cannon of Howard Baker's office. Baker was on his way back from Tennessee, and his wife, Joy, was having severe stomach pains and might require hospitalization. He was scheduled to appear at a major fund-raising dinner for Representative Stewart McKinney of Connecticut. Howard wanted to know if I could fill in for him if Joy's condition was diagnosed as serious. I would be able to fly up to Connecticut and return the same evening. I quickly agreed to be available.

I awaited further developments later in the day. Late that afternoon, Cannon came by my office to explain that because of bad weather in New York and Connecticut, I probably would not be able to get back to Washington that night, and that Baker didn't want me to make that sacrifice on such short notice.

I called Diane to explain Baker's dilemma and the travel difficulties. My call proved to be a mistake.

We had become concerned about reports and advisory warnings from the police that the "Silver Gang" was on the rampage in northern Virginia again. The gang was a highly professional and well-organized band of thieves who burglarized homes in search of silverware. Assault and rape had accompanied their latest break-ins.

Ordinarily, the side door to our house would have been unlocked for our sons when they came home from school. Today all of the doors were locked. Diane was just arriving home from George Washington University, where she is a fine-arts student, and heard the phone ringing.

Our sons had both keys to the house. She tried climbing through the kitchen window, but a chair that ordinarily would have been under the kitchen window was missing. She tried to step lightly on a large glass-topped kitchen table. The phone kept shrieking. The table suddenly tipped and shattered on the floor into large, thirty-pound shards of glass —any one of which could have amputated her leg or foot. As it happened, she landed on the base of the chrome stand and injured only her pride.

When she picked up the phone she was in tears. "Billy, you won't believe what has just happened. . . ."

The incident itself, on a scale of misfortunes, was rather minor. But it came on the heels of our refrigerator's breaking down over the weekend while I was in California. All of the fresh and frozen food had spoiled, so we had been living on soups and McDonald's takeouts all week. In addition, we had been without heat in the house for over ten days right during an early-spring cold snap—even Senators can't get immediate home-repair service. No heat. No food. Now, no kitchen table.

It was not the most appropriate time to tell Diane that I was about to catch a plane for Connecticut in the name of duty, particularly now when she was under pressure to complete her work for an art show in which she had been selected to participate. I could rationalize that Diane was accustomed to those last-minute calls I made to tell her that I would not be home for dinner because Congress would be in session late that evening. (There had been hundreds of such calls during my years in the House.) But no one ever really adjusts to the anguish that is suffered when the hope for a quiet meal together, after its careful planning and preparation, is shattered by the shrill ring of the telephone.

Diane, embarrassed, hurt, and angry with herself and the concatenation of events that had led to the destruction of a table she'd treasured, said, "I'm okay. I'm not hurt. Don't worry. I think it's important that you help Howard out under the circumstances. . . ."

She was being noble, the dutiful political wife. Good soldier. Good sport.

I was profoundly disgusted with myself: not for having made the call, but rather for planning to leave again after having just returned from a long trip—and I wasn't running for any office! And yet, once I knew that she was not physically injured, I was prepared to ignore the psychic scars that my absence would inflict. It is a story writ large but in silence on the wife and family of every politician.

We are constantly playing to a large audience in the grandstand, ignoring the interests and needs of our families in the pursuit of some higher cause. It is a false god before which we fall down, and we're lucky enough if we have a family to which we can come home and repent.

I didn't go to Connecticut that night. Howard Baker wouldn't allow it. I could not have gone anyway. Fog mercifully sealed off ambition and obligation at the Washington airport.

APRIL 3, 1979

A FINAL MEETING WAS scheduled before the Armed Services Committee in order to "mark up"—draft and act upon the final language of—a bill: the supplemental request of the Defense Department for the fiscal year 1979. Defense Secretary Harold Brown and Deputy Secretary William Perry were scheduled to testify. They are two of the brightest men in the current Administration.

The major question to be resolved was the Department's support for the purchase of the four large destroyers that Iran had cancelled. The Department had originally requested additional funds to purchase two of the four ships in the supplemental request. The Committee was considering adding enough money to purchase all four and wanted to secure the testimony of Brown and Perry in support of such a proposal.

Actually, Chairman John Stennis and John Tower were trying to help me avoid more bad news for the State of Maine.

If all four ships were not included in the supplemental request, then it was clear that the Defense Department would request that the remaining two ships be funded in the fiscal 1980 budget—of which we would begin consideration in a matter of weeks. In order to stay within the President's budget goals, the Department would cut other parts of its shipbuilding program. In all likelihood, the cut would come out of my hide or that of Maine's Bath Iron Works and the frigate program. It was unfair, because Bath Iron Works is one of the few shipbuilding yards that actually complete ships ahead of schedule, thereby saving the government millions of dollars. But power politics is not played by the Marquis of Queensberry's rules of fairness. Position and self-interest prevail.

The Defense Department was not about to cancel shipbuilding contracts in the home state of the Chairman of the Committee—and certainly not in favor of ships built in the state of a freshman member of the Republican Party. It would never entertain any argument I might advance that the frigates would be more appropriate for the Navy's needs than the Iranian destroyers. Merit would not be measured against might. Of course, there was no guarantee that I could show superior merit.

I was between that proverbial rock and a hard place; but I had been there before.

In the summer of 1975, *The New York Times* reported that a "deal" had been consummated behind closed doors between Defense Department and Belgian officials involving the sale of F-16s to Belgium. The news report said the United States had offered to purchase $30 million worth of new Belgian-made machine guns as a "sweetener" to encourage Belgium to purchase the F-16 over the French-built Mirage. The Maremont Corporation, which has a plant located in Biddeford, Maine, had been the principal manufacturer of these weapons and had been scheduled to receive the $30-million contract. More than six hundred jobs were at stake if the contract was not awarded to the company.

Administration officials issued a strong denial of the news report. Their denials were not reassuring.

Shortly thereafter, at a reception being hosted by Nelson Rockefeller at his summer home in Seal Harbor, Maine, I asked the Vice President if he could arrange for President Ford to meet with me and the mayors of Biddeford-Saco so that we could discuss the issues with the man who had the ultimate authority.

Rockefeller contacted me two days later and said Ford would meet with me; but he indicated, in an indirect way, that he believed the decision had been made and would not be reversed.

During the meeting, which took place in the Oval Office of the White House, President Ford assured me and the visiting mayors that no "deal" had been made and that on the basis of his review of Maremont's past performance, the company not only could compete, but could prevail.

It was a spark of hope. The cobwebs of suspicion and cynicism that were starting to gather in my mind were brushed away. Rockefeller must have been given bad information, I thought.

The joy was short-lived. The Army, after "competitive" testing of the two weapons systems, selected the Belgian-made machine gun. The objective criteria utilized by the Army were rate of fire, level of performance and cost effectiveness. The Maine company was required to produce a weapon 60 percent of whose parts would have to be interchangeable with the machine guns that were already in the Army's inventory. No such requirement was placed upon the Belgian-made weapon. Upon investigation, we found that the Army had failed to abide by its own regulations and criteria. Whereas an official statement was made that the Belgian gun fired at a more rapid rate than did the Maine-made weapon, and therefore had a greater kill ratio, the Army's criteria specified that the ideal rate of fire was seven and a half rounds per second —exactly that achieved by the Maremont Company—and that a higher rate was a waste of ammunition. The Army concluded that the bolt assembly on the Maine gun jammed at more frequent intervals than did that on the Belgian one—overlooking test results which showed that the barrel of the Belgian gun developed cracks after sixty thousand rounds.

Finally, I had been told that the comparative cost of the weapons would be a very important factor in the decision. The cost of the Belgian weapon was nearly double that of the Maine-produced gun! The Army nullified the dramatic disparity by including the cost of ammunition over the life cycle of the weapons.

I was outraged by what I considered to be palpable deceit. I even joined the District of Columbia Bar so that I could take an active role in the lawsuit the Maremont Company decided to file against the Defense Department. Damn it, we would fight City Hall!

Well, we won a preliminary restraining order that prevented the Defense Department from signing any agreements pursuant to the award, but the victory, like the court decision, was only temporary. There was a limit to what the Maremont Company wanted to spend on legal fees and court costs (it would have been necessary to carry the matter to the Supreme Court). There was also a time factor: if the contract could not in fact be awarded to Maremont within a matter of a few months, it would have to lay off the six hundred people who were employed on the production line. We might score a legal victory after many months of battle, but it would be a Pyrrhic one. Finally, there was the political reality facing the parent company, located in Chicago, Illinois: this was only one contract of many that the company had with the U.S. government. It was important to the people of Maine, but it was less so to the remote board of directors, who had a much larger stake in the company's future relations with the Defense Department.

So a white flag was raised. The Maine delegation received from the Army an ocean of compliments for our tenacity and determination in representing our state. Some minor contracts were awarded to Maremont to prevent large-scale layoffs. City Hall had won again.

I was disappointed with the armistice, but even more so with the way in which it was achieved—under the banner of fairness, the aegis of objectivity and equity. It was, as *The New York Times* had originally reported, a "deal." The fix was on from the very first, in spite of all the denials. President Ford, in my judgment, had not been fully informed of the facts. He would not have raised my hopes when he didn't have to. In fact, I later learned that some of his staff were dismayed at his optimism over Maremont's chances. Any objective person would probably conclude that it was a good deal for our country—the sale of $2 billion worth of airplanes in return for a $30-million contract for machine guns. Yes, a pretty good trade. But it would have been better to say so openly rather than wrap a false veil of honor around the whole process. . . .

I decided to support the Defense Department's request to purchase the ships originally contracted for by Iran. We, as John Tower argued, were falling way below an acceptable level of ships to protect vital sea-lanes. The ships could be purchased at a saving to the taxpayers of $200 million per ship. Secretary Brown testified he wanted the ships. In short, a strong case could be made on the merits.

And yet, I did not make my decision on the merits alone. There were other factors that I could not blot out. Maine had been serving as a depository for bad news in recent months: the Air Force was about to inflict extreme economic adversity by reducing a major air base by more than 80 percent; the state had run out of oil during a long cold snap and in February had had to borrow two million gallons of fuel from the Defense Department; the Nuclear Regulatory Commission had ordered the shutdown of Maine Yankee, which supplies 35 percent of the electrical power in the state; the Commodities Futures Trading Commission had just cancelled April and May contracts for potatoes (allegedly because the potatoes currently being delivered were damaged or below grade upon arrival), thereby inflicting hardship on an industry that could ill afford it; eligibility for food stamps was being revised in a manner that would impact severely upon the state—now regarded by the federal government as the "poorest" state in the country on a per capita income basis. . . . The list went on. And now the potential loss of contracts in a major shipbuilding yard! I wondered exactly how much more acquiescence the people whom I am supposed to represent could stand.

My support for the supplemental budget request did not go unchallenged.

Several days later, I was riding over to the Capitol on the subway with Don Riegle and I asked him what the Budget Committee would do with or to the supplemental request.

"Take out the Iranian ships, of course. Don't tell me you voted for them."

"Yes, I did."

"Well, Bill, I was telling some friends of mine it would take at least six months before the Defense Department got to you. Looks like they've done it in three. What's in it for you?"

"Don," I replied, "they are going to include the Iranian ships in either the supplemental or the fiscal '80 request which we'll take up in a few weeks. If it comes out of the '80 budget, it's possible that my state could lose some contracts.

"By the way, Don, don't get too self-righteous. I recall the time you were in the House and running for the Senate and the Justice Department had requested authority to admit thousands of Vietnamese refugees into the country, those who had supported the United States and were in danger of being slaughtered, and you opposed it because Michigan was suffering high unemployment problems."

"Not exactly," he countered. "I said that every American should get exactly the same benefits we were about to give to the refugees." He then added with a smile, "In any event, you must admit that my position had wider application and was not as parochial as yours."

"All depends on whose self-interest is at stake, Don. Whose ox is getting gored. Yours was then. Mine is now."

We are friends, and we parted on good terms without any rancor. But his comments stung and stayed with me for some time.

APRIL 4, 1979

A HIGH SCHOOL MARCHING BAND from Millinocket, Maine, known as the Pink Panthers came to town today. The students were bubbling with pride and enthusiasm. Even the downpour could not dampen their spirits and joy at being in the nation's capital. They wore brown windbreaker jackets with pink-striped jersey sleeves and necks. They flocked around, begging me to pose with them for photographs (the official photographer failed to come and take a group shot). The students had Polaroid cameras and Instamatics. I spent nearly a half an hour posing with them and then left for a luncheon with some experts in the field of economics to discuss the role of wage and price controls as an instrument to fight inflation. They were unanimous and vociferous in their denunciation of artificial controls.

I received a call later in the afternoon from the Chairman of the Armed Services Committee, John Stennis, who asked me to call Ed Muskie and secure his assistance in sustaining the funding of the supplemental request. I called Ed immediately.

I spent the rest of the afternoon on the Senate floor serving as the Assistant Minority Whip. I tried to concentrate on the debate taking place, but a headline in the morning *Bangor Daily News* kept flickering like summer lightning in the corner of my mind: COHEN WARY OF DICKEY-LINCOLN. The story as written was accurate. A number of environmental groups wanted me to introduce a bill to ''deauthorize'' (discontinue) the funding for a controversial hydroelectric project in northern Maine. I was prepared to fight to terminate the project when it came to the floor as part of the general Public Works Appropriation Bill in June. I was reluctant, however, to try to deauthorize a project that had been fathered by Ed Muskie, since he was the second-ranking member on the Environment and Public Works Committee. Assuming that I could have hearings scheduled on a deauthorization proposal (unlikely), if I lost by a large margin in the Committee (likely), it would be virtually impossible to turn the vote around on the Senate floor. Those members who had voted against deauthorizing a project would be locked into voting for it when the appropriation bill came to the floor.

Unfortunately, the headline implied that I was backing away from my campaign commitment to fight against the Dickey project. Most people do not read beyond the first few paragraphs of a news story, and the headline tends to prejudice the reader with its tone. I knew that the phones in my district offices would be ringing with protests and charges of betrayal. They were.

Exactly one week has passed since the Three Mile Island mishap in Harrisburg. The congressional reaction was predictable. Opponents of nuclear energy called for a moratorium on all further plant construction. Advocates of nuclear power were shaken by the dimensions of the catastrophe that had nearly occurred and called for greater regulation.

One Senator said Harrisburg had been to nuclear power what the Tet offensive was to Vietnam—the beginning of the end.

APRIL 5, 1979

JESSE HELMS IS a tall, ramrod-rigid conservative Senator from North Carolina. He has become a household word to those who believe that we have gone from riches to rags as a nation because of a spendthrift and morally bankrupt liberal mentality that has seeped through and permeated our political and social philosophy from the New Deal to the Great Society.

He tends to see most issues in bold primary colors. No "pale pastels" occupy any of the walls of his philosophy. No clouds of doubt cast shadows over his convictions. He enjoys, in Mark Twain's words, the "calm confidence of a Christian holding four aces."

As a legislator, Jesse is consistent and predictable in his voting habits —just as are those who reside at the opposite end of the political spectrum. But while his political adversaries know that Helms will be forever rolling a rock down on their comfortable assumptions, they can never be certain from what direction or angle the rock will come.

He will usually inform the Senate leadership during the course of debate that he has a number of amendments to offer to pending legislation without revealing the nature or content of the amendments. This will prevent his opponents from researching and organizing arguments against the amendments or allowing special-interest groups to contact and lobby other members of the Senate.

This afternoon, Senator Helms carried off his offering of an amendment with the surprise and success of the attack on Pearl Harbor. His amendment to the legislation creating a new Department of Education would deprive the federal courts of jurisdiction over any cases involving voluntary prayer in public schools. A motion to table Helms's amendment failed on a tie vote of 43 to 43. The Senate was in a virtual state of shock! How could this be?

The Senate was going to be forced to vote "up or down" on an issue that has hung like a ragged wound in the minds of millions of Americans ever since the Supreme Court banned prayer in public schools in 1964.

The vote wasn't even close: 47 to 37. Twenty-nine Senators were running for re-election in 1980, and few of them wanted the burden of explaining how they could be against children's praying, voluntarily, in public schools.

But Helms's victory was not secure. Senator Abraham Ribicoff of Connecticut voted in favor of the Helms amendment so that he would be in the parliamentary position of being able to move to reconsider the vote. Before Helms could be recognized to call for a vote on Ribicoff's motion, Majority Leader Robert Byrd moved to recess until Monday morning. Proponents of the bill were staggered by the solid blow of the Helms amendment and wanted time over the weekend to collect their senses and some votes.

APRIL 6, 1979

ON MY WAY from the Capitol today, just as I started to get into my car and drive out to Langley High School in Virginia to watch Kevin play his first baseball game of the season, a large woman dressed in jeans and a red sweat shirt called out to me.

"Hey, mister. Hey, mister, wait a minute!"

She jogged toward my car. Her face was lined with anxiety. I thought she was lost or looking for directions. She was carrying a sheet of green paper rolled in her fist. "Have you seen Jesus of Nazareth?" she asked. "No, I haven't," I responded somewhat matter-of-factly.

I got into the car and drove off. I noticed that the woman stopped a young couple walking up the steps to the Senate Building and asked them the same question. They just smiled at each other and shook their heads.

Such encounters are not unusual on Capitol Hill. We have our share of Mad Hatters and misanthropes, although some critics have suggested that not all of the dispossessed are found on the outside of our hallowed halls.

There is one man who can be seen during the spring and summer months walking around the Capitol grounds wearing a beard, top hat and black cutaway coat. He responds to the name of Abe.

Another harmless old man waits daily near the subway cars on the House or Senate side (or occasionally in front of the dining room) passing out his personally typed copyrighted essays on the subjects of God, government and man.

"Did you read my last essay, Bill? You know, the one about Effort and Excellence?"

"I read it, Joe. I thought the analogy to a golf swing was just right. It was a good piece. Keep it up."

I've been saying nearly the same thing for six years. He continues to beam with pleasure at the compliment no matter how often it is replayed.

Then there is Crazy Pete. He is a gaunt, tense, bespectacled man whose black hair (what remains of it) looks as if it had been cut with a pair of rusty garden shears. He walks hunched over, wearing a tattered dark overcoat, muttering to himself. He reminds me of a coiled spring that is slightly twisted. There is an odd camber to his walk that yields a sidewinder sort of gait.

The Capitol Hill police often tease him as he leaves one of the office buildings muttering his deep rage to himself. He will whirl around and gnash at them with angry threats.

He is the type of person who will one day explode into violence, and someone will ask, "Why wasn't he locked up?"

APRIL 7, 1979

I SPENT this Saturday morning visiting with Diane at the art festival held outdoors in one of the parking lots near George Washington University. This is an important day for her. She has started down the long road to building a career of her own, establishing her own identity and creative talents beyond those of mother and political wife. She has subordinated her own need to flourish for nearly twenty years, and that need is rising like sap.

After lunch, I took Chris to his soccer game. He is one of only two boys on the team who are not German. The wind was not blowing up to 50 mph, as it did during Kevin's baseball game last night, but the players still looked as if they were standing in a wind tunnel.

That evening one of Kevin's schoolmates who lives down our street was hosting a party for a band from New York. Cars lined the entire length of the street on both sides. As the party broke up, it became clear that many of the students had been drinking heavily. At least two young men were lying passed out on our front lawn after having regurgitated whatever spirits had invaded their systems for the evening. Others were running up and down the street shrieking. After a half hour of indulgence, I finally got dressed and went outside to ask them to please quiet down.

I then threw caution to the winds and tried, through my powers of persuasion (my words rolled out like thin strips of gauze), to stop two rather large young men from rolling one of the three-hundred-pound boulders that line our neighbor's lawn out into the middle of the road. The bigger one, a future draft choice for mauler of the year, promptly offered to alter my face!

I was angry enough to take up the challenge (Who knows? I thought: perhaps his jacket just makes him look that big in the dark, or perhaps the alcohol has affected his faculties), but maturity and better judgment prevailed. I had broken my jaw twice during college athletic days. A cracked mandible was a handicap that I could forgo at this point in my life.

Position also tempered instinct. A variety of headlines that could flow from a rash act on my part quickly slipped across my thoughts.

SENATOR CLUBS VISITING STUDENT MUSICIAN! or (more likely) SENATOR INJURED BY STUDENT FOLLOWING DRINKING SPREE!

So the rock was rolled into the street. Later, Kevin (Where was he when I needed him?) and a friend rolled it back onto the lawn.

Finally, around 2:30 A.M., peace settled over our street.

APRIL 9, 1979

THE WEEKEND HAD BEEN a busy one for the proponents of the Department of Education. They concocted a scheme to strip the Helms amendment from the Department of Education bill and yet cover the flanks of those members running for re-election in 1980 who did not want to be on record as opposing prayer in public schools.

They brought a new bill, S. 450, sponsored by Senator Dennis DeConcini, to the Senate floor that involved the jurisdiction of federal courts. Robert Byrd argued that this was the appropriate vehicle to which a prayer amendment should be attached, and in fact, he would do the honor himself and offer the amendment. Jesse Helms was not deceived by this fast shuffle of the legislative deck. He knew intuitively that a card was being dealt from the bottom.

Earlier he had declined Robert Byrd's invitation to offer the prayer amendment to the DeConcini bill.

"However, I will say to the Senate that I know this could be interpreted as giving a lot of Senators an out. They can go home and say, 'Well, I voted for it on the DeConcini bill, which is a more appropriate vehicle,' and that sort of thing.

"I hope Senators will not make that mistake. To the limit of my capability, I will say to the able Senator from West Virginia, I will try to make it clear all across the country just what occurred on the Senate floor. Senators should not seek to avoid the responsibility of voting for a prayer amendment that has a good chance of survival. It may not have a chance of survival on the DeConcini bill, which I think the Senator from West Virginia will acknowledge, because there is great doubt that the House will even have an opportunity to vote on it once it goes to the House Judiciary Committee."

The Byrd amendment passed 51 to 40.

Then the Department of Education bill was taken up again. The proponents argued that the prayer amendment, if it stayed in the bill, would kill the bill and must be removed. Those who favored the restoration of prayer in public schools had placed their convictions on record with the prior vote. Now they could enter the lofty realm reserved for statesmen and responsible legislators by removing the noxious provision from the bill. This bit of rhetorical legerdemain, coupled with a little gentle persuasion by Vice President Mondale of some recalcitrant Democrats, resulted in the prayer amendment's being stripped from the Department of Education legislation.

Helms knew that the handwriting on the wall was not a forgery. The DeConcini bill would be buried deeper than Davy Jones' locker in the dead sea of the House Judiciary Committee's inactive files. It didn't have a prayer of becoming law.

April 11, 1979

The Senate was not in session today. The Easter recess had begun. As newspapers across the country would note, more than a hundred Congressmen had taken to the skies on flights to various parts of the world. The swallows do not even arrive in Capistrano with the regularity with which members of Congress leave for the far reaches of the globe in nonelection years. One television network tried to film all the members who were boarding flights on military planes at Andrews Air Force Base. The television crew received something less than a warm welcome.

Senator Jacob Javits, who with Frank Church, the Chairman of the Foreign Relations Committee, led a delegation to China, tried to place the trips (always called junkets) into perspective.

"We spend billions of dollars in preparing for war. To suggest that we should not spend thousands for peace is absurd."

His words, which made eminent good sense, fell like dry leaves on the public's palate. No one could dispute that it is important to meet with leaders of foreign governments and to view on-site the social and economic systems of other countries. But because of the past, and flagrant, abuses of trips that entailed little work and lots of leisure in exotic vacation spots, every trip is now brushed with the dark color of "junket" and taxpayer rip-off.

And the timing seems all wrong. Gasoline prices at the pumps are testing the very fabric of civil obedience. The nation is terrified about nuclear "meltdowns." Food prices are soaring. Inflation is at double-digit levels. The Senate voted to allow higher outside earnings, and the House was considering a $50-per-day tax deduction. . . . The news accounts of the congressional travel plans rubbed like shards of glass in an oozing wound.

Late in the afternoon, after testifying before a Senate subcommittee against the construction of a large hydroelectric power plant in northern Maine, I received a call from a *Time* magazine reporter.

"Senator Cohen. A lot of people are saying that this is a do-nothing Congress. How do you respond to that charge?"

I had anticipated the question. The Ninety-sixth Congress was not blazing any new records for passing legislation. In fact, we seemed to be setting new records for *not* adopting legislation. We had passed only eight bills, none of any major significance, which was half the number of the previous Congress. Although 4,197 bills had been introduced, this was 2,737 fewer than had been offered in the Ninety-fifth Congress in the time period. We had cast 105 recorded votes, half the number of the previous year. Even the *Congressional Record* contained nearly 2,500 fewer pages this year.

I responded to the question with mock gravity: "You could say that, but you would be wrong." The phrase, taken from the Nixon days in the White House, floated straight over his head. When I realized that he was actually quoting me, I became serious quickly. Nothing is more painful than reading your witticisms in the cold print of tomorrow's papers. They hang like the stale smell of cigar smoke in a closed room.

"No, it's not a question of being a do-nothing Congress," I said. "Congress is actually reflecting the mood of the country, which no longer wants to see a cascade of laws flowing from Mount Washington. They don't want more laws. They want us to revise or remove existing laws which are unnecessary or unworkable. They no longer accept the doctrine of 'Publish or Perish' in politics. They realize we have become a nation of too many laws—which are either unenforced or overenforced. As a result, we are breeding contempt for the rule of law. So I look upon the lull in legislative activity as a positive sign rather than a negative one that Congress isn't doing anything. A great deal more time is being spent on committee hearings, oversight, trying to make government work more efficiently, trying to formulate a sunset law that will eliminate unnecessary law. . . ."

I did not mention that it was common sentiment that Majority Leader Byrd did not want to take up many controversial bills. He had not scheduled any Friday sessions since January, in order to allow those running for re-election to return to their states to campaign over the long weekends. The country's mood of not wanting a hyperactive Congress coincided nicely with his plans to do everything he could to minimize the risk to vulnerable Democratic Senators.

At 5, several other Republican Senators and I arrived at the White House to meet with Zbigniew Brzezinski, the President's National Security Adviser. We met in the Roosevelt Room and gathered around a large conference table. Finger hors d'oeuvre and coffee sat on a table awaiting our self-service.

Brzezinski breezed in a few minutes after 5 and after grabbing a small plateful of sandwiches, sat at the head of the table and suggested that he give us an overview of foreign policy for the first half hour or so before he opened it up to our questions.

He is a trim, sharp-faced man. His hair is cut in a pompadour style that gives his face an arrowlike angularity. He speaks with a clipped, authoritarian accent that sounds more Prussian than Polish.

Brzezinski is a word merchant. Phrases slip easily from him and jump from thought to thought like a flat rock that skims and hop-skips the surface of lake water. He is not orotund in expression like Kissinger, but neither is he as profound. In fact, it seems rather obvious that he sees Kissinger as a rival.

In his discourse on the Administration's foreign-policy achievements and objectives, he took subtle shots at Kissinger.

"We are much better off under SALT II than under SALT I, which committed us to inferior numbers of weapons systems. Now we have achieved equal aggregates.

"In the past, we have placed too much emphasis on hardware and too little on human interest and intelligence. We have been too busy trying to suppress change rather than trying to adjust to and accommodate it."

This was an obvious reference to the fall of the Shah and Iran to the Islamic revolution and the myopia of the previous presidential advisers.

Brzezinski painted a positive picture under the Carter Administration.

"During the last two years, the United States has accomplished tangible benefits in foreign policy. First, there is the Panama Canal Treaty. We now have a more mature, more flexible, more differentiated posture in Latin America. For the first time, we have no slogan to describe our relationship with Latin America. . . .

"Secondly, the Egyptian–Israeli peace treaty is a major diplomatic achievement of this Administration.

"Third, we have established diplomatic relations with the People's Republic of China. This was not a case of mere expediency, but was long-range in planning and had an immediate anti-Soviet impact. . . ."

Brzezinski went on to cite three other major areas of achievement: the international-fuel-cycle evaluation program ("it may not yield any benefits, but it is important that other nations are interested''); the effort to shape a common front with developing countries (he did not explain what victories were achieved under this broad goal); and a long-term defense program with our NATO allies.

When he finally opened the session to questions, Brzezinski shared his time, if not gladly, at least generously. It was clear that he would have preferred to discourse with columnist James Reston of *The New York Times* on his world visions rather than walk a group of hardheaded Republican Senators through the labyrinth of his thought processes.

Once again, we were offered the rose-colored picture that President Carter had painted for us last month.

"Watergate and Vietnam are behind us. Our position in the Third World countries is far better. In the Far East, we have for the first time good relations with China and Japan simultaneously.

"Yes, there are two short-range problems—the arc of crisis along the Indian Ocean, and South Africa. But we are starting to address these. . . ."

He was long on generalities and short on specifics.

"Dr. Brzezinski," he was asked, "exactly how do we identify legitimate United States interests in this world of change? Exactly what would we do to protect Saudi Arabia from going the way of Iran? . . ."

His response was: "Those are difficult questions to answer and have to be considered on a case-by-case basis."

I returned home, showered and changed clothes. Diane and I had been invited to the McLean, Virginia, home of Henry and Jessica Catto. Henry was Chief of Protocol at the White House under President Ford. They are staunch supporters of fellow Texan George Bush and were hosting a dinner for him tonight. Bush was in the process of preparing to run for the Republican nomination for President.

The guest list was heavily weighted with nationally known journalists and their wives. Henry Kissinger was also invited, but he arrived late. When he did, though, he immediately started talking about the first volume of his memoirs, which he had just completed.

He is not one to listen to light talk at a party. Guests are always eager to seek out his opinions on world issues, and he is not reluctant to respond.

"When I go to college campuses today, it is an entirely different attitude that I see. There is little moral outrage about the Vietnam war. They want to know why we lost.

"You know, if I had to consider sending my son into a war knowing that one hand would be tied behind his back, that we were not committed to win, I don't know what I would tell him. . . ."

When we left for home later that evening, Kissinger was still sitting at the dinner table discoursing—the sun around which all the planets were revolving.

APRIL 13, 1979

DIANE NEEDED time to finish her paintings as part of her final assignment for the semester. I decided to take the boys to Rehoboth Beach in Delaware for a few days.

It rained the entire weekend. The wind whipped up huge white caps on the Atlantic. I spent most of the time reading John Irving's *The World According to Garp,* while Kevin studied for school exams. Chris, the indomitable explorer in the family, walked the rain-soaked beaches all weekend. The three of us had not spent that much time together without interruption since I had become involved in politics. We experimented with different restaurants. Diane and I want our sons to be comfortable in ordering a variety of food. Kevin has a habit of eating McDonald's hamburgers when he's on his own. When he dines out with me, he always orders filet mignon—a habit I hope to break.

On the way home, the torsion bar in my sports car snapped, dropping the right fender onto the front tire and causing it to blow out. The torsion bar had become a victim of rust and corrosion. We narrowly missed becoming new highway statistics.

To compound our troubles, someone had removed the jack from the car. When I finally managed to change the tire, we started the long ride home with the front fender rubbing against the tire, emitting blue smoke and a rubber scream for most of the 135 miles. It was a long trip home. The tension sent a severe jolt of pain from my neck muscles into my head.

Garp only reinforced my own notions about life's fickleness—the dramatic shift from joy to sorrow and tragedy that the tick of a second can bring.

APRIL 17, 1979

ON TUESDAY, I flew from Boston to Augusta, Maine, where I addressed the Maine White House Conference on Libraries. I stayed on the platform to listen to the speaker who followed me—an articulate librarian from New Hampshire. I had not anticipated that he would talk for more than thirty minutes and started to squirm as each minute beyond the half-hour margin I had allowed myself ticked off.

I arrived nearly forty minutes late for a press conference that I had scheduled at the State Capitol.

Among the many questions that were asked came one I had anticipated. A young reporter from one of the wire services stood up and in the most cynical reportorial manner that she could muster said, "In view of the fact that you received large contributions from the oil companies, how do you intend to vote on windfall profits?"

I considered a lengthy answer, pointing out that the contributions I had received made up a small fraction of the total money I had raised and spent. I thought of emphasizing that my vote had never been for sale and never would be, that anyone who supported me financially was making an investment in good government and not special treatment. . . .

I decided against making a speech (it usually appears too defensive) and replied, "I intend to support a windfall-profits tax."

The reporter had an obligation to ask what a number of constituents had written me about in letters. Her question raised one of the fundamental problems in our current system of financing congressional campaigns. It also gave evidence of the pervasive, though fallacious, notion that the only special interests in our nation are negative or evil forces which conspire against the best interests of the country.

Several weeks ago, when I was returning to Washington from Maine, a young flight attendant asked in a lyrical Southern accent, "You're a Senator? Tell me, are you bothered much by all those special-interest groups that I read about, all those lobbyists?"

I imagined that the vision she had of Congress was that of a temple of the people invaded by spores of special interests or money changers emptying their bags into the pockets of public servants in exchange for votes. It is not an accurate account of the role played by lobbyists in Washington, but a visitor to the Capitol would not find the vision entirely distinct from reality. Surface impressions tend to be lasting.

There are, by the best estimate under a weak and unworkable 1946 lobby disclosure law, approximately fifteen thousand lobbyists in Washington. Lobbying is one of the major growth industries in the city that spends nearly a billion dollars each year. Another billion dollars is spent on the direct-mail lobbying technique that generates massive letter-writing campaigns to Congressmen. Lobbyists have a legitimate function under our system of government and serve a useful purpose—the transmission of their companies' or clients' views to officials responsible for making decisions that will affect them. They are agents of principals who have the constitutionally guaranteed right to petition their government.

This sounds orderly and entirely aboveboard in principle. Of course, our history books are heavy with examples that the theory has been abused in practice—the Korean bribery scandal involving Tongsun Park being the most recent disclosure.*

But in recent years there is a brazenness that seems to have taken hold of the process, an arrogance and disdain that makes a pathetic mockery of the legislative process.

The halls of Congress have become so crowded with professional lobbyists that Congressmen often are forced to push their way through the throng to reach the chamber to vote. Indeed, a few years ago it became necessary to rope off the hallway leading from the steps of the House to the floor so that the members could pass through and cast their votes before the allotted fifteen-minute time period expired.

I recall that as a new member of Congress, when the bells rang announcing that a vote was in progress, I would usually jog from the Longworth (later the Cannon) Building across to the Capitol and take the front steps two at a time (on good days, three) only to confront a sea of faces urging me to vote according to their respective interests.

"Bill, this is a 'yes' vote for you. It will help the small businessmen of your state."

"No," another would say, "labor and the committee want a 'No' vote."

If the vote was on an important piece of legislation, you would find

---

* In February, 1980, the FBI revealed that it had been conducting an investigation into political corruption that included members of Congress. FBI agents had posed as wealthy Arabs who were prepared to (and did) pay large sums of money to Congressmen in exchange for personal favors or special privileges. Eight members of Congress, including one Senator, allegedly were involved in the scandal. Although only a small fraction of the total congressional membership was said to be implicated, the stain had spread, in the public's eye, to nearly all of Capitol Hill.

some lobbyists in the galleries pointing their thumbs up or down—emperors signaling for the life or death of a bill.

In the beginning, I pretended my ears were stuffed with wax and walked through the crowd without looking to the right or left. It was a much too proud and pious posture and evidence of a corresponding arrogance.

I decided that an easier route was to enter the Capitol on the first floor and then walk up the side stairs, thereby avoiding the east entrance to the floor.

I don't know if any votes are ever changed by the pleas and importunings that reverberate and ricochet around our hallowed halls. Perhaps a few Congressmen who are confused or uninformed on a given vote are influenced by the upright or inverted thumbs. But it does give the impression that an auction is going on for the highest bid and that the merits of the legislation and the welfare of the public are thrown out in the process. . . .

I looked directly at the flight attendant and said, "Actually, I am rarely lobbied by anyone in Washington. The only people who lobby me are airline attendants who want me to vote to protect their free or reduced fares to foreign countries from being taxed as income by the IRS."

I said this lightly and without malice. I wanted to make a point that is so often overlooked: everyone is or has a special interest. Farmers calling for higher parity or price supports; colleges and churches urging the retention of the charitable tax deduction; homeowners who deduct interest paid on mortgages; recording artists who want royalties from radio stations that play their songs; public-interest groups that want reimbursement for their legal fees; students and strikers who demand the right to food stamps—and flight attendants who receive free or low-cost travel as tax-free compensation in kind.

No group is inherently evil or ill-willed. Each acts out of narrow self-interest or from a particular social and economic philosophy to get its share (or more) at the federal feeding ground—following the maxim that "Who does not demand, does not receive."

APRIL 23, 1979

ONE of the legacies of the Watergate episode was the creation of a Congressional mechanism to introduce some rationality and order into our budgetary and appropriations process. The national budget and national debt were growing at an exponential rate, and there seemed to be no inclination to change the haphazard and irresponsible manner in which we were spending the taxpayers' dollars and mortgaging the futures of our children.

One of the most obvious causes of the explosion in federal spending was the lack of any congressional discipline. The system was vulnerable to the lobbying strength and technique of every interest group in America. I recall the tension I felt during my first term in the House of Representatives during consideration of the Housing and Urban Development (HUD) appropriations bill. Once general debate on the bill was concluded, it was in order for any member to offer an amendment, provided it was germane (related to the purposes and provisions of the bill). Representative Robert Giaimo of Connecticut (now Chairman of the House Budget Committee) offered an amendment to increase the appropriation by $500 million. Less than an hour was devoted to debating his amendment. Less than an hour, and I was being asked to vote up or down on an increase of a half a billion dollars (more than the entire budget for the State of Maine) for providing better housing for the poor and the elderly! I knew what the political consequences were if I voted "No." A campaign brochure produced by my next opponent would appear and declare in bold print: "Cohen voted No for decent housing for the most disadvantaged in our society—our senior citizens and people on low or fixed incomes." The brochure would be circulated to every senior-citizen center, nursing home and low-income housing project in the State. I would be forced to justify a seemingly heartless and inhumane vote: "Yes, I did vote against the amendment, because I am concerned that we must start balancing the budget: we must . . ."

I decided to vote against the amendment and risk the political wrath of my constituents. The campaign brochure appeared in due course, and its language matched my expectation almost verbatim. I discovered that it is much easier to vote against spending bills and amendments in the noble cause of fiscal responsibility than it is to explain and justify the vote during a congressional campaign. Everyone is scornful of Congress' reckless spending habits until a red pencil is applied to a program in which they have a direct or indirect interest.

Prior to 1974, each appropriations bill was considered separately and its substance usually increased during the amendment process without any idea or concern about the bills that were to follow or the total amount that we would spend by the end of the appropriations process.

Richard Nixon decided to extend the fiscal discipline that Congress was unwilling to impose upon itself. He simply started to impound (refuse to spend) funds that Congress had appropriated. The interest groups were outraged. Congress was outraged. There was talk of including an article of impeachment against Nixon for his impoundment activities, which, it was asserted, constituted an illegal breach of the separation of powers. But outrage was not the equivalent of folly. No Congressman wanted to be associated with any effort to remove a President from office on the ground that he was imposing some fiscal restraints upon an irresponsible Congress.

As Nixon's power started to dissipate under the sweltering heat of the Watergate investigation, Congress became proportionately bolder.

The Congressional Budget and Impoundment Act of 1974 marked Congress' determination to regain control of its constitutional power of the purse. The Budget Act created committees in the House and Senate that would have the principal responsibility for developing a comprehensive budget policy each year. Each session, a series of concurrent resolutions on the budget would be adopted. The first resolution to be adopted each May would establish spending and revenue targets. In September, a second resolution would be adopted that would either affirm or revise the targets after taking into account any interim fiscal or economic developments. The second resolution, if adopted, became binding on the Congress.

Today marked the first day of debate on the budget for the fiscal year beginning on October 1. One of the key areas of controversy will be the projected deficit. Last November, President Carter set a goal of containing the deficit to a limit of $30 billion. The political climate will not tolerate exceeding the $30-billion mark, although a number of Democratic liberals are unhappy about the prospect of having a bridle slipped over Congress' head. Republicans have been talking of reducing the deficit well below that of the Carter proposal. Some conservative Democrats do not want Republicans to run away with the issue of fiscal restraint.

The chest-beating and declarations of war on big spending may be good for public consumption, but may be hard to reconcile with the schizophrenic demands of the public itself—reduction of the budget and retention (and expansion) of the existing programs. It is clear that more money will be needed to beef up our military posture and programs. The price of food is escalating and so is the need for increasing the funding of the food-stamp program for the poor. Housing costs are exceeding the grasp of low- and middle-income groups; pressure will be on to increase the funding for housing programs. Ted Kennedy is putting pressure on Carter to institute a costly national health-insurance program. . . .

In addition, many economists believe (and they are right) that Carter underestimated the inflation and unemployment rates for the coming fiscal year. The Congressional Budget Office estimates that Congress will have to actually cut $10 billion more from programs than Carter proposed just to achieve a $30-billion deficit.

Today we began the debate to see whether Congress could resist the political temptation of preaching restraint while practicing profligacy.

APRIL 25, 1979

THE SUPPLEMENTAL BILL for defense appropriations was on the floor today. The major item of controversy was the appropriation to purchase the four ships that Iran had cancelled on its contract. Don Riegle had announced in a "Dear Colleague" letter to all members of the Senate that he would lead the fight to delete funds for two of the ships.

In his effort to cut the supplemental request, Don pressed too hard. His letter suggested that the decision to purchase the Iranian destroyers was little more than a bail-out for Litton Industries in Mississippi, located in the homeland of Chairman John Stennis.

It was a point that no doubt crossed the private thoughts of many members. But the statement of it in bold print was a direct challenge to the integrity of the Armed Services Committee and its Chairman. The letter had crossed the fine line of advocacy into the realm of a one-man effort to salvage the integrity of the Senate.

John Stennis did not treat Riegle's challenge lightly. He is a man from the old school of oratory. He does not use a prepared text. He is a deep-throated, table-thumping, animated debater. He knows just when to drop his voice, scan the Senate chamber from right to left, and with his right hand clenched into a tight fist, move into his next line of defense with a roar that comes deep from the gut of confidence and conviction. Even those who disagree with Stennis look upon him with respect and admiration.

Riegle's effort was rejected 26 to 62.

DONALD W. RIEGLE, JR.
MICHIGAN

United States Senate

WASHINGTON, D.C. 20510

April 25, 1979

Dear Colleague:

This letter is being hand-delivered to your office this
morning in order to provide basic information on the
continuing controversy concerning the four Iranian ships
at issue in the FY'79 budget supplemental now on the
Senate floor.

At 3:00 p.m. this afternoon, the Senate will take up my
amendment to delete the Iranian ships from the FY'79 urgent
supplemental. The Senate Budget Committee, after long and
vigorous discussion, deleted the four ships from the FY'79
supplemental by a vote of 11 to 9. However, due to a
calculation error by the Budget Committee staff, funding for
only two of the four ships was actually removed, and so I
will be seeking your support today to again remove funds for
the remaining two ships.

Here is the relevant background. In 1974, the Shah of Iran
ordered four Spruance class destroyers from the Ingalls
Shipbuilding Division of Litton Industries. The ships were
ordered with special modifications such as heavy air-condition-
ing, for operation in the Persian Gulf.

With the downfall of the Shah, the new Iranian government
cancelled its order for the four ships, presently under
construction in Pascagoula, Mississippi. They range in work-
completed from 40% for the ship furtherest along to 10% for
the ship least far along. The Iranian destroyers are intended
to defend a fleet against attack from the air.

They are being equipped with the Navy's outdated TARTAR air
defense system -- including radar, fire control, guns and
missiles. With the advent of the Soviet Backfire bomber and
advances in Soviet missile technology, the Navy several years
ago decided to shift procurement to the far more sophisticated
AEGIS air defense system. An AEGIS-equipped destroyer is
capable of much more accurate attack on many more targets than
the TARTAR ships. Security classifications prevent me from
emphasizing adequately the tremendous advance that AEGIS offers
over TARTAR, but I strongly urge you to inquire if you want
the specifics.

190 ROLL CALL

PAGE TWO

Four years ago in 1975, the Senate Armed Services Committee
considered a request for a nuclear frigate equipped with the
TARTAR air defense system similar to the ships ordered by
the Shah. The Committee, under the Chairmanship of Senator
Stennis, flatly refused the request and stated in its Committee
Report:

> "The Committee has carefully considered this
> request and believes it inappropriate to build any
> ship, and especially a nuclear ship, with a weapons
> system that is clearly inadequate to meet the projected
> threat within a relatively short time period after
> delivery of the ship."

In addition, the Defense Department's five-year plan presented
early this year made no provision for any additional ships
of this type. Yet suddenly, these out-moded ships have become
the centerpiece of the Defense request in the urgent
supplemental.

Plainly put, the sudden pressure for these ships is clearly
a bail-out for the shipbuilder and an effort to keep some
2,000 shipworkers busy in Mississippi. The Navy, while
obviously anxious to accommodate Chairman Stennis' very strong
interest in these ships, is also quite willing to accept four
"free" ships that circumvent the normal budget process by their
being slipped into the supplemental. For its part, the
Administration seems to care more about holding down the highly
visible FY'80 deficit -- and less about the immediate FY'79
deficit upon which few eyes are focused.

If we buy these ships we will be spending $1.3 billion for
outmoded ships we don't need, and for which the Defense
Department had made no previous request.

At a time of budget austerity -- with the Budget Committee making
deep cuts in virtually every budget category except Defense --
the $1.3 billion request for Iranian ships is clearly
unjustified.

Every defense dollar spent ought to go for top priority items
that enhance our security. The American people will be justly
outraged if we knowingly waste money this way during a period
of high inflation and high taxes; when there is a need to
scrutinize how each and every federal dollar is spent.

PAGE THREE

The people will see this as more of the same old pork-barrel
politics. And it will add insult to injury when they find
out that $580 million of the $1.3 billion will actually be
given back to Iran.

In my view, this $1.3 billion bail-out is a symptom of why
we keep spending more federal money and getting less for it.
As Chairman of the Senate Subcommittee on Economic Stabilization
I don't think we can afford any more of these "special cases"
which carry billion dollar price tags. It was why I and most
of the other Members of the Budget Committee made many painful
budget cuts in order to achieve a FY'81 balanced budget.

In the future, I intend to challenge any authorization or
appropriation bill that contains these Iranian ships, so if a
future effort is made to retain them, there will be future votes
to delete them.

In closing, let me say that it is entirely feasible to salvage
the construction work already completed by reprogramming
certain other justified ship requirements (currently in the
five-year plan) in a manner that can both save money and provide
us with the up-to-date weapons technology we need, and I will
present one such option during the floor debate today.

Thank you for your patience in reading this information. I
hope you will support the bi-partisan majority of the Budget
Committee who voted to delete all four ships from the supplemental.

Sincerely,

Donald W. Riegle, Jr.

DWR/lb

Today also marked the beginning of a pattern of work that had become all too familiar in the House. We began the day at 9 A.M. and
concluded at 12:56 A.M.

APRIL 26, 1979

THE GOVERNMENTAL AFFAIRS COMMITTEE HELD a closed-session briefing for members with Special Trade Representative Robert Strauss.* A

* Strauss was made Ambassador at Large shortly thereafter to help with the negotiations between Egypt and Israel.

public hearing was to begin on legislation to implement the Multilateral Trade Agreements, and Chairman Ribicoff thought it was important for us to ask Strauss questions that he might not be at liberty to discuss publicly for fear of generating adverse reaction from nations who were signatories to the Agreements.

Strauss had become President Carter's fireman, responding to practically every alarm that rang inside the Administration. He is smooth, smart, and sassy. He has the tongue and toughness of a mule skinner.

When Strauss approached me behind the members' dais, he slapped me on the back and said, "Bill, we need your help on this bill."

"Bob, you've already got Muskie; you don't need me."

"—— Muskie, I need *you*," Strauss retorted. He flashed a smile and moved on to the next member.

When Strauss assumed his position at the witness table, he managed to deflect tough questions with an earthy humor. One member wanted to know why Strauss had not demanded more in the way of concessions to protect some of our domestic industries. Strauss responded, "Senator, it's sort of like making love with a gorilla. You can't always tell the gorilla that you've had enough and you want to stop. . . ."

When my turn came to question him, I noted that the trade agreements, while in the overall interest of the nation, impacted most severely on New England industries. I pointed out that the Administration had not been particularly sensitive to the textile, shoe and clothespin industries.

I left the meeting before we went into public session principally because I had some work to do in the office. But secondarily, I wanted to impress upon the negotiators that I was not satisfied with their efforts as far as my region was concerned, and that they could not count on my vote for the Agreements. It was clear that the Senate would vote overwhelmingly for the Agreements, but I hoped that I might make the Administration a little more sensitive to Maine's needs in the future.

APRIL 27, 1979

I ATTENDED the memorial service for Marvella Bayh (Indiana Senator Birch Bayh's wife, who had had cancer) at the National Cathedral. It became a media event. The program had reprinted some of Marvella's thoughts when she knew that her life's hourglass could no longer be inverted.

"When they told me there was treatment but no cure at this time, I dropped to my knees," she said. "Two things from out of my past, when I went to church as a child, came back to me. Number one, 'Where can I go but to the Lord?' and number two, 'I am weak but He is strong.'

"The third feeling I had was, 'When life comes down to basics, really how little control we all have over our own lives.' And it also came to me how, even if we live to be 100, how really short life here is. And therefore, it's important to enjoy it and not rush so fast and take time to smell the roses. . . ."

April 28, 1979

Tonight I attended the 65th Annual Dinner of the White House Press Correspondents Association as the guest of Marvin Stone, the editor of *U.S. News and World Report.* Ordinarily, the President is the featured speaker of the evening. Last year President Carter sent his press secretary, Jody Powell, in his stead, and Powell took the opportunity to lecture the White House correspondents on the responsibilities and burdens of the presidency and the media's insensitivity to Carter's initiatives and accomplishments. It was a strategic miscalculation of enormous dimensions and left a wound that continued to ooze openly with many members of the press corps.

Carter had to make amends this year. He had to come and cauterize the wound. He did it well with a string of witty, self-effacing and critical one-liners—an open admission that he had made a mistake last year.

"I'm here substituting for Jody Powell. [Pause.] You remember [pause] Jody Powell? [Laughter.]

"His speech last year obviously affected your treatment of me since then. I want to thank you. [Pause.] Thanks a lot!"

Carter also took the opportunity to quell the silly speculation surrounding his new hairstyle of wearing the part on the left instead of the right. Pundits had been having a field day with gossipy columns. Was the President trying to hide incipient baldness? Was it the first sign of a cover-up? Male menopause? Mid-life crisis? What was to follow—an open shirt, gold chains and a Kawasaki motorcycle?

Carter treated his personal choice as a political decision. "I discovered John Connally's secret. . . . I noticed a few months ago that he parts his hair on the left side, and I decided, all by myself, to remove the insidious Republican advantage with a bold stroke of the comb. You probably surmised that this shift from right to left is only for the primaries and then, for the general elections—you guessed it—right down the middle. . . ."

It was a superb performance by the President and did a great deal to mollify the antagonisms that a breach of protocol and ritual had engendered.

During the dinner, Marvin Stone arranged for me to sit next to China's new ambassador to the United States, Chai Xemin.

I asked Ambassador Chai what he thought of the proposed SALT II treaty.

"As Teng Hsiao-ping has said, you will have to do whatever you feel is in your political interest to do. We maintain that the Soviets cannot be trusted."

Why do you think the Soviets did not move against China when you invaded the border of Vietnam?" I asked.

"They were afraid to. They could not afford to move troops from Europe for a short battle and did not want to risk a long-term war in China for fear they would be vulnerable to an attack in Europe. Also, they would have internal difficulties with a protracted war."

"What about Soviet expressions of reducing tensions with China?" I queried.

"We are always ready to talk to them, but we do not trust them," Ambassador Chai declared.

"Senator Cohen, how do you feel about SALT?" Chai asked.

"I am undecided," I responded. "The Soviets have a stronger conventional army than the United States, and they are now equal in strategic weapons. I am concerned about the trends and what they mean for the future."

"I agree," he said simply.

April 30, 1979

TODAY the Senate Select Committee on Ethics began public hearings on charges against Herman Talmadge of Georgia. The hallway on the first floor of the Dirksen Senate Office Building could have been the vestibule of a movie theater on opening day of a box-office special. A crowd started to gather early in the morning. The line of spectators snaked down the corridor. Each person, before entering the hearing room, had to pass through a portable archway that contained a metal detector. Armed Capitol Hill police were present to ensure order and control. The hallway was charged with excitement. A United States Senator was on public trial before his colleagues. The papers had been filled with allegations of deceit, false reports, illegal gifts, secret bank accounts, and money stuffed in an old overcoat.

The Washington Post contained a photograph of a handsome young man, Daniel Minchew, the former administrative assistant to Talmadge who was the chief witness against his former employer. He looked like a clothes model in a fashion magazine. Next to him sat a laughing Herman Talmadge who was leaning back in his judge's chair, the picture of confidence.

A "Dear Colleague" letter from Talmadge had been released this morning outlining his defense against the charges, brought mainly on the basis of Minchew's allegations. It was obvious that Talmadge subscribed to the philosophy that a good defense is a good offense. He came out swinging.

> We will show that Daniel Minchew is without credibility. You will have evidence proving:
> —that Minchew lied under oath to this Committee;
> —that Minchew lied to financial institutions from which he borrowed money;
> —that Minchew lied repeatedly to the Department of Justice;
> —that Minchew failed three FBI lie detector tests;
> —that even his own hired polygrapher agreed that his answers to the FBI were deceptive;
> —that Daniel Minchew lied to the Internal Revenue Service again and again.

> You will also have before you evidence:
> —that Minchew had a poor reputation for veracity and honesty;
> —that his travel agency license was revoked because he misused funds due the airlines;
> —that he was hounded by creditors;
> —that he failed to pay his debts;
> —that he bounced checks.

Mr. Chairman and Members of the Committee, to find me guilty of
complicity in the Riggs account you would have to accept the word of
a proven liar, cheat and embezzler.

The photograph of Talmadge in the left-hand corner of his press
release showed a younger and more vigorous-looking Senator than the
one that appeared in *The Washington Post*. It was a photograph taken in
the prime of his political life, long before his current personal crisis.

At 12:30, I was scheduled to appear before the Education Research
Fund luncheon held at the Ramada Inn in Rosslyn, Virginia. I had been
asked to give a speech outlining the "case against a new department of
education." I arrived at the luncheon under the mistaken notion that the
audience was opposed to creating a new cabinet-level department. To my
surprise, I learned that those in attendance were strongly in favor of the
bill that was on the Senate floor for a final vote that afternoon. I felt like
an Israeli in a PLO camp, but decided there was no alternative under the
circumstances but to make the strongest case I could against the creation
of yet another government department.

My missionary work at noon proved to be no more effective than the
effort to defeat the legislation in the Senate later that day. The final vote
was 72–21 in favor of the new department.

MAY 1, 1979

TODAY the Permanent Subcommittee on Investigations began public
hearings involving a government employee who may have engaged in a
conflict of interest.

The former director of the Bureau of Engraving and Printing (BEP),
a division of the Treasury Department that is responsible for the printing
of our currency, has spent more than thirty years in the Bureau, working
his way from a pressman's position to the top. During a period approximately nine months prior to his retirement, he was offered the top executive position with the American Bank Note Company (ABN), one of the
largest manufacturers of specialty presses and counterfeit-detection
equipment in the world.

The ABN Company had a long-standing business relationship with the BEP and had a close working relationship with the director. At the time of the offer, ABN was in the process of negotiating the sale of a major counterfeit-detection system to BEP. In addition, some equipment that had been leased to the BEP was not working according to standards, and its inefficiency was producing higher operating costs to the BEP.

Although the director rejected the offer, he undertook at ABN's request the selection of office space for a branch office of ABN in the Washington area. According to the evidence, the director not only selected the office, but made some modifications in the floor plan. Several months later, he announced his retirement from BEP and signed a contract with ABN for nearly twice his government salary and located in the office space he had previously picked out for ABN. When he retired from BEP, he persuaded his office manager and one of his top engineers to join ABN with him.

On the face of the facts that had been developed by the subcommittee staff, the director appeared to have engaged in conduct that contravened a conflict-of-interest statute. In fact, a grand jury was investigating the matter at that very moment.

Our subcommittee had a job to do, an obligation to determine whether the director had engaged in improper activities while a government employee. Had he walked through the revolving door of government service into the plush office of a corporation that continued to negotiate lucrative contracts with the government—indeed, with the very agency that he had formerly served? Had he exploited his public position for private gain?

On the surface, there appeared to be wrongdoing. The occurrence or appearance of impropriety, however, might dissolve when all the witnesses had testified and all of the evidence was secured.

The danger inherent in such a congressional-committee investigation is that the person under scrutiny will not survive with his reputation intact or unstained. He will wriggle like a wet insect caught in a beam of white light. Acts of innocence or error when magnified under the microscope of the committee and the klieg lights of the national television networks will emerge as calculated wrongdoing, the product of personal greed and avarice.

The camera will wait until a Senator raises the volume of his voice with dramatic indignation and then zoom in on the witness, who will respond either in anger or with contrition. That evening, the millions of viewers will see only a few seconds on the news—the dramatic confrontation between the righteous inquisitor and the guilt-laden violator of the public trust.

We assume the worst, and many times we find it. But good reputations are also sometimes destroyed in the process.*

---

* A federal grand jury subsequently indicted the director on criminal charges. The U.S. District Court for the District of Columbia later dismissed the indictments on the ground that they were legally defective.

CHAPTER 12

MOST PEOPLE who visit the Senate or House are rather shocked by how few members are actually on the floor engaged in vigorous debate or sitting in rapt attention. If a fistful of legislators are on hand at any given time, it's probably an extraordinary day. A booklet is handed out to gallery visitors which seeks to explain the light attendance.

IF YOUR SENATOR IS NOT IN THE SENATE CHAMBER . . .

At the time of your visit to the Senate Chamber there may be comparatively few Senators on the Floor—and your own Senator may not be present. Much of the Senate's time must be devoted to items of routine business which have been thoroughly studied and discussed in committee and therefore can be disposed of by a small number of Senators.

The Majority and Minority Leaders (or other Senators acting for them) are always present to guide legislation and to protect party interests. A bell system keeps Senators not on the Floor advised of the legislative situation. Party Whips are ready at a moment's notice to call their Colleagues to the Chamber when vital issues are about to be decided.

Senators are among the busiest individuals having a multitude of responsibilities requiring their personal attention. If your Senator is not on the Floor, or in his office attending to the many problems and requests of his constituents, he is probably engaged in a committee hearing or investigation.

To insure the efficient accomplishment of its work, the Senate has created 15 permanent standing committees. Bills, resolutions, and other matters requiring action by the Senate normally are referred to the appropriate committee for initial examination and subsequent re-

port. Each Senator is a member of at least two standing committees
and also of several subcommittees. In addition, assignments to special, select, and joint committees (or commissions) are spread among
the membership.

The booklet does not mention that we might also be at lunch or
possibly in the gym—where I occasionally go when there is little legislative activity on the floor or when I choose to skip lunch for the day.

The fact is that most of the work is done in the committees: witnesses
are called; advice as to pending legislation is accepted or rejected. Eventually the bill is "marked up"—reworded and approved for final vote—
and sent to the full Senate. But even in the committee rooms, visitors or
witnesses will rarely find more than a few Senators present. Many take
the Senators' absences personally or as an insulting lack of interest. The
actual reason is a simple law of physics. Atoms may be split; legislators,
at least in this life, may not. At any given moment, a Senator may very
well have three or four meetings going on simultaneously. He and his
staff try to set priorities in terms of the sequence with which he will make
his rounds. Chances are he will stay at one meeting only long enough to
ask a few pertinent questions and then, extracting a 3×5 card on which
his schedule is typed, have to attend another hearing or meeting. Usually
a different event is scheduled for every thirty minutes; rarely is more than
one hour devoted to a single meeting or event. A Senator's day is subject
to the dictates of that 3×5 card.

There are two consequences that flow directly from the scatter-gun
schedule of a Senator. He can gain only a superficial understanding of the
legislation being considered by the committees. Secondly, he becomes
practically hostage to staff members of the committee. These are the
bright young men and women who fill the marbled corridors of the Senate
Office Buildings and who have taken charge of the legislative process.
They are part of the new elite that has engulfed Washington. They are
graduates of law schools or hold master's and doctoral degrees. Many
drive expensive cars and can be seen dining at some of Washington's
most fashionable restaurants. They draft the laws that will change the
shape of America to conform to their visions of equity, the environment
and the life-styles of the future. Only in the presence of Senators do the
committee staffers fall back into the shadows. Their retirement from the
center of control is temporary only—the Senators will move quickly on

the treadmill toward another engagement. The staff members are quite accustomed to running the committees according to their plans. They prepare opening statements for the chairmen of the committees to read at the committee hearings; they conduct preliminary interviews of witnesses and prepare written questions which Senators use in examining the witnesses during open hearings.

During the second day of the conflict-of-interest hearings, I was handed a note by a staff member suggesting that we were getting off the track into irrelevant matters. I took the note and simply set it aside and continued my questions.

On the third day, I was chairing the hearing, because Sam Nunn could not be present and there were no other members in attendance. I spent a significant part of the time examining the witnesses on points that had little direct bearing on the conflict-of-interest charges involved. I was handed a note that said the majority and minority staffs agreed that "this line of questioning is going nowhere."

At that point, I tore the note into shreds and asked, "Under whose authority did that vote occur?"

I overreacted to the staff's recommendation to move along with the hearings. The questioning was fading off into the irrelevant, but I was rebelling against the established reality of staff domination of the Committee. I made my point. I also made some enemies in the process.

At noon I cohosted a luncheon with Senator Paul Tsongas of Massachusetts for Bill Rodgers, the winner of the Boston Marathon. Rodgers had been invited by President Carter to attend an official state dinner at the White House. The winner of the Boston Marathon in the women's division was Joan Benoit of Portland, Maine. She had set a world record with her victory but had been completely overlooked by the White House. I had written a letter of protest to President Carter and released it to the press. She received a belated invitation to the dinner. The official White House statement indicated that Joan was invited as a result of communications with Senator Edmund Muskie's office.

Late in the afternoon, I learned that Ed had been putting pressure on Democratic Senators not to sponsor or support the bill that I had filed to deauthorize the Dickey-Lincoln hydroelectric project. I decided that I had better start contacting every member personally if I was going to avoid a major defeat when the project came up for appropriations.

MAY 4, 1979

TODAY I held a joint conference with former Delaware Governor Russell Peterson, who is the president of the National Audubon Society. We called the conference to announce my decision to file legislation to "de-authorize" the Dickey-Lincoln Hydroelectric Project located in northern Maine.

Environmentalists were strongly opposed to its construction because of the massive damage to one of the last free-flowing rivers in the Northeast. Eighty-eight thousand acres of timberland would have to be flooded and another four hundred thousand taken out of use to permit construction of one of the largest dams in the world. In addition, there were serious questions about the economic benefits that would be derived from the dam as compared with its significant costs—over $1 billion.

But the people of Maine were divided on its desirability. While rich in natural beauty, Maine is a poor state economically. Oil costs have been rising dramatically. There is opposition to the construction of an oil refinery along the northeastern coast of the state. Questions concerning the safety of nuclear power are causing many to reassess their previous opposition to the dam. A former Maine Governor expressed opposition to the project. Maine's present Governor is in favor.

The issue becomes more complicated when national political considerations are taken into account. Public-works projects are the mother's milk of politics. For years, a politician's success has been measured in terms of how many highway projects, bridge constructions, harbor dredgings, or power projects would be delivered to his state. His voting record or philosophy was incidental to his "clout" in producing tangible benefits to his constituents. In Washington, it is called pork-barrel politics. It may be condemned or vilified by editorial boards and cartoonists across the country, but anyone who becomes too outraged about the morals and manners displayed at the feeding ground will find reformation of the system a task worthy of Hercules.

Jimmy Carter found this out early in his career as President. One of his first initiatives was to denounce the waste in large public-works projects. He proposed the elimination of seventeen major water projects because of their extravagant expense and limited benefit. His proposal garnered some accolades for courage and fiscal prudence from various newspapers and virtually none from Congress. It was no contest from the beginning. The President might occupy a bully pulpit, but Congress held the power of the purse. Carter had to capitulate in order to gain any support for his other programs. Just as "human rights" as the centerpiece of his foreign policy has been plucked off and replaced with a more mature and pragmatic approach to geopolitical strategies, so the President's wail over wasteful pork-barrel politics has been muffled and reduced to a faint whisper.

His budget request includes over $710,000 for further planning of the Dickey-Lincoln dam. Ed Muskie, as Chairman of the Budget Committee and second-ranking member of the Subcommittee on Public Works, was largely responsible for securing the President's support.

I did not expect the Subcommittee to be particularly receptive to my opposition to the dam. It was clear that the Chairman, Bennett Johnston of Louisiana, had been well briefed by Muskie or his staff on the arguments in favor of construction. It was also clear that the Subcommittee would not consider deleting funding for the project.

I knew that my only chance to terminate the funding would be on the Senate floor—and when it came to persuading my colleagues to vote against the Chairman of the Budget Committee, the odds were long indeed.

At first, I had resisted the idea of attempting to defeat the project by deauthorizing Dickey. If successful, this would permanently terminate the project. If it was unsuccessful, I ran the risk of locking members into voting for continuing requests for appropriation of planning and construction money.

Environmental groups who had supported my candidacy for the Senate wanted to take that risk.

As soon as the conference was over, the speculation leaped into print. The media "hype" was on for a major confrontation. "Cohen Throws Down Gauntlet to Muskie"—a test of effectiveness in the Senate.

It was preposterous that this was being construed as a test of my influence in the Senate over that of Muskie. He had served twenty years in that body. I had been a member for four months. Not many members wanted to incur the Chairman of the Budget Committee's wrath. (Actually, his position on the Public Works Subcommittee was of greater concern.) I had no control over the characterization by the editorial writers. And I knew that my failure would be painted as a major defeat of a young upstart at the hands of an old master.

I could live with defeat. But I didn't want the media to distort my motives or working relationship with Muskie by turning the issue into a personal battle.

MAY 7, 1979

I HAD lunch today with a Senator from the West.

"Never have I seen people so cynical," he said. "For the first time in my life, and I'm only forty-six, I'm getting cynical about the public as well. No matter how hard you try, no matter how much effort you make, they want to know who's paid you off, what interest group has a line on you. Frankly, I'm tempted to say I've had it. The job isn't worth it.

"A group of us should get together and just take on some issues without waffling, without regard to the political consequences.

"If it's energy, let's go with deregulation and urge production full steam ahead.

"If it's inflation, let's make the cuts necessary.

"These may not be the right answers, but we just can't afford to drift anymore. We can't play it cute and try to duck the issue until it becomes so hot we're forced to do something.

"Look at Carter. He tells the Congress he wants deregulation. Out in Iowa he says if Congress continues controls, he won't veto it.

"He tells the Congress we need nuclear energy and tells a crowd of demonstrators, 'but only as a last resort.'

"Bill, we can't afford to have a man as weak as Carter anymore who keeps cutting and weaving his programs and policies to suit the occasion."

MAY 8, 1979

AT A luncheon today, I noticed that Senator Paul Laxalt seemed tense and exercised. Nevada was suffering a 46-percent loss of revenue as a result of the gas shortage in California.

"I am going to my state on Thursday and propose that we establish a state-operated purchasing agency to buy oil. No one has any answers

—we can't get them. I think we should have an independent audit of the oil companies' reserves."

I agreed with Paul, but his suggestion was not greeted with universal acceptance. His proposal to establish a state-controlled petroleum-purchasing agency flew in the face of doctrinaire concepts of the free-enterprise system. The lowered eyes of several conservative members reflected their disapproval. But they remained silent. Paul was one of their most respected spokesmen, and while they might disagree with his proposal, they also knew that the economic fabric of his state was unraveling and that riot-angry people wanted more than a recitation of philosophy. Their fortunes and futures were being extinguished. They wanted some answers and some action.*

It is a dangerous time for America. One Senator became agitated as he listened to the negative comments being made about President Carter's gas-rationing plan. He stood up and said, "This meeting sounds like a Tower of Babel. I'm going to vote for the rationing plan because I'm a politician. We've got to do something."

MAY 9, 1979

DURING AN ARMED SERVICES COMMITTEE MEETING, I received a call from the White House. I left the hearing room to take the call. It was from Zbigniew Brzezinski.

"The President wanted me to call you personally to let you know that the announcement of the SALT agreement will take place this afternoon. [I had known that from the morning news.] If there is any information you need, please don't hesitate to call. I thought we had a good session recently."

"Yes, and we will probably have to have several more," I responded.

"This is the beginning of an important national debate, and President Carter wanted me to be sure to alert you to the schedule."

"Yes, it certainly is," I said matter-of-factly.

Brzezinski seemed to be waiting for some signal from me on how I felt about the treaty. I gave none.

---

* Almost immediately after Laxalt publicly proposed the creation of the state-owned purchasing agency, gas supplies became more plentiful in Nevada.

Shortly after the call, I was given a message that I had two visitors outside waiting to see me.

"We are not here to ask for anything, Bill. Just a courtesy call."

It's the standard line used by everyone. The conversation starts out as inane chitchat. "How's the family? How do you like the Senate? What a great victory! We're proud of you. . . ." Invariably, there is some bill that is of concern to them—"Just want to alert you; perhaps I should talk to your legislative assistant."

I spoke with Muskie on the floor of the Senate. He had just returned from a trip to Europe. Over the weekend, the newspapers had carried stories that the vote on Dickey-Lincoln would serve as a test of our influence in the Senate. It made for good reading, but was not particularly helpful as far as my relations with Ed were concerned. I explained to him that I was not embarked on a "kamikaze" mission and had no delusions about my influence in the Senate after five months. He said, "Bill, don't worry about it. I understand."

MAY 10, 1979

AT 11 A.M. I attended a hearing before the Military Appropriations Subcommittee. Although not a member of the committee, I was allowed to question Pentagon witnesses on the procedure they had followed in recommending that Loring Air Force Base be reduced in personnel and operations.

Later, on the Senate floor, John Stennis put his arm around me and walked me over to the cloakroom of the Democrats.

"Son, you've got to help move that supplemental bill in the House. If they don't approve it, then it will be a knock-down-drag-out fight in the fiscal '80 budget."

"Yes, Mr. Chairman," I replied, "a lot of blood will be spilled. I assume mostly mine. But I don't have any influence with the White House on this one."

"Well, see if you can't call someone on the House Armed Services Committee. You know we want to avoid a fight. . . ."

I was on my way that afternoon to the West Coast to give a series of speeches in San Francisco and Los Angeles, with a stop in Dallas on my return to Washington. Before leaving, though, I called several Republican members of the House to solicit their support for the action taken by the Senate on the supplemental bill.

During my flight that afternoon, the House of Representatives overwhelmingly rejected President Carter's gas-rationing plan, 246–159. At least 100 Democrats defected from the Administration plan. President Carter said he was shocked and embarrassed for our nation's government and that this was "one of the most gutless Congresses" he had worked with. Of course, it was only the second Congress he had worked with, and he had not had much more support in or success with the first one.

MAY 11, 1979

A MAJOR STORY WAS reported in the *San Francisco Chronicle* on the Senate hearings on Herman Talmadge.

Bold headlines shouted: EASY MONEY FOR U.S. SENATORS. Photographs of Senators Adlai Stevenson of Illinois and Quentin Burdick of North Dakota accompanied the text. Under Stevenson's photograph appeared the quote "It should be changed." Under Burdick's were the words "He collected the maximum."

The story implied in the first paragraph that most, if not all, Senators had been abusing their expense accounts for personal advantage. It also suggested hypocrisy on the part of those who accused Talmadge of sloppy bookkeeping practices when committee members had very little idea how their own accounts were managed. The latter point was not controvertible. Few Senators have a personal comprehension of the accounting practices demanded by rules they have promulgated themselves over the years. Administrative assistants or business managers are hired for this purpose. There is simply no time available to be an office manager or accountant as well as a legislator. One study indicated a Congressman has only seventeen minutes a day for constructive, or at least, uninterrupted, thought. And yet there is no explanation we can offer to a cynical press or public for neglect of our bookkeeping. We are almost completely vulnerable to the mistakes or misdeeds of our staffs—and we are held totally accountable for them.

What struck me about the article—in addition to the innuendo that we were all guilty of some abuse of public funds—was the manner in which the quotes were placed under the photographs. It appeared that Stevenson, the Chairman of the Ethics Committee, while collecting the maximum amount of expense allowance with supporting documentation, was calling for change and reform, while the Burdick photograph contained the quote "He collected the maximum." The words hung like a convict's number.

May 14, 1979

At 8:15 a.m. I spoke to employees of the Steak and Ale restaurant chain in Dallas, Texas. Their political-action committee had supported me in the campaign, and they had invited me to address the group concerning the political process, the role of a Congressman and their responsibility to become actively involved in communicating their views to the Representatives and Senators.

At the conclusion of my talk, one of the employees asked, "Senator Cohen, if you want us to participate actively in the process, why are you a cosponsor of S. 623?"

I wasn't familiar with the bill by number, but suspected it was a bill calling for a limited public financing of congressional campaigns. That was exactly what she had in mind.

"Why do you encourage us to take an active role in the political process and then support public financing?"

"Because you can be active as an industry without having the appearance of purchasing public policy with campaign funds. There is nothing I dislike more than fund raising, and yet there is nothing more important to a political campaign. I would like to see a system of limited spending ceilings and contributions so a cloud of suspicion would not be cast over every vote of mine by people saying that a special interest has purchased it. I want to vote to retain the tip credit,* for example, because it is sound policy—not because you have supported my campaign financially."

The answer was not entirely satisfactory.

"How do you explain that twenty percent fewer people checked off the one dollar on tax returns?"

"By the same forces of apathy, indifference, cynicism that cause forty percent of the people to stay at home on Election Day. People no longer feel that they can change the system or that the system is worth changing."

* The tip credit permits the employer of a regularly tipped employee, such as a waiter or waitress, to credit tips for up to 40 percent of the minimum wage for that employee's pay.

May 15, 1979

TONIGHT, Bob and Elizabeth Dole were hosting the dinner for the Republican Trust Fund. As we drove to their condominium in the Watergate, I mentioned to Diane that I thought Congressman Phil Crane (who was running for the Republican presidential nomination) was being unfairly crucified for some statement he allegedly made in college, more than twenty-five years ago, about desiring to make love to scores of women.

"Hell, even if he said it, it was just some silly fantasy that any young man might express."

Diane brought another perspective to bear immediately.

"No, Bill, that's just another example of the double standard in our society. If a woman had made that statement, she'd be labeled a whore. I think it will hurt him, and particularly with women."

Diane believes passionately in her right, and that of every woman, to stand on an equal footing with men.

During the debate on the Equal Rights Amendment extension, I was unsure whether it was appropriate to extend the time period for ratification by the states. One night shortly before the debate began, Diane helped remove some of my doubts.

"Billy, we have two handsome, healthy sons who are going to survive and succeed during their lifetimes. If we had had daughters instead of sons, wouldn't you have wanted them to have the same rights and opportunities? When you wonder whether you are being fair extending the period, ask whether it is fair to have a few legislators prevent votes from coming out of committee; ask whether seven years is enough time to reverse almost two hundred years of bias. The same people who are opposed to extension of the ERA would have been opposed to women having the right to vote. Why was it necessary to amend the Constitution to give women the right to vote? Why wasn't the Fourteenth Amendment enough? It's not just symbolic.

"So when you think about fairness, think about how long women have had to fight just to get what you, as a man, take for granted—every day."

MAY 17, 1979

DIANE AND I AND THE BOYS ATTENDED a dinner sponsored by the Maine State Society—Maine people who have been "transplanted" to the Washington area. There were more than four hundred people in attendance tonight to feast on Maine lobsters. An evangelical minister gave an impassioned invocation and invited everyone to visit a war memorial that gave bronzed testimony to the fact that a Maine fighting unit lost more men in the Civil War than any similar unit. It was evidence of great sacrifice; but its appropriateness to this occasion escaped me.

Seven young ladies ("Ambassadors") representing Maine products gave a brief description of the clothes and jewelry they were wearing, where the finery and stones could be purchased or how much the potato or blueberry crops or fish catch produced in income for the State. The M.C. announced the presence of dignitaries; the Ambassadors drew tickets for the 150 door prizes, which consisted of Maine-made gifts and trips to Maine resorts or fishing camps.

Then the plates of steaming lobsters were brought out. The shells were expertly cracked by everyone (nearly) and the white interiors dipped in butter. Slightly messy, but delicious.

Maine's Governor was present. He gave a long account of the bad press he had received for suggesting that the media were preoccupied with trivial matters such as André the Seal's annual spring trek from Marblehead, Massachusetts, to Rockport, Maine.

MAY 18, 1979

AT 7:40 A.M. I caught a Delta flight to Bangor. I was scheduled to hold a press conference with the local media before heading to northern Maine to deliver a speech to the Life Underwriters Annual Convention. I was not looking forward to the trip. I was suffering from an inner-ear infection —a chronic problem that I have had since 1974, when a small plane in which I was riding was forced to make a rapid descent because of a violent thunderstorm. I had a head cold at the time, and the pressure change was so rapid that it popped the crystal on my watch. It also completely sealed my Eustachian tube, just prior to a statewide telecast that I was to make explaining my vote to recommend that impeachment proceedings be brought against Richard Nixon.

I landed in Bangor and walked into the glare of the television cameras.

"Senator, what do you think of the congressional proposal of requiring car owners to keep their cars off the road one day of the week?"

"Well, the Senate is not actively considering this proposal. It has some flaws, certainly, and would have to contain a number of exceptions or exemptions—for doctors and medical personnel; for utilities and emergency service vehicles, and other types of special occupations. But I think it is probably an improvement over the President's plan. My own preference would be an odd-even plan now employed by California. If people do not panic, I believe the system can work. . . ."

That evening, the story of my interview ran: "Congressional plan for removing cars from highways one day a week receives support from Senator Cohen. . . ."

Immediately following the press conference, I drove to St. Joseph's Hospital, where my uncle was recovering from surgery. He looked ten years older than when I saw him a few months ago. The tumor that was removed, along with his gall bladder, was malignant. A calm had settled over him like the white sheet that covered his thin body. I stayed only ten minutes, then rushed to catch a plane to Presque Isle on a small commuter flight. The lack of a pressurized cabin caused my ears to ache.

I stepped off the plane and could barely hear anything. Off to an interview at a local television station.

"What, if anything, did the hearings on Loring Air Force Base accomplish? What can you tell the people of Aroostook County?"

"Do you really believe you can stop the construction of the Dickey-Lincoln Dam? . . ."

Following the interview, I drove to my district office in Presque Isle for an hourlong interview with King Harvey, owner of the *Fort Fairfield Review*. He is a tough-minded, seasoned, cynical man who requires only one thing from politicians: honest and direct answers to hard questions. I learned from my first interview with him more than seven years ago never to hedge or play word games with him. I have never regretted the decision.

During the interview, my Washington office alerted me to calls that were coming in from a Boston radio station. The wire services were carrying stories about the large percentage of millionaires in the Senate:

at least twenty-five of the members were among that select circle of wealth. The financial statements that were being made available to the public also revealed that whatever political success I might have achieved, I was not heavily endowed with financial assets. The radio station was referring to me as one of the paupers of the Senate and wanted me to call and discuss my financial status.

It was a call that I could "afford" to forgo. I do not consider my lack of financial success or security as a badge of honor.

At 7, I left to address the Maine Life Underwriters. I received a Certificate of Appreciation and a basket of Aroostook County products, including a five-pound bag of potatoes.

After my speech, I left on a private plane for Portland. The weather was poor. Visibility was virtually nonexistent and the ceiling lower to the ground than a dachshund's belly. Somehow the pilots managed to descend through the fog blanket and touch down on a runway that became visible less than ten seconds before we landed.

It was nearly midnight. My head was pounding. The fluid in my ears felt as if it had solidified into a concrete tube.

MAY 19, 1979

AT 9:30 A.M., I fired the starting gun at a ten-mile event sponsored by the Connecticut Mutual Life Insurance Company to raise money for heart-disease research and to promote running as a means of maintaining physical fitness. The gun misfired three times.

I left to address the graduating class at the University of Southern Maine. The event had been scheduled to be outdoors, but the steady drizzle and threatening clouds forced the crowd of nearly five thousand into the Portland Expo Building.

For twenty minutes, I spoke to the students and their parents about the need to confront the new realities of our addiction to oil and overreliance upon foreign sources for our energy requirements.

"Conservation is not some pejorative word that we associate with bird-watchers or butterfly chasers who are naive about economic necessities. Conservation of energy is a moral imperative that is a responsibility of every citizen in this country.

"We are going to have to conserve what we waste and dissipate, and what we have to abandon is the notion that we are entitled to some other nation's resources at prices that we can afford to pay because we as Americans have a divine right to them. . . ."

I concluded my message with a poem written by Archibald MacLeish.

Ours is a strange time in America.

Women, when the towns are still,
hear a far-off thrill of thunder
under the edges of the night and rise
and touch their children . . . but the house
is silent and there was no thunder.

Young men, heavy with the need to sleep,
lie sleepless and blame all the clocks
that count the night out . . . but the stroke
that woke them was not iron.
      Nearer than
night they hear the heart's foreboding.

We do not know for what we wait—
Gale in the elm tops or the dear
sun's rising on a gentle day—
evil or good. We cannot say.
Only that the time draws nearer.

Those who wait for time to take them
find within fulfilling time
not what they hoped but what they feared.
The bold go toward their time;
      they make
its meaning answer to the mind.

After the ceremonies, which lasted two hours, I went to a lunch with Bob Monks, a successful entrepreneur, and Charlie and Susan Wing, the founders of Cornerstones, a school they operate in Brunswick, Maine, teaching people how to construct affordable new homes or to retrofit older ones, maximizing nature's gifts in a postindustrial age of dwindling fossil fuels. Bob was one of the first to encourage me to run for Congress. He provided financial as well as moral support. He had been unsuccessful in two attempts for the Senate—once against Margaret Chase Smith in

1972, and the other against Ed Muskie in 1976. He is a brilliant young man with a sense of high moral purpose that he inherited from his father, an Episcopal minister. But his fate is that of longing for public office while his talent is really in the field of private entrepreneurial success. I wanted him to meet Charlie and advise him on how to develop or protect his ideas on energy conservation, which were starting to receive nationwide attention.

At 3, I was on a commuter flight which eventually landed in Bangor after two intermediate stops.

I stopped to visit with my parents for a half an hour, then showered, changed clothes and left to address the Annual Convention of the Maine National Guard.

The dinner was buffet style. The line of guests moved slowly, and my hope for an early departure faded as the schedule slipped. I had a long prepared text which, under the deteriorating circumstances, would have inflicted an intolerable amount of pain on the audience. Patriotic as those in attendance were, I was satisfied that they would not have been impressed with a recitation of one of John Adams' letters to Abigail.

So I left the speech in the briefcase and talked about energy, American weakness and the threat to our survival as the beacon of hope for freedom-loving people.

I met my brother, Bob, and his wife, Pam, later for drinks. I hadn't talked with them in nearly a year.

MAY 22, 1979

EARLY IN THE MORNING, I met with a group of contractors to discuss issues of interest to them: the Alaska Lands bill, energy, ERISA (the Employee Retirement Income Security Act), and the regulatory overkill of the Mine Safety Administration and the Occupational Safety and Health Administration.

At 10, the Governmental Affairs Committee convened to "mark up" a bill to carry a new agency called the International Development Cooperation Administration. I opposed this measure for the same reasons I had voted against creating a new Department of Education—the expansion of government agencies in the name of reform and reorganization. After casting a negative vote, I left to attend an Armed Services Committee hearing on the Navy's shipbuilding program.

At the Republican Policy Luncheon, a note of levity was unexpectedly introduced by one of my freshman colleagues. After we finished eating and started to receive the weekly reports from the ranking Republican members of the various Senate committees, my friend asked, "Can't anything be done about getting a hold on the daily schedule? I mean, there's no way we can tell our families what time we'll be home for dinner on any given night. At least in the House, Tip O'Neill set a schedule whereby we could plan our days and nights. . . ."

The inquiry was greeted with a general undertone of laughter and snickering which suggested it was something of a perennial problem to which he would just have to adjust. Finally, one Senator said, "Hell, we've tried everything with Byrd to plan the schedule with some regularity and rationality." Then he smiled and added jokingly, "We even thought of getting him a mistress!"

The implausibility of the thought produced an eruption of chuckles and guffaws.

My friend waited for the laughter to subside and quipped, "Whose?" It was the perfect riposte. The members roared their approval of his skill at repartee. We finally had to be gaveled to silence with an admonition that a lady (Nancy Kassebaum) was present.

After the luncheon, we moved to the Senate floor for a roll-call vote on whether to convert a $50-million loan to Turkey to an outright grant. The Greek community and its supporters in Congress were opposed to granting any sort of financial relief to Turkey because of Turkey's invasion of Cyprus several years ago. Congress had voted to cut off military aid to Turkey because American-made weapons were used during the invasion, in violation of our laws. This had produced a bitter reaction by the Turkish government and opened a deep wound with one of our traditionally strongest NATO allies. In the past, I had voted to impose an arms embargo on Turkey and then voted to lift it with the hope that that would serve as an incentive for Turkey to enter into negotiations to resolve the refugee problem on Cyprus.

Turkey was now on the brink of financial collapse—it had a 50-percent inflation rate and 20 percent unemployment, with 50 percent of its productive capacity idle. The $50-million grant would not do much to reduce the danger of the current government's toppling, but it was vital to start to repair the lesion that we had opened in a moment of domestic political anger. The vote carried 64 to 32.*

---

* The House of Representatives subsequently refused to provide Turkey with a grant of $50 million. It insisted that any relief must come in the form of a loan.

Following the vote, I attended an Armed Services meeting and offered a motion to delete all funding for the mobile MX missile which the Administration testified it wanted to protect our ICBM force. I deliberately took an extreme position on this to highlight the folly of funding the research and development of the MX missile while deferring a decision on how the missile would be hidden or launched.

Halfway through the meeting, I received a call from my office. Trade Representative Bob Strauss and Agriculture Secretary Bob Bergland were holding a meeting in the hearing room of the House Ways and Means Committee on the subject of shoe imports. The state of Maine was being particularly hard hit by the export of leather and the flood of cheaply produced shoes coming into the country from Japan and Korea. My staff insisted that I forgo the Armed Services meeting and express my concern directly to Strauss.

Strauss was customarily blunt with questions offered by New England representatives:

"What can I do with Korea? Not a damned thing. Been around politics a long time, and I learned to give the unvarnished truth. Ain't going to promise you something I can't deliver. . . ."

"What are you going to do to help save the domestic shoe industry from this kind of unfair competition?" I asked Strauss.

"Only thing we can do—subsidize the shoe industry during the short term. . . ."

I returned to the Armed Services Committee and apologized for my absence. John Culver didn't let my apology go unchallenged.

"Oh, that's all right, Bill. Shoes are more important than the destruction of the world."

"Well, John, as a matter of fact, there's a higher kill rate in Maine as the result of this Administration's policies. . . ."

Carl Levin of Michigan interrupted me: "We're going to hit the Russians with shoes instead of missiles."

"As I recall, Khrushchev did use a shoe to bang the table at the United Nations. . . ."

Chairman John Stennis cut off the bickering before it got out of hand.

There is always a constant shuffle of members into and out of committee hearings. But I learned from that exchange that it is preferable to come and go in silence rather than try to explain the urgency or priorities that you assign to your schedule.

MAY 23, 1979

SECRETARY OF DEFENSE HAROLD BROWN'S OFFICE CALLED to invite Diane and me to join the Secretary in the President's box at the Kennedy Center. The Stuttgart Ballet was performing tonight. I declined the invitation. I had declined a working dinner at the White House on Monday. The Administration was pressing too hard on SALT. Its sudden interest in extending social invitations was clumsy.

At 10:30, I attended an Armed Services Committee meeting. I offered a motion to force the Administration to make a decision on the basing mode for the missile. The substance of the motion would require the so-called vertical multiple protection shelter (MPS) unless the President certified that an alternative was militarily superior and as cost-effective.

Howard Cannon of Nevada objected to the narrowness of my language. John Tower supported it. The Committee broke for lunch around noon.

I checked with the Senate Republican staff and was told there would be nothing controversial on the floor and no votes were expected for several hours. I decided to get some exercise.

No sooner had I worked up a sweat in the Senate gym than someone called for a roll-call vote on a minor resolution. I hit the shower, literally jumped into my clothes and dashed to the floor. Everyone knew where I had been. My hair was soaking wet.

After voting, I went to a Wednesday Group luncheon. Prior to asking the members for a report on the activities in their respective committees, we talked politics.

Malcolm Wallop of Wyoming was curious about Kennedy's actions. "Bill, do you think Kennedy will refuse the draft or run for President?"

"I think he'll continue to refuse the draft and continue to run," I responded. "I don't believe Carter will be a candidate." (How wrong I was.)

"I disagree," another Senator interjected. "Rosalynn is tough as nails. She's fifty percent of the Presidency. He'll run. . . ."

Someone else repeated a rumor that had been floated recently: Thurgood Marshall would resign from the Supreme Court, Walter Mondale would be appointed to his seat on the bench and Kennedy would run as Carter's Vice President, thereby gaining four more years away from Chappaquiddick while under the righteous cloak of Carter. . . .

At 2 P.M. I met with some students from Maine and then returned to the Committee on Armed Services. Scoop Jackson offered a substitute to my amendment, but Howard Cannon still objected to the language. I offered to combine the essence of my amendment with that of Scoop's, and at that point Chairman Stennis sent us out of the room to negotiate. After twenty minutes we reached a compromise and returned to the Committee. Carl Levin of Michigan and Jim Exon of Nebraska insisted on seeing the compromise in writing and objected to any vote until the next day.

May 24, 1979—Rocky II

TONIGHT, Diane and I attended a Republican black-tie dinner in memory of Nelson Rockefeller. The event was held in the spacious ballroom of the Washington Hilton Hotel. A din pervaded the elegant ballroom, as men and women in high fashion exchanged exuberant greetings.

As we approached our table, one of the "paying guests" said excitedly, "Did you hear that the House Administration Committee killed the public-financing bill seventeen to eight? Now, there's a turkey that deserved to be shot down. . . ."

"No," I replied, "I hadn't heard that."

I decided to say nothing by way of amplification or challenge. I was a supporter of public financing for Congressional elections and did not see it as an assault upon the Republican Party. I had no idea who the man was, and he obviously wasn't aware that I was one of the principal cosponsors of the bill in the Senate. I concluded that a confrontation would make for an unpleasant evening at a very small table.

The brutality of politics is never more evident than in a moment of repose, when its dynamism is at rest during a funeral or a memorial banquet for one of its departed participants.

I can still recall the 1964 Republican Convention in San Francisco when Rockefeller haters booed so long and loud that he was unable to complete his speech to the delegates. Then, during the 1976 Republican Convention in Kansas City, Rockefeller had been reduced to a pathetic parody, pictured gleefully holding on to a convention-floor telephone that had been yanked from its socket. Henry Kissinger sat in the large hall in a silence that did not admit the sound of even one hand clapping. He hung like a dark, brooding presence that everyone wanted to go away. His name was not mentioned during the three-day affair. His presence was at the sufferance of delegates who were belligerent toward and contemptuous of him.

Tonight, all the swords were sheathed. The old warriors took off their helmets and breastplates and paid tribute to the adversary they had tried to dismember over the years for his liberalism and apostasy. A film was projected onto a large screen that captured highlights in Rockefeller's life which verified that he was a man of action and passion. Then came tributes from all the presidential aspirants for 1980—John Anderson, Howard Baker, George Bush, John Connally, Phil Crane, Bob Dole, and Ronald Reagan.

Former President Ford took the podium to the band's blare of the "Michigan Fight Song." He praised Rockefeller and expressed regret that he had not fully appreciated the strength of the Ford-Rockefeller team. Ford had dumped Rockefeller—or acquiesced in his decision not to run for Vice President in 1976—because Rockefeller was anathema to conservative supporters of Ronald Reagan.

Kissinger was the master of ceremonies. He was, in referring to Rockefeller, characteristically melancholy, nearly maudlin and barely comprehensible. The public-address system was unable to project his low monotone throughout the large ballroom.

It was not a happy event. The false gaiety and exaggerated claims of affection tasted like a tin coin attempting to pass for gold under a molar bite.

Rockefeller would not have arranged a party that was so dull, and so full of empty platitudes.

May 28, 1979

THE HEAVENS WENT dark gray and started to weep. It was Memorial Day, and I was scheduled to make an address at the Augusta Veterans' Memorial Cemetery. The downpour forced everyone into a small chapel which quickly became overheated.

During the hour-and-a-half drive from Bangor to Augusta, I found my thoughts moving with the cadence of the windshield wipers as they clicked across the glass. Eight years ago, I had delivered my first Memo-

rial Day speech in a small rural Maine town. On the way back to Bangor,
I jotted down some thoughts that kept surfacing that day.

> *Memorial Day is a moment*
> *when celebration and sadness*
> *are joined hand in hand*
> *in a strident brass band march*
> *on every Main Street*
> *at 10 A.M.*
>
> *It is a holiday weekend*
> *filled with pain*
> *and potted flowers*
> *for some,*
> *you know the ones,*
> *who circle through manicured lawns*
> *in a quiet drone,*
> *searching for those now gone*
> *sunk in brevity,*
> *carved in stone.*
>
> *A time for families*
> *to gather from distant coasts*
> *and drop tears over the memory*
> *of tall ghosts,*
> *sons or brothers*
> *who gave their green for all*
> *and forever.*
>
> *Then there is the parade*
> *where balloons and miniature flags*
> *are held by babies*
> *resting on their fathers' height*
> *and the shirt-sleeved crowd*
> *rejoices at the sight*
> *of some friend who steps left*
> *when the sergeant barks right.*
>
> *A veteran from some ancient war*
> *steps proudly to a patriotic beat and blare,*
> *his frozen face, the subject once*
> *of an artist's special grace,*
> *strapped in a metal disc*
> *that gave thin shelter*
> *against the risk*
> *of destruction.*

By the reviewing stand
pass ROTC units, then
a local high school band,
and there, in the very rear,
dressed in blue shirts and bright scarves,
comes the smallest group,
the youngest troop.
Cub scouts, with
blushing flower faces
and embarrassed grins,
unsure of their presence,
of their particular
significance.
Is it simply the promise
of a continuing nation
or is it instead
a subtler solace to those
who mourn their dead,
that these sons of others
will one day answer
a written call
and stand ready to fall
in some foreign land
in the name of freedom?

I really don't know,
I only ask because today
my son was somewhere
in that parade
and I couldn't bear to
go.

I wondered whether I should recite those lines today. Would the rain-drenched parents understand the sorrow I felt inside?. . .

As I approached the podium, I overheard a member of the women's auxiliary say, "It's hot in here—hot enough to faint."

I dismissed any notion of reciting poetry and instead rushed through a speech I had written as an alternative. In eight minutes, I managed to quote from John Adams, Winston Churchill, Oliver Wendell Holmes and Robert T. Ingersoll.

MAY 31, 1979

MY OFFICE CALLED to tell me that the *Washington Post* was running a
two-page story on my father's futile effort to save his bakery from local
urban-renewal planners. . . .

My father has owned and operated a small family bakery on Hancock
Street in Bangor for nearly fifty years. The bakery was the last building
standing on Hancock Street, a dilapidated area that had been leveled
pursuant to a federal urban-renewal program. There was little justification
for the City of Bangor to take my father's bakery under its eminent-
domain powers. He had torn down his old place fifteen years ago and
replaced it with a concrete-block, brick-faced building that was in full
compliance with all the city's codes. City officials, however, had concluded that the general real estate in the area would be more desirable to
a future land developer without the presence of the bakery. Thus, the life
and livelihood of one man had to be bulldozed under in the name of
progress. On the surface, perhaps that seemed fair enough. One man and
his family who derived their living from the bakery should not stand in
the way of the future. But what was fundamentally unfair was the terms
under which the individual yielded his life's investment to society's majority.

Under the urban-renewal program, the City was not required to pay
him the replacement value of his business—only the "fair market value."
He was required to go into debt to build a new bakery at inflationary costs
and then find himself in a position of being forced to pay taxes on the new
building's inflated value.

I thought the City was treating one of its hardest-working citizens in
a shabby manner—particularly since those who owned the dilapidated
apartment houses ("slumlords") all made a profit under the program. But
my lips were sealed by virtue of my position. To have complained publicly about the treatment my father was receiving would have prompted
charges of "favoritism" or congressional interference. I receive an average of 1,500 letters a week from my constituents, many of whom ask me
to intervene on their behalf against arbitrary, capricious or unfair treatment by some federal or local government agency. When it came time to
assist my father, I was forced to stand aside in silence. For several long
weeks during his negotiations with the City of Bangor, I seriously contem-

plated resigning my seat in the Senate and undertaking his case as a private attorney in a lawsuit. But a lawsuit would take months to litigate fully, and his bakery would have been torn down long before he would ever have been accorded a full measure of justice by twelve of his community peers.

The experience left me a great deal more sensitive to the sense of helplessness that individuals feel when they are up against "City Hall."

JUNE 6, 1979

MY CAR WAS down and out again. I walked over to Dennis DeConcini's house and caught a ride to the office. I wanted to attend the weekly Prayer Breakfast meeting this morning to hear my freshman colleague Al Simpson of Wyoming. Each week members of the Senate gather in the Vandenberg Room on the first floor of the Senate side of the Capitol to spend an hour in fellowship and prayer. Usually a member of the Senate will discuss his background and religious experiences and beliefs.

Just before the meeting began, John Stennis came over to me and said, "You be sure to come to our meeting at ten, now."

"Mr. Chairman," I said, "have I ever missed a meeting yet?"

"No, sir—come to think of it, you haven't. But today is especially important. There is some language in that bill that practically has your name on it.* I don't expect any problems, but you never can tell."

"Don't worry, Mr. Chairman, I'll be there."

After breakfast, Al Simpson began his address to the group. He is a tall, slat-thin, slightly stoop-shouldered man who wears half glasses that slip down to the end of his nose. He peers over them with a perpetual squint.

After telling two lightly irreverent stories, Al described how he had careened through life experiencing its pleasures, pains, anxieties, and ambitions. He came to a point when he could look in the mirror and say, "I forgive you." For him, self-love was the beginning of general love for

---

* I had offered an amendment on behalf of Ed Muskie and myself to the Military Construction Authorization Bill that would mandate the retention of Loring Air Force Base at full strength.

others. Life became a mystery to be experienced and not a problem to be solved. . . .

It was one of the most moving talks I had heard—light and spicy at times, but his words reflected an inner serenity that I envied.

One member said, "Al, I wish your father [former Senator Milward Simpson of Wyoming], who served here with great distinction, could have heard your words today. He would have been lifted into ecstasy."

Simpson responded with characteristic humor: "Oh, don't worry. He has. He's heard it all before.

"You know, let me tell you what happened to me one day while practicing law. I heard that a close friend of mine had died. I was shocked. I was with him just the day before, appraising some property. I sat down and wrote a letter—it was beautifully written, really. Mailed it to his wife. The next day I was in a nearby town and read in the paper that he wasn't dead, only in serious condition. I called my friend's house and said if a letter comes, don't open it. It's not important—just return it to me. Well, of course, they just ripped it right open and read every word. His wife was truly grateful for what I had said. But right that day I learned a hell of a lesson. Why is it that when we love somebody, we don't tell that person while he's alive and breathing? Why do we always wait until our friends are dead before we tell them that we love them?"

At noon, I attended a luncheon sponsored by Strom Thurmond for our Ambassador to Saudi Arabia, John C. West. We were told the Saudis were in a fragile position, subject to blackmail by the PLO and terrorist attacks. The United States was not in a position, if Iran was any example, to provide much protection or assistance.

One Senator reflected the frustration of many when he said, "They've got to fish or cut bait—one way or the other. They can't continue to have it both ways. Every time there is an OPEC meeting, the price is raised. They're going to have to decide where they stand. . . . The point is, if they do, they invite political suicide, because the United States not only is not about to intervene—the fact is it would be futile if we did."

On my way back to the office, I ran into Jack Javits, who was heading for another committee meeting.

"Bill, what are they doing on the floor? I've been in committee hearings since nine."

"Jack" I said, "I haven't the slightest idea."

"That's the story of this place, isn't it?" he laughed. "There are just too many balls that we have to juggle at one time."

JUNE 10, 1979

I BOARDED an Eastern Air Lines flight to Boston at 8:20 A.M. I had chartered a private plane to fly from Boston to the coastal community of Belfast, where the Veterans of Foreign Wars were holding their annual convention.

The fog and haze along the coast was thicker than Washington's summer smog. The pilot, Harry Winger, was skeptical that we would be able to land and said we might be wasting a trip. I suggested that we fly to Belfast and hope the fog lifted before we arrived.

The fog didn't move. There were no personnel at the small airport to give us any guidance. The plane's instruments took us directly over the runway, but we could see nothing from the air.

Fresh in the pilot's memory (and mine) was the crash of a small commuter airplane two weeks ago off the fogbound coast of Rockland that had killed fifteen passengers.

"Bill, we're right at the minimum, and we are directly over the airport. Can you see anything down there? If the fog starts to darken up, that's a good sign."

"No, I can't see a damn thing."

"Well, that's it. I'm not going to drop any lower. Where to?"

In addition to delivering a speech, I was scheduled to meet with an eighty-two-year-old man who had been waiting for years to talk to me, and then with Richard Saltonstall, the new owner of the *Belfast Republican Journal.* I knew the veterans would be upset by my absence, but there would be other conventions to attend. I would call the eighty-two-year-old man and apologize. The luncheon could be reset.

A year before, during my campaign for the Senate, or as a member of the House and thus constantly on the campaign trail, I might have tried to persuade the pilot to make a second pass or to drop below the minimum to see if we could break through the fog. Several hundred people were waiting to hear me preach or pontificate and they would talk to several hundred more, and I wouldn't have wanted to risk inviting their reproach for my absence. I had taken risks on many occasions before. Only once in six and a half years did I miss an event because of bad flying weather, and that was because a Delta Airlines flight could not land in northern Maine during a major snowstorm. But I knew that Harry Winger would not yield to any importunings. And for the first time during my service in Congress, I didn't feel the pressure to take the risk. I could make up the loss of support during the next five years.

"Okay, Harry. Let's get out of here."

We turned south and flew to another small airport in southern Maine. I was scheduled to address the graduating class at Kennebunk High School later in the day.

I was exhausted by the time I touched down on a Delta flight at Washington's National Airport late that evening.

JUNE 11, 1979

A MEETING WAS scheduled in my office at 10 A.M. with Dan Tate, the White House deputy assistant for congressional liaison. He arrived about twenty minutes late, a little nervous and somewhat ill-at-ease.

"Senator, I'm not here for any specific purpose. Just wanted to introduce myself and say hello."

It was a standard courtesy call, an attempt to reduce barriers and open a line of communication. It was an indication of the Administration's political ineptitude that such a meeting had not been arranged until nearly six months after the Ninety-sixth Congress convened.

"Well," I responded, "I don't have anything on my mind."

I deliberately avoided initiating any discussion on issues or programs that I was concerned about. Tate's job, I surmised, was to probe for members' hard points or soft spots in the hope of securing future support for the SALT treaty. I didn't want to send any signals that I was prepared to engage in any horse trading.

"But as long as you're here, let me tell you how disappointed I am with President Carter on the decontrol of oil prices. First he came out and said it is imperative that we move to a gradual decontrol of prices. I came out in support of his program. Then when he was out in Idaho a few weeks ago, he said, 'If Congress wants to extend price controls, I won't veto their action.' How in hell am I supposed to persuade my constituents that it's necessary to decontrol prices?''

"Senator," Tate said apologetically, shaking his head, "the staff has talked with him and he deeply regrets having said that."

At noon, I went to the floor to see if I was needed to take part in the discussion of the Military Authorization Bill. Only Chairman John Stennis and John Tower were there. Stennis was speaking as I approached Tower.

"John, do you need me to say anything on the bill?''

"No," Tower responded with a grin. "I think we can handle it without you."

"Okay. I'm going over to get some exercise. If you need me, just call over. . . .''

Although we were talking barely above a whisper, Stennis turned toward us and said, "Mr. President, if we could have a little order here, the two Senators who are talking would be able to hear me compliment them for their fine work on the committee. . . .''

No one was listening to the Chairman except those in the galleries, and it was unlikely that they had any notion of what Stennis was saying. But he is from the old school of etiquette that demands respect, and he was correct in lightly rapping our knuckles for talking during his presentation.

Later in the afternoon, I had a light lunch with Professor Chris Potholm of Bowdoin College, a member of my staff and top campaign strategist. I took him on a tour of the old Senate chambers. A policeman spotted me in the area, where the general public is not allowed, giving a demonstration of the incredible acoustics in the chamber and said, "Excuse me, but are you are a member of the Architect's staff?''

"No, sir," I mustered with some annoyance. "I'm a member of the Senate.''

Six months in the Senate and I still was mistaken for a Senate employee. I was wearing a blue blazer and light slacks that had a little too much flare. Or so I rationalized.

The officer immediately became apologetic, almost obsequious.

"Sir, I'm sorry. I should have recognized you. Would you like to take your guest to the gallery?''

My annoyance turned to embarrassment. He had made an honest mistake, and he didn't have to bow and scrape or seek absolution. But stories are legion of the fate that has befallen Hill employees who have failed to pay due respect to Senators.

   John Stennis is a man who holds the respect of his colleagues. He was shot by a would-be robber several years ago and spent months recovering from the attack. Richard Nixon wanted Stennis to serve as a censor of his tape recordings, so as to certify the validity of his claims that the information that had been deleted involved matters of national security. The idea was rejected—but not because Stennis did not have the trust of his colleagues.
   Stennis, for all his Southern charm and ostensible deference to the members of the Committee, is essentially an autocratic father. Like any chairman, he sets the agenda for committee deliberations, grants approval to subcommittee chairmen for special hearings or for travel to domestic or foreign locations, and controls the debate in the full committee. His support for programs or amendments that members offer is often crucial to their success. Their success will translate into political success at home —clout, as the folks like to say. In return for his support, he builds credits from the members, which he stores for future recall and use. But unlike other chairmen, he tries to restrict the scope of debate to dampen the fires of emotional confrontation, to mold a consensus on almost every issue in order to avoid a partisan or ideological split. The defense and security of the country should not depend upon party affiliation. And so he scrupulously tries to avoid a majority-versus-minority confrontation. He especially discourages committee reports containing "minority views." Anyone who dissents on a particular bill usually files his "individual views."
   He can be abrupt with anyone who challenges his control over Committee proceedings. Once during a debate on an amendment I offered to the Military Authorization Bill to force the Administration to make a decision on the MX missile, I sought to respond to a question that had been raised by another member. I raised my hand and said, "Mr. Chairman, Mr. Chairman." Stennis looked at me and said, "No, we've heard enough from you today. Let's hear from counsel on this matter now."
   Had I been in the House or, indeed, on any other committee in the Senate, I would have raised hell at the suggestion that I defer to a staff member to give his interpretation of an amendment that I had offered. But nothing would have been gained by openly questioning his authority.

I let the insult lie in the deep bed of the Chairman's power and prerogative. His habit was something that I could not challenge or change—not without appearing disrespectfully surly or sassy.

Today, just as I was starting to engage in a vigorous debate with Sam Nunn on the need to reinstitute draft registration and classification, Stennis interrupted: "This is unusual, gentlemen, but important." He then leaned over and started whispering to Harry Byrd, Jr., of Virginia. My momentum evaporated.

Everyone in the room knew what he was doing and just started to laugh. I mocked the Chairman lightly to John Tower.

"Now, Ah apologize fo' the interruption, but you go right ahead and pick up where you left off. . . ." Tower just laughed. Fortunately, the Chairman didn't hear me.

We never did resume the debate. Finally, after the vote was taken, 12–5 in favor of the legislation, Stennis said, "Well, we've had a wonderful discussion on this heah bill. . . ."

Again, everyone started to laugh. I laughed loudest. Stennis turned to me in seriousness: "Cohen, what's so funny?"

JUNE 12, 1979

"SUNSET." It has become the current shibboleth of Capitol Hill, invoked by liberal and conservative alike. A pleasant-sounding word for a death sentence to be imposed on every agency and program unless Congress, by positive action and approval, allows it to be born again. It marks the latest attempt to gain control over the explosion of federal programs.

Today, John Glenn was chairing a Governmental Affairs Subcommittee hearing on the proposed sunset legislation. Among the witnesses were spokesmen for the national Chamber of Commerce. While they offered general support for the legislation as it applied to programs, they were strongly opposed to applying the guillotine blade to existing tax credits or deductions (called "tax expenditures") that had been written into the Tax Code over the years. Glenn ripped into the witnesses for having sent an inflammatory and irresponsible letter to his constituents in Ohio on the legislation. The Chamber had attacked the Congress' use of the words "tax expenditure" as a synonym for "tax revenue" and the underlying assumption that the federal treasury had a divine right to the taxpayer's money and that the burden of proof would be upon the taxpayers to demonstrate why they should be permitted to keep that money in the form of a deduction from or credit against their income taxes. Glenn didn't like the Chamber's double standard and bluntly said so.

At 12:30, I attended the weekly Policy Luncheon. A number of us had been working under the leadership of Jack Javits to develop some new economic policies, to constitute a Positive Action Program. I suggested that we change the name in order to avoid having the press pick up its acronym and call it "Republican PAP."

At 2 I returned to my office to meet with a group of small businessmen who wanted to talk about forthcoming legislation. I prefer, if possible, to know in advance what specific legislation any group is concerned about, since it allows my staff to thoroughly research its status in the legislative branch. They refused to give me or my staff any indication of any bills with which they were concerned. Apparently, they thought a surprise attack would be more productive for them.

As I walked into my office, the group was already seated around my desk.

"We're going to put you on the spot," their spokesman said rather enthusiastically.

"Maybe you will, maybe you won't," I responded, failing to contain my disdain for the underlying assumption that I was somehow an adversary who had to be taken by surprise.

"We want some yes or no answers," he insisted.

"I don't answer yes-or-no questions," I replied. "Life and politics are a little more complicated than yes or no. If you want me to express an opinion, it will be a full one—so you won't put down a simple checkmark on your question-and-answer sheet and then at a later time say that I misled you. . . ."

I had anticipated what issues would be of interest to them and had researched the materials with the assistance of my staff the night before. But I resented the notion that I was not to be armed with knowledge in advance. I was a solid friend of the small-business community (99 percent of all business in Maine is small business) and needed no aggressive challenges questioning the sincerity of my interest.

"Where do you stand on sunset, health insurance, inflation, balanced budgets, local control, decontrol of prices? . . ."

The secrecy was so unnecessary. . . .

I returned to the Senate floor to listen to the debate on whether the United States should give recognition to the elections in Rhodesia. . . .

JUNE 13, 1979

I DELIVERED a brief speech on the Senate floor on the economic choices facing our country and inserted in the *Congressional Record* an article written by Congressman Jack Kemp.

The "morning hour" concluded by 10 A.M. Dale Bumpers of Arkansas obtained recognition to speak and delivered an impassioned speech on an amendment (to delete funding for an aircraft carrier) to the Military Authorization Procurement Bill that was pending. He was angry at the request that was made and granted by John Stennis last night that only Sam Nunn's amendment on the subject of the registration of young men for military service would be in order today. He spoke for twenty minutes in a loud and lyrical manner, mixing a folksy humor with hard facts about the astronomical costs of aircraft carriers and their vulnerability to attack in wartime.

In the meantime, Mark Hatfield of Oregon approached me on the floor and asked me not to offer an amendment that I had drafted as a substitute for Sam Nunn's. Mark wanted the opportunity to defeat Nunn on an "up or down" basis. He invited me into the Republican cloakroom to review his negotiating strategy with Nunn.

Hatfield was willing to take up the registration question as a separate bill after the House had acted but before there was a House–Senate conference. This would give the Senate an opportunity to debate and vote on the issue before being faced with a conference report on the Defense Procurement Bill and forced to vote up or down. This sounded reasonable enough except that Hatfield would not agree to a specific time limit on debate. In the absence of an agreement to limit the time for debate, no Senator can be precluded from engaging in a filibuster and thereby dragging out the debate for days or even weeks. Debate can be terminated by a vote for cloture, but the Senate is generally reluctant to invoke this procedure. On an issue as controversial as registration, which would be seen by many as the first step toward a return to the draft, it was unlikely that the Senate would act to terminate debate. Thus, Hatfield was still preserving his option to filibuster. I expected Nunn to reject the offer or suggest an alternative. Under Hatfield's proposal, Senate action would be controlled by the House. Secondly, unless Hatfield agreed to a time limit, it was possible that because of a filibuster a vote would never be taken. With the SALT II treaty ratification scheduled to take most of the fall months, Hatfield would be in control. I walked back onto the floor certain that the strategy would not work.

Nunn was under pressure from Stennis to work out a compromise and prevent Hatfield and George McGovern from delaying action on the Military Procurement Authorization Bill that was pending.

Nunn listened to Hatfield's proposal and then said, "Mark, as I understand it, you would be willing to take up the registration issue as a separate bill provided the House passes it so that we can debate the issue before a House–Senate conference, but you are not agreeing to a time limit on debate."

"That's right, Sam. Not at this time."

"What would be the chances of agreeing to a time limit?" Nunn pressed.

"I think they would be good. I'm sure we can work it out," Hatfield responded.

To my surprise, Sam accepted Hatfield's proposal. Even Hatfield was surprised. If the House failed to act, the pressure for consideration of the bill by the Senate was off. If the House passed the bill, Hatfield had, by implication, agreed he would not filibuster but nevertheless could debate the issue for days. He was elated.

In the meantime, Bob Dole and I indicated that we would be filing a bill that would force the Administration to report to the Congress the exact state of our military preparedness.

At noon, Peter and Judi Dawkins, two of our closest friends, came to Capitol Hill for lunch. Pete is considered one of West Point's most outstanding graduates; he not only had won the Heismann trophy for excellence in football, but was also a Rhodes scholar. He is presently a colonel in the Army and had just received his doctoral degree at Princeton. He was driving back to Fort Campbell, Kentucky, where he commanded a brigade in the 101st Airborne Division. We spent the afternoon touring the Capitol and visiting with some of my friends in the Senate.

JUNE 14, 1979

LAST NIGHT I HAD a long talk with Diane about the frequent recurrence of throat infections and loss of voice that I had experienced since the latter part of my campaign for the Senate. Diane was sympathetic, but insisted that the time had come to have an operation on my nose to correct a deviated septum, which forced me to breathe constantly through my mouth. I took her advice and called to arrange to enter the Maine Medical Center in Portland in two weeks for the surgery.

I anticipated there would be some difficulty in explaining the nature of the operation to my constituents. My press secretary drafted a release that stated quite clinically that I would enter the hospital to have a deviated septum corrected. I objected to the wording.

"Tom, it sounds like I've either got a sexual problem or a sewer system in my nose. Why don't you rewrite it to state that it is a minor operation to correct a problem of recurring laryngitis?"

"Bill, if the release says that, everyone will speculate that you've got cancer of the throat," he countered.

We compromised. At an appropriate time we would issue a statement that said I would undergo minor surgery to eliminate a nasal blockage that was producing recurring throat infections.

JUNE 17, 1979

FATHER'S DAY. Chris and Diane treated me to breakfast in bed. They served my favorite—blueberry pancakes. We called Kevin in Los Angeles, where he had flown yesterday. He had a job on the West Coast for the summer. He had left our nest for the first time in his sixteen years. He would be with us for two more years, but we knew things would never be quite the same again.

After breakfast, I left for the airport to return to Maine. I had to deliver a commencement speech at a high school in the afternoon and one to the annual meeting of "Girls' State" that evening.

At the airport, a young man approached me and said, "Senator Cohen, can I ask you a question?"

"Well, it'll have to be quick. I'm late," I snapped.

"Who are you supporting for President?"

"No one," I responded. "Who are you supporting?"

"George Bush. I hope you will too. . . ."

I passed through the metal-detector gate without looking back at the young man. I had been too quick with him, but I was in a foul mood. I didn't want to get on that plane today. I'm not given to sentimentality, but this was the seventh consecutive Father's Day that I was on an airplane heading somewhere other than home with my family, and I was brooding about it.

Just before takeoff, a man came to the rear of the plane, where I usually sit, and said, "Hello, Senator." My temporary anonymity having been blown, I tried to avoid eye contact with anyone. I had two speeches to work on and I didn't want to be interrupted.

A few minutes after we were airborne, the woman sitting next to me, said, "Excuse me. He called you Senator. Are you?"

"Yes," I smiled, and then returned to the pile of papers in my lap.

"What's your name?" she asked.

"Cohen," I said without elaboration.

"Cowlin?"

"No, it's Bill Cohen. I'm from Maine." Again, I tried to get back to the speeches.

"Then you must be one of us," she persisted.

"Pardon?"

"You must be Jewish," she concluded.

"Half," I said.

"Oh, wonderful. I'm whole. . . ."

June 18, 1979

Today, President Carter signed the SALT II treaty in Vienna. Brezhnev issued a warning that the Senate should not tamper with the treaty.

At 8:30 P.M. we gathered on the Senate floor to prepare to walk to the House chamber to listen to President Carter address a joint session of Congress. Whether one approved or disapproved of the treaty, this was a historic day, but there was no excitement in the air. We gathered together out of duty rather than enthusiasm to welcome home the leader of our country.

As we entered the House, I noticed that the right-hand side of the chamber, where Republicans sit, was virtually empty. Absence under the circumstances was a flagrant act of disrespect. Pages had to be utilized to fill the seats and reduce the embarrassment to the President.

The Sergeant at Arms bellowed out his familiar litany.

"Mistah Speakah, the Members of the United States Senate." Those in the chamber stood and applauded politely.

As soon as we were seated, the Diplomatic Corps was led onto the floor with the same fanfare. It occurred to me that I could have been standing in a medieval palace listening to trumpets herald the arrival of a delegation of knights. . . .

Finally, the klieg lights installed in the chamber by the television networks became intensely bright. It was the signal that President Carter was about to walk through the center doors and onto the floor.

"Mistah Speakah, the President of the United States."

The President looked thin and tired. He had arrived in Washington only two hours earlier. He was wearing a dark blue suit and white shirt. He was given the usual standing ovation when he entered the chamber and again when Speaker Tip O'Neill introduced him.

He used no TelePrompTer tonight. His speech was well prepared and well delivered (as one member gratuitously added later, "for him").

But what was unusual was the silence that greeted him during the speech. He was applauded on five or six occasions, and then only when he talked of "peace through strength." Ordinarily, a President can count on being interrupted fifteen to twenty times. That tradition was broken.

He converted few, if any, members with his speech. More importantly, he inspired even fewer.

JUNE 20, 1979

SIX A.M. The gas lines of California had arrived in Washington with a vengeance. Diane and Chris were leaving for Maine this morning. While she finished packing I drove her car to the nearest gas station to fill the tank. The line was already forty cars long. The sun was barely up, and no coffee-and-doughnut shops were open. The people in line were upset about the inconvenience, but were surprisingly calm. They were also cynical as to the causes of the "shortage"—manipulation by the oil companies.

After a two-hour-and-fifteen-minute wait in line, I finally made it to the gasoline troughs. Diane was on her way by 9 A.M.

I made a brief speech on the Senate floor calling for cooperation from the oil industry to satisfy the public as to the true status of our stocks and reserves.

Then I attended a Governmental Affairs Committee hearing on reform of our regulatory agencies. After forty-five minutes, I left to participate in another subcommittee meeting on legislative gerrymandering.

At a luncheon today, one of my freshman colleagues informed us that he had just introduced a bill to relieve radio and television stations of paperwork associated with federal licensing requirements. With a completely straight face, a sort of dreamy-eyed innocence, he related how he had sent out a questionnaire to all the radio and television stations in his state and discovered that his proposal was overwhelmingly popular.

The other members chided him good-naturedly and offered to bestow on him the "shooting-the-fish-in-the-barrel award." While they were lightly mocking in their comments, some also indicated they might follow suit and ingratiate themselves with their own local radio and television stations.

Jack Javits is one of the most respected members of the Senate. He is perhaps its most intellectually gifted member and hardest worker. He is not given to wasting time on frivolities or even indulging in light banter. He is completely serious about his work and is taken by others in exactly the same fashion.

Today, he addressed the issue of SALT II. He laid out the criteria that would determine his vote.

"Would the treaty leave the United States worse off than we currently are?

"Would the treaty itself place us in an inferior position?"

"Is the treaty reasonably verifiable?"

Someone asked Javits what he thought about televising the debate in the Senate. Several members expressed their strong disapproval and conviction that it would only lead to posturing and grandstanding by presidential candidates.

But Javits dismissed their apprehensions.

"Just consider how the 'squawk boxes' in our offices have changed things. When I'm on the floor giving a speech and no one is present, it really doesn't matter. I'm not alone—people are listening to what I have to say all over the Capitol. Televising the debates will be an educational experience for the American people. . . ."

Around 7 P.M. I was working in the office when the phone rang. It was Howard Baker's office. He was due to speak in Atlanta tomorrow and had a conflict with an important piece of legislation on the floor in the morning. Could I possibly fill in for him? I had a full schedule the next day myself, including a speech in the evening to the National Restaurant Association.

I spent the next hour trying to make contact with my staff to have them contact the various people scheduled to meet with me the next day and finally called Baker's office to say that I could substitute for him provided that was acceptable to the people in Atlanta. Then, minutes later, I received a call from an officer of the American Credit Bureau Association. He was delighted that I could come to Atlanta. His enthusiasm and genuine relief was flattering. He had no idea about my speaking ability (or lack of it) or whether in fact I was prepared to speak on a subject of interest to the Association. I was a warm senatorial body willing to come to Georgia in the morning.

I tried to reach Diane until midnight. She had not arrived in Maine. She had made it as far as Rhode Island but couldn't get gas until the next day.

JUNE 22, 1979

THE FABRIC of civil order was starting to fray. Independent truckers were on strike because of the high cost of fuel. One trucker who did not join the strike was shot and killed by a sniper as he drove his rig on the highway. Arson and vandalism had erupted. . . .

Ed Muskie had said nothing on the subject of energy for the past two months. Today, in Portland, Maine, he delivered a major speech on energy, criticizing President Carter's program and challenging Congress to come up with a better one.

JUNE 25, 1979

LAST WEEK the magazine *U.S. News and World Report* contained an article that declared that rudeness in America had reached epidemic proportions.

Today, the white gloves of senatorial etiquette and courtesy were stained by the spreading pool of impatience and belligerence.

Lowell Weicker stands six feet six inches tall and weighs approximately 230 pounds. He is a large man who opted early in life to walk loudly and swing a big club. In a moment of high energy or stress, he could bellow down the walls of Jericho or the new Hart Senate Office Building. He introduced an amendment to delete $13 million in loan guarantees for the Wheeling-Pittsburgh Steel Corporation to construct a new rail mill. The plant was located in Pennsylvania—the state of Senator John Heinz, a fellow Republican.

Heinz secured recognition to speak and implied that Weicker was motivated by the base instinct of protecting a competing company headquartered in Connecticut. He started to bait Weicker with questions that carried some unkind innuendos.

Weicker roared like a bull elephant. "Anyone who would make such a statement is either devious or an idiot. The gentleman from Pennsylvania qualifies on both counts."

Heinz invoked a point of personal privilege under the Senate rules, but was ignored by Weicker and the presiding officer. He finally cited Senate Rule 19, which forbids Senators to "impute to another Senator any conduct or motive unworthy or unbecoming of a Senator."

Weicker was forced to sit down and remain silent—a posture he or any other Senator is not readily accustomed to—until he was able to secure unanimous consent of the Senate to speak.

If the presiding officer rules that a Senator has violated the rule, he may order the offending Senator to take his seat, and he may not proceed without leave of the Senate.

Weicker was ordered to sit down while Heinz asked that Weicker's remarks be taken down and read into the record again. But the Senate reporter had left the chamber in order to have his notes transcribed for the *Congressional Record*.

In the meantime, Majority Leader Robert Byrd stepped in and tried to soothe the ruffled feathers, saying he could understand why Heinz would take umbrage at Weicker's remarks. "Many times we say in heated debate what later we wish had not been said."

Weicker finally secured permission to speak and said he would agree to strike the words from the *Record* if "the Senator takes umbrage, and I would if I were he. . . ."

Heinz in turn offered to apologize if Weicker felt that his integrity had been questioned by Heinz's remarks. Weicker would not apologize, but did agree to strike his words from the *Congressional Record*. Then Heinz and Weicker shook hands. The offending words never appeared in the *Congressional Record*.

At noon, I delivered a speech to the Young Governors' Conference and then had lunch with Elliot Richardson to discuss his progress with the Law of the Sea Conference and his future political plans.

Later in the afternoon, Bob Dole and I offered an amendment to increase the appropriation for Selective Service. It did not occur to me that senatorial courtesy required that I should have contacted Sam Nunn, because this might have an impact upon his registration proposal. When someone called this to my attention, I rushed to the cloakroom to call Nunn's office. He was in the middle of an interview and could not take the call, so I alerted his staff to the amendment.

It was not necessary for him to be on the floor. Chairman John Stennis rose in opposition to our amendment, as did the Chairman of the Appropriations Committee, Warren Magnuson of Washington. Mark Hatfield was also opposed to it. Hatfield is a deeply religious man, and he is fundamentally opposed to any activation of the torpid Selective Service System, since it might enhance or help promote a militaristic mood in the country and thereby increase the chances of our getting involved in a conflict or war.

"Bill, don't offer this now. This is our fallback position if we lose on the registration issue. Don't give it away now."

"Mark, I'm not giving anything away. I think we ought to give Selective Service the money it needs to do the job we've given it," I said.

"I am opposed to even having any Selective Service System. I don't want to appropriate any money for it, not to mention an add-on of $1.1 million to this supplemental appropriation," Hatfield insisted.

"Well, if that's your position, then I intend to oppose you when Nunn's bill comes to the floor. . . ."

I felt my anger flare up as if it were a cup of brandy touched by a match. But the flame died almost immediately. Mark Hatfield is not a man of cunning but of deep conviction. I was not angry with him because his beliefs ran counter to my own on this issue. I was annoyed that he assumed that my amendment was simply his fallback position, something to be accepted as a last resort.

I knew that with a broad crosscut of the Senate's ideological spectrum opposed to our amendment, there was little choice but to save it for another day. A motion to table our amendment carried on a voice vote, and neither Dole nor I insisted on pushing it to a recorded vote which we were certain to lose.

JUNE 27, 1979

HOWARD BAKER HELD a press conference this morning to announce that he could not and would not support the SALT II treaty in its present form. Substantive amendments would have to be adopted before it could be considered acceptable.

Baker was under pressure to make a decision. The longer he waited, the more pressure was being generated by proponents and opponents. Delay would only have the effect of increasing the political overtones of the decision. Proponents argued that if he supported the treaty he would be considered a statesman—a title that would serve him well in a general election—and should he oppose the treaty, it would mark a cave-in to conservatives who were angry over his vote to ratify the treaty on the Panama Canal.

An early decision would not erase the speculation that he had yielded to political pressure from the right, but he would avoid the appearance of vacillating or of waiting until it was expedient to vote for or against the treaty. In fact, Baker could quite correctly state that political considerations were not a factor in his decision, since a large majority of the American people were said to be in favor of SALT II.

The fact is that Baker had genuine doubts about the equitability and verifiability of the treaty, and he was making the best of a tough decision by making that decision early.

I had read and studied enough about SALT to conclude that it was unequal in its terms. Yet I still held out some hope that something would surface, some revelations would come to the attention of the American people to convince them that we were negotiating out of fear rather than with confidence and that the voices who had spoken so fervently about the need to allow the Soviets to catch up and achieve parity were the same as those who now said we must have SALT because we cannot as a free society compete against the determination and the discipline of a totalitarian state.

Because I was a freshman member of the Senate, there was no pressure on me to make an early decision. I knew at that time that I would not support the treaty unless it was amended, but I was content to speak about the problems that I had with it without slamming the door on its possible ratification.

The Governmental Affairs Committee was holding hearings this morning on the serious problem of the loss of privacy in the age of the computer.

Confidential information, the most personal and sensitive revelations that we make to physicians to enable them to diagnose and treat medical problems, was being disseminated on a wholesale and indiscriminate basis to third parties—insurance companies, credit companies, government agencies, law-enforcement personnel—and used to embarrass, discredit or harass us. Our lives were being committed to a computer tape and stored in the cold calculations of impersonal corporate machines. Reputations were being ruined—an entire multimillion-dollar industry had sprung into existence that was engaged in theft, fraud and sale of confidential information—and only a handful of people came to the hearing.

JUNE 28, 1979

THE FOURTH OF JULY RECESS period came two days early. I flew to Portland to meet with Dr. William Maxwell, who was to perform the surgery on my nose the next day. Diane picked me up at the airport and drove me to Dr. Maxwell's office. He reviewed the medical procedure and explained the risk involved—the possible perforation of my nasal membrane, which would leave me with a whistle in my nose every time I breathed. It was also possible that even with the operation my breathing might not improve.

I had complete confidence in Maxwell, who is regarded as one of the finest specialists in his field. He also treated me for laryngitis during the last stages of my campaign for the Senate. Despite the risk inherent in this surgery, I decided to go through with the operation. Several people who had had the operation warned me of the pain they had suffered. "Be sure that you have general anesthesia, Bill. Don't let the doctor con you into staying awake under a local. You'll regret it. . . ."

We left his office and went to McDonald's. Not exactly what I had always envisioned as my last supper, but I had not been in a hospital since I was five years old and I didn't know what, or if, I would be fed.

After checking into the hospital, I filled out the medical consent forms that relieved the hospital of all liability—including, I suspected, an appendectomy, if it was deemed necessary in my doctor's best medical judgment. I donned a pair of pajamas I had just purchased at a local department store. They were about three inches above my ankles, I discovered. It was either the pajamas or the house johnny, so I opted for the pajamas.

JUNE 29, 1979

THE OPERATION WAS a success. No black eyes. Nose as big as it was before the operation. Same shape (alas). The difference was that for the first time in my life I could breathe. The doctor had to caution me not to abuse my newfound skill—I was flaring my nostrils, inhaling deeply and in danger of passing as an advertisement for a popular nasal decongestant.

I spent the day recovering from the effects of the anesthesia and taking pain-killers. Diane and Chris came in to view the patient. They picked up my spirits. That evening, I read Macaulay's *Critical and Historical Essays*. Forty pages jumped over the fence in my mind and wafted me into the netherworld of sleep.

JULY 2, 1979

MY OFFICE RELEASED the statement that I had undergone minor surgery. I had wanted to wait until I was out of the hospital because I didn't want to see a lot of visitors or receive phone calls. The papers carried the story. Ed Muskie's press secretary called the office and said, "I understand your boss just had a nose job." One woman called and asked, "Did they get it all? . . . I mean did they get all the cancer?"

I spent the week on the Maine coast sitting in the sun. The chug of lobster boats penetrated the morning mist, as they moved in constant pattern and pursuit of their clawed catch. Sandpipers scurried about the beaches like a tiny regiment or band along the edge of each new wave, picking food from the bubbling sand.

The harmony of this unending struggle was obvious even in the fog that swept in and softened the sound of bobbing buoys and haunting horns. It has always been therapeutic for me here. The ocean reduces the enormity of events and the seeming complexities of political problems. Standing in the spray of an incoming tide is nearly a religious experience —a reminder of the existence of a power much greater than ourselves and a beauty too perfect to be conceived or produced by man.

CHAPTER 13

AFTER HALF A YEAR in office, many of the notions I held about the House and the Senate had been confirmed. The Ninety-sixth Session of Congress was hardly under way, but patterns of conduct were becoming familiar. The differences between the two legislative houses began to loom large.

The Congress of the United States is theoretically composed of two coequal bodies, the House and the Senate. The rate of pay is the same for members of each body, each individual is technically called a "Congressman," and each house contributes approximately the same amount to the total legislative output. The House may have an edge in tax matters, because of its constitutional right to initiate all revenue-raising measures; conversely, the Senate's role in foreign affairs is larger, because of its treaty ratification and confirmation powers, among others. But there is a rough equivalence.

In spite of all the appearances of parity, however, the two institutions are wildly dissimilar—and never more obviously than when they are in session.

Although its rules are far more carefully structured, the gallery observer in the House will witness very little that is orderly. What purports to be the main event—the "gentleman" or "gentlewoman" speaking in the "well" of the House—actually appears to be little more than a sideshow. The overall effect is that of a service-club meeting gone amok: Some members are answering their mail; others are chatting in small knots in the aisles; a few are gazing into space; fewer still are involved in frenzied debate; even fewer appear to be listening—and most are not there, except when the bells ring for a vote. When a key issue or the occasional spirited debate captures the attention of the majority, the chamber is filled with whistles, huzzahs, groans. When they choose to participate, House members are not shy.

In fact, the decibel level on the House floor has reached such proportions that the current House Minority Leader, Representative John J. Rhodes of Arizona, once felt impelled to mention, in a letter to the Republican membership, that "emotional displays of non-approbation do not enhance the image of the Minority, nor promote constructive debate, a key part of the legislative process. . . .

"So, may I ask that we all refrain from vociferous expressions of disapproval of positions on legislation before the House by members with whom we might disagree while the presentation is in progress. . . . Or, to put it another way, the basic lack of merit of many of the arguments of the opposition will become even more apparent without the accompaniment of raucous noises from our side."

The Senate, by contrast, is almost totally unstructured. Amendments can be added to bills at will, regardless of their relevance. Unlimited debate is an article of holy writ, and only in the most extreme cases will cloture be invoked to stem the stream of verbiage. The Senators sit at individually assigned desks, rather than in randomly selected chairs, as is the case in the House. While their attention to the speakers who drone on at astonishing length may not be rapt, it is at least polite. Rather than doze or converse, a Senator will usually leave the floor. The Senate is a gentlemen's club, and no matter how loathsome one Senator may think his adversary in debate, he will invariably refer to him as "the distinguished Senator from ———."

In addition to ambience, the House and Senate differ markedly in self-identification. House members tend to see themselves as legislative craftsmen, laboring diligently and productively—albeit anonymously—for the public good. After a few years of service, they come to regard the average Senator much less charitably—as a bloated vessel of wind, reeling under the weight of his own self-importance.

Senators, not surprisingly, cherish an image of themselves as the molders of large ideas and shapers of global policy. To them, the Senate is the center of the political universe; they subscribe to the notion of the upper chamber as "the world's greatest deliberative body." Their colleagues on the other side of the Capitol are regarded as plodding technicians, with modest goals and insufficient vision. If Senators see themselves as architects of great cathedrals, they assign to House members the role of bricklayers.

Ultimately, all generalities are technically inaccurate, and so are those just ascribed to the House and the Senate. But there is a germ of truth in all of them.

Senators do have a larger impact on the shaping of public opinion, since they are a smaller, more highly visible body, with virtually no restrictions on subject matter and no limits on debate. Almost every Senator is at least a minor celebrity, recognizable to the public and with an access to the news media that is the envy of his brethren on the other side of the Capitol. Moreover, the Senate has raised the fist-pounding, oath-hurling—and televised—committee investigation to an art form, something the House (with the exception of the Nixon impeachment inquiry and a few other rare instances) has been unable to duplicate.

It is no small wonder that many well-balanced individuals who reach the Senate become puffed-up peacocks, with egos of majestic proportions. In an environment in which the subway to the Capitol will grind to a halt and roar up to fetch them at the press of a button, in which debate is larded with grandiloquent compliments, in which a paid Senate employee dozes by a bank of automatic elevators waiting for the opportunity to inform the unwashed that they are "for Senators only," it is difficult to keep one's self in perspective.

Except in their own districts, the members of the House are not celebrities. During the ten or more months each year that they must spend in the Washington area, they find no glow of recognition on the faces of salesclerks, waiters and many employees of the institution in which they serve. In most ways, they must deal with life's realities in the same fashion as the average citizen, and this fact, plus the necessity of chronic campaigning for a position that becomes vacant every two years, has the virtue of creating a becoming humility on the part of most members who are not committee chairmen or part of the leadership.

There are prudent, younger members of the House who work toward carving out an area of expertise in the committees on which they serve and also tend solicitously to the needs of their constituents. They understand (unlike youthful Senators) that they cannot bull their way into every important national debate because of the strictures of the institution in which they serve. In time, if they are favored by good health and a responsive electorate, they can rise to a position of modest influence in selected areas, and by the time that moment arrives, they ordinarily have the capacity to perform well.

The nature of the two institutions dictates that a Representative will almost invariably be better informed in his area of specialty than a Senator, simply because most Senators are spread far too thin. It is not unusual for a Senator to have to move among ten committees and subcommittees in the course of his legislative work, whereas a Representative may have one or two committees and perhaps an additional three or four subcommittees. In a conference committee, called to resolve differences between the House and Senate versions of legislation, a talented Representative will usually best a talented Senator, in spite of the fact that the Senator is literally trailed by platoons of staff experts, simply because the Representative is usually more familiar with the nuances of the subject matter.

With a term that is brief and a staff that ranges in size between one-half and one-fifth that of his Senate colleagues, a House member must by necessity involve himself in the problems of his constituents and be responsive to their views on issues.

Serious Representatives mull carefully the thought embodied in the words of Edmund Burke to the voters of Bristol, England: "Your representative owes you, not his industry only, but his judgment; and he betrays you instead of serving you if he sacrifices it to your opinion." Burke's words are contrasted with those of former Representative Clem Miller, who wrote: ". . . the first duty of a Congressman is to the area he represents."

Representatives, the members of the "people's house," experience directly the conflicting pulls created by the classic roles of trustee and instructed delegate. Unlike Senators, who are insulated from constituent opinions by physical barriers (large staffs and multiroom offices) and mechanical marvels (such as Autopens, which mindlessly sign their mail), House members are expected to see constituent visitors and read and sign their own mail—and most of the conscientious members do so. Moreover, the Representative is a chronic campaigner, rushing home breathlessly on most weekends to explain his views to the Lions, the Elks, the Republican or Democratic clubs, and countless other groups who want a piece of his weekend—and are offended if he declines. Less is expected of a Senator, who is presumed by his constituents to be busier mulling global issues, and whose leisurely six-year term gives him the luxury of four or five as a statesman, and just one or two seeking votes. Survival dictates that the Representative's ear must be kept to the ground constantly, and many House members tilt toward Clem Miller's evaluation of their duty. Senators, on the other hand, are incorrigibly Burkean the vast majority of the time, and as a practical matter, it is rare that a single issue will spell the end of a senatorial career. But single-issue constituencies are more organized and militant today than ever before. "Hit lists" are being drawn up by organizations that want to eliminate those seen as apostates. Senator Dick Clark of Iowa was on such a list in 1978 and was defeated. Conservative organizations have expanded the list to include George McGovern of South Dakota, John Culver of Iowa, Birch Bayh of Indiana, Frank Church of Idaho, and Gary Hart of Colorado. Single-issue groups are not confined to only one end of the ideological spectrum. Environmentalists, for example, publish their list of personae non gratae whom they label the "Dirty Dozen." The 1980 elections will prove whether these groups are effective in their aim.

JULY 5, 1979

PRESIDENT CARTER'S SPEECH to the nation is cancelled. Reports abound that he had nothing of substance to say to the American people on the subject of energy. A fire storm of criticism erupts and he plunges even further in the polls. It reminded people of his decision to send the Sixth Fleet to Iran as a show of force and then his cancelling the decision before it was even executed.

JULY 9, 1979

CONGRESS RECONVENED. An air of uncertainty hung over humid Washington. President Carter had been on a retreat at Camp David for ten days, trying to gain a perspective on events that were shaking the very foundation of his Administration. Everything was going wrong. His approval rating slipped below that of Richard Nixon at the height of Watergate.

JULY 10, 1979

AT 5:30 A.M. the clock shrieked for me to get up. It would take me more than forty-five minutes to get to the baseball practice field at 7 A.M. Once a year, Republican Congressmen battle the Democrats in an exhibition game sponsored by Sears, Roebuck. The baseball commissioner, Bowie Kuhn, is usually in attendance, along with the national TV networks. Republicans have won 14 out of the last 17 games, but the Democrats are getting younger recruits with each new Congress. The Republican team, on the other hand, seems to be in need of orthopedic assistance to hang together for the full seven innings.

I have pitched for the Republicans for the past seven years. Wildness is the best pitch in my repertoire. I am referred to (at the age of thirty-nine) as the "youngster on the mound from Maine." Willie Stargell, hero of the Pittsburgh Pirates, is only thirty-eight and called the Grand Old Man of baseball. There is something to be said about the theory of relativity. The weight of years and the force of gravity take their toll. Usually, it takes three weeks following the game before I can move my right arm without severe pain.

At a luncheon today, several of those who were invited to Camp David to meet with President Carter described the experience.

"Incredible," one said. "The man is completely depressed. I've never seen anything like it. It was really bizarre. . . ."

"Yes," another interrupted. "He spoke about the malaise that is sweeping the country, that the country was going to hell with all of the divorces and breakups. He said it was typified by *People* magazine, which glorified all the misfits as heroes. . . . Finally, he got around to talking about energy—which was the reason he invited us up there."

JULY 11, 1979

CHICKEN LITTLES WERE everywhere. Skylab was falling. The morning news report said it might hit Maine. I stayed in the office to keep in touch with federal and state agencies in the event disaster struck.

At noon, I stopped by a luncheon held for the National Youth Science Camp. Four students from Maine were in attendance. After posing with the students and ingesting the meal, I returned to the office to meet with the Canadian Ambassador to discuss subjects that were of growing concern to and potential conflict between the people of Maine and Canada.

The meeting lasted only a half hour. The Governmental Affairs Committee was holding a hearing on the 1980 Census. I wanted to voice a complaint with the Director about the failure to designate Franco-Americans as a recognized minority.

While I was attending this hearing, my resolution to reject the HEW report on Home Health Care was passed on the Senate floor by "unanimous consent." It was the first time an Executive Department report had been officially rejected by Congress since the Civil War. And it wasn't even necessary for me to be present. The request for approval of the measure, as reported out of the Finance Committee, was made. No objection was heard. The gavel fell. A small moment in history was recorded with little notice.

I returned to the office to meet with the Future Homemakers of America to tell them what it was like to be a Senator.

Sometimes, it was as chaotic and unpredictable as the tumbling descent of Skylab—which landed in Australia.

JULY 12, 1979

AT NOON, I attended a luncheon sponsored by Richard Lugar, a disarmingly soft-spoken and intelligent Senator from Indiana. The guests at the luncheon included J. Willard Marriott and some executive members of the Chamber of Commerce. When invited to express my thoughts about the prospects for promoting the virtues of the free-enterprise system, I took the opportunity to criticize the Chamber's tendency to send out newsletters containing highly provocative and occasionally erroneous descriptions of legislation that was pending in Congress.

"Whenever you engage in that kind of overstatement, you undercut your credibility, in my judgment. I think you've got to be more balanced in your approach. For example, the American Enterprise Institute discussed the issue in a scholarly and intelligent fashion. . . ."

I was referring to the Chamber's attack on the concept of the sunset legislation pending before the Governmental Affairs Committee. It may be that there are legitimate arguments against applying it to tax credits or deductions that have been written into the tax code over the years. But the Chamber chose to resort to arguments that were calculated to inflame its members rather than inform them. Its position papers made it sound as if the government, if it adopted such a proposal, were decapitating an American tradition: that a tax deduction, once enshrined in law, could never terminate without an express revocation by Congress itself.

"Well," came the response, "sometimes we do have to state our position in tough, provocative ways. We've got to mobilize our members into action against what we feel is wrong, and we can't get too sophisticated about it if we want them to respond and get involved. . . ."

After the lunch, on my way out, one of the executives from the Chamber showed me a note that had been handed to him by another Senator.

"Cohen is not speaking for me or a lot of others. Keep charging."

JULY 13, 1979

I ATTENDED a four-hour meeting of Republican members of the Armed Services Committee. The subject was SALT II. Extensive issue papers and bibliographies of reading material were presented to us to help prepare us for the hearings. Because of the complexity and volume of the material that had to be digested, we were advised to try to narrow our focus to one or two areas of concern and rely upon others to develop expertise on other points.

Following the meeting, I returned to my office to be interviewed by CBS correspondent Bruce Morton. He was doing a "Where Are They Now?" piece for his network. I thought I would be asked to pontificate on the wearisome subject of the "lessons of Watergate." Instead, Morton wanted to know what the experience had done to me as a person.

"Did your experience on the House Judiciary Committee change your life?" he asked.

"Yes," I said, without elaboration.

"How?" came his spartan rejoinder, not giving me any verbal ropes to pull me toward a specific direction.

I went into a long, rambling discussion about what it had meant for me politically, the value of the inordinate exposure to the public. Morton wanted to know what changes had taken place in the private world of my thoughts, what imprint the finger of history had left on my soul. He might have asked how a spectacular sunset or sorrow changes your life. It does, of course, but there is no way to explain it in the glare of klieg lights. And no desire to do so.

JULY 18, 1979

IT TOOK this country 186 years to reach the point of spending $100 billion in a single year by authorization and appropriation of the United States Congress. Fourteen years later, on our bicentennial anniversary, Congress had quadrupled the budget. This year the budget will soar to $506 billion, with a $40.1-billion deficit and an accumulated national debt of $834 billion. There is a widespread feeling that no one is in charge, that we have lost control of our economy and are losing that of our destiny.

Today's debate over whether we should complete construction of the new Hart Senate Office Building seems to reflect the anger and polarization that is so virulent throughout the country.

Democrat Bennett Johnston, a conservative Senator from Louisiana, had been requested to serve as the chairman of the Senate Office Building Commission—a thankless job which might produce a chestful of Purple Hearts for his valor, but was unlikely to win many bouquets from his colleagues or constituents.

His combat duty today was to defend an additional $57.4 million to continue the work on a building that had been labeled the Taj Mahal, the Palace of Versailles, a monument to government extravagance and waste. Johnston had recommended a cutback in many of the frills in the plans—including teakwood paneling, rooftop restaurant, multimedia hearing room—at a saving of more than $3 million. But less than ten hours after his recommendation was made, the Senate Appropriations Committee had restored most of the items cut on the basis that the paneling provided less expensive maintenance and the restaurant was for the use of tourists and constituents, not Senators.

John Chafee, a former Governor of Rhode Island, was leading a blistering attack against the building, pointing out that in 1972 the building was to cost $48 million. Seven years later, the cost estimate had jumped to $142 million.

John Danforth of Missouri leaped into the debate and suggested there was a parallel to what was happening with our economy.

"It seems to me we are conceding to the people of this country, 'Folks, we do not have any control over anything in America, much less even on how to build an office building in our own backyard.' "

Johnston took great offense at Danforth's statement that we ought to leave the steel girders to rust in the sun and dissipate $70 million of the taxpayers' money already spent on construction.

"Listen, I do not take a back seat to you or any of you on a balanced budget. . . . Look, do not call me a big, profligate spender. . . ."

The mood in the chamber turned into a sour malignity. The presiding officer called attention to the Senate Rules requiring Senators to speak to the Chair and to refer to the other Senators in the third person.

Majority Leader Robert Byrd, who was listening to the debate on his "squawk box," rushed onto the floor and came to Johnston's defense. He reminded everyone that the Senate Rules existed "in order that acerbities might be avoided and the debate might not get too personal."

Tempers cooled somewhat, but the debate remained vigorous. Chafee and Danforth noted the explosive growth of congressional staffs and office space in the past decade. We add staff so that we can undertake more work, then purchase or build more office space to house the staff, and then add more staff again in an unending spiral. . . .

Lowell Weicker finally rose to support Johnston, and scored Chafee and Danforth in the process: "The easiest thing in the world is to demagogue against politics or politicians. Whenever an editorial writer wants readership, he takes a shot at politicians. That is sure to get favorable letters to the editor.

"Whenever a radio or television commentator wants listeners/viewers, he blasts Washington.

"Whenever a politician wants to get a bit of favorable publicity, he does the same thing: he harangues against politicians.

"I suggest to my colleagues today that I think it time a few of us expressed pride in our profession and thus in representative democracy. There is no such thing as Washington. There is no such thing as Hartford. There is representative democracy, there are representatives of people. . . .

"Now let us talk about facilities. Every day, I hear about all the 'perks' we have, how we are ripping off the taxpayers. I just came back from getting my hair cut—not free, what hair there is, not free. Thirteen dollars. Not free. I pay what everybody else pays for some of the lousiest food in the world—served right here in the Capitol. Indeed, more than is warranted.

"And no, I do not use taxpayer-funded facilities for exercise. I belong to my own club, I play my own tennis, I pay my own way.

"But just to get a little headline, a little more publicity, sell a few more papers, have a few more people watching the tube, it is easy to refer to this great palace, this great monument.

"But that is not reality. Pretty soon we are going to chew ourselves up around here. All the institutions of this country, be it government, be it the media, be it business—we are just going to chew each other up, devour ourselves.

"Do you want to take your constituents through the present annex office facilities? Has any one of you on this floor taken your constituents through there? Has the Senator from Missouri taken them through, or the Senator from Rhode Island? No, you take them through the Capitol, through the rotunda. You take them into the Senate chamber. These belong to the people of the United States and are matters of pride. But not the annex.

"Since when have they wanted the cheapest? There is more here than just the mortar, the stone, the flesh, and the blood. There is, or should be, the element of excellence.

"Do you want to talk about buildings? Do you want to know what money is spent on? Without the bat of an eye, right after we heard all the squawking in the Appropriations Committee yesterday, along comes a $20-million federal building for Knoxville, Tennessee, for an energy exposition. Nobody said boo. One hundred million dollars for the winter Olympic facilities in Lake Placid, New York; nobody objects.

"The John F. Kennedy Center in Boston—does anybody want to ask the cost of that?

"All of these are buildings for voters and are okay. But not Washington, the seat of government. There is a safe target to bad-mouth.

"Well, I will not remain silent during exercises in self-destruction."

The vote on Johnston's amendment ended in a tie, 47–47, and therefore failed. After a series of parliamentary maneuvers, however, the approval to appropriate the money to continue with the building was given by a margin of 3 votes.

Those who opposed construction of the building would have to wait another year to see what inflation, miscalculations, and construction delays would do to the new ceiling of $142 million.

JULY 19, 1979

GEORGE MCGOVERN APPROACHED me on the floor.

"Bill, I think I made a mistake in that vote on Dickey-Lincoln. I've been doing more research on it, and I'll take a much closer look if it comes up again."

On July 17, I offered an amendment to the Public Works Appropriations Bill to delete any further funding for the Dickey-Lincoln Hydroelectric Dam in Maine. Muskie waged a vigorous defense of the project. The timing of the vote could not have been worse from my perspective, as President Carter had just called upon Congress and the country to dedicate ourselves to exploring and developing alternative sources of energy. My amendment was defeated 52 to 46.

McGovern's statement was one of the more redeeming moments that I had experienced in the Senate—not because it brought me possibly one vote closer to a victory on a particular issue, but because it came completely without solicitation. It reaffirmed an essential decency and conscientiousness on the part of members that transcends partisanship and pettiness on issues of importance. George McGovern's character and candor were put on quiet display for me today.

JULY 20, 1979

LAST MONDAY, President Carter finally came down from Camp David and made a nationally televised speech about the energy crisis that confronted and challenged us. He promised strong and decisive leadership. For a full four days, Congress seemed prepared to support and rally behind the President. Today, that support evaporated. Carter had asked for the resignation of energy czar James Schlesinger. This was expected. But he also fired HEW Secretary Joseph Califano and Treasury Secretary Michael Blumenthal. Transportation Secretary Brock Adams tried to impose the conditions under which he would continue to serve in the Carter Administration, so he departed also. Finally, Griffin Bell, the Attorney General, who had long indicated he wanted to return to private life, was unfairly lumped into the pile of those Carter believed were incompetent or ineffective. The result was devastating. The President was seen as having adopted an indiscriminate purge mentality instead of a prudent approach to restructuring his Cabinet. Having done so little to shape and control policy within his Administration, he now was seen as having done too much.

The comments in the cloakroom in the Senate were caustic. "He's suffering from mental fatigue. They've cut down the trees and left all the monkeys."

The statement was somewhat unfair and spiced with obvious partisanship. But it was clear that Carter wanted to appear decisive and succeeded only in inviting derision. He had squandered what little goodwill existed for him on Capitol Hill.

JULY 23, 1979

THE HEARINGS on the SALT II agreement began today before the Armed Services Committee. Secretary of Defense Harold Brown was the leadoff witness. He had already testified before the Foreign Relations Committee and was not expected to deviate from his prior testimony or strong position in favor of the treaty. The question was, could the members of the Committee, who generally are considered to be more hawkish and military-minded than their Foreign Relations Committee colleagues, shoot any holes in his testimony? Did we have friends in the Pentagon or the intelligence community who had leaked sensitive and damaging information that would dissolve, or at least create doubts about, the validity of Brown's testimony?

The hearing was being held in the Caucus Room of the Russell Senate Office Building—the scene of so many historic Senate investigations. It is a massive, high-ceilinged room that is nearly as large as the Senate chamber. Whenever it is used as a hearing room, there seems to be a pervasive sense of excitement and history hanging in the atmosphere. Today was no exception. The network television crews had rolled in their unblinking "cyclopses" and heavy-cabled equipment early in the morning. Four long tables, running perpendicular to the green-baize-covered dais, were filled with newspaper reporters and journalists. A legion of support personnel from the Pentagon were present to add documentary and moral support to the Secretary. The remainder of the room was filled by Senate staff employees and members of the general public who were in support of or opposed to SALT.

The presence and pressure of so many eyes and minds on the proceedings are a positive and healthy contribution to the legislative process. The members come well prepared. They know that words and conduct will be seriously scrutinized by commentators and constituents. There is, of course, the opportunity to play the demagogue or do some histrionic strutting, but what might play well for the "hometown folks" runs the risk of being censured by the broad spectrum of the American people who witness the proceedings in their homes. A Senator is supposed to do more than merely reflect the interests or parochialism of his state. He is one of a hundred, reflecting the interests of the entire country. This duty is reinforced by the decorum of the Caucus Room, the glare of the television lights and the poised pens of reporters.

Harold Brown is one of the most brilliant men ever to hold the position of Secretary of Defense. He is a physicist and former president of the California Institute of Technology. He is also a seasoned congressional witness who knows that the flight of time is a witness' greatest friend. To bring order out of what otherwise would be chaos, the Senate committees operate under the "ten-minute rule." Each member has exactly ten minutes to question or parry with a witness. Then the chairman will call upon another member, alternating between Republican and Democratic members. After each member has had an opportunity to question, the process starts over again, top to bottom. A skilled witness knows that he can string out his answers to two or three questions per Senator and exhaust the ten minutes easily. Harold Brown is a master at it. He speaks slowly, in long, convoluted sentences that are often laced with technical terms or words of art.

For example, Brown might state that our current doctrine of deterrence includes the targeting of our intercontinental missiles at Soviet industrial-urban centers. This might prompt a Senator to inquire whether that phrase means the civilian population centers of the Soviet Union. Brown will respond, "No." The confused Senator will then ask for an explanation, which Brown will attempt to provide. The clock has ticked off five minutes of time. I do not suggest that Brown always engages in a "filibuster," but he has perfected the art of dealing with a hostile or unsympathetic interrogator. In addition, Brown has a way of seeming to grope for just the right phrase or word, a struggle for coherent precision which conveys an effort to be honest rather than an attempt to obfuscate.

One other factor runs in favor of a witness: the pressure of the Senate schedule itself and a usual lack of continuity in the line of interrogation. Most Senators are unwilling to be interrupted by or yield to a colleague who might wish to follow up on a line of questioning they have pursued or tripped over. Obviously, a matter of ego is involved. But beyond ego is the reality that once the ten minutes of time has expired, a Senator may have to wait as long as two or three hours before he can question the witness again. In the meantime, he will usually have to leave the hearing room to attend other hearings or meetings. He will not be able to gain a sense of the conflicts or ambiguities that develop during the course of the day. He therefore wants to extract answers to those questions which are most pressing in his mind. Because a Senator usually wants to ask more than one or two questions, an experienced witness knows that a scatter-gun approach will be adopted that lends itself to superficiality instead of penetration.

Sitting next to last on the seniority scale on the Armed Services Committee, I had to wait four hours before my turn came to question Harold Brown. I was determined to avoid the trap of asking open-ended questions. I took nearly five minutes drawing a tortured analogy with two heavyweight contestants who are considered equal because they can be said to have the same number of weapons but are distinctly unequal in their size, skills and destructive power. I suggested Brown was using "fig-leaf phrases to cover naked ambiguities" and questioned his candor when he refused to submit to the Committee the working documents the Joint Chiefs of Staff had kept during the SALT negotiations.

It was not an effective presentation on my part. The whole procedure became a source of frustration for me rather than an opportunity for acquiring information. The dance of the legislative process was too slow, too rigid and structured. It was little more than a race against the clock. I treated Brown as an adversary rather than a vehicle for information. There was little profit in my approach.

JULY 25, 1979

THE JOINT CHIEFS OF STAFF WERE testifying for the second day. I inadvertently managed to set off some fireworks when I asked the witnesses to be as brief as possible in their responses to my questions. I suggested that "Time tends to fly much quicker on this side of the table than yours." Chairman Stennis, who had been distracted from the proceedings and was talking to the chief counsel to the Committee, suddenly whirled in his chair and said, "What did you say, please?"

"I hoped he could make his answers as brief as possible so that we can ask more questions."

The Chairman replied, "You made some reference to this side of the table. I hope you did not mean to say that you have been cut short?"

"Not at all. With lengthy answers, the ten minutes tends to expire rather quickly."

Stennis does try to run his Committee with as little partisanship as possible. He thought I was being critical of his integrity. Electricity suddenly crackled in the hearing room. It was as if a fuse to an explosive had just been touched by fire. But as soon as he realized that my comments were directed to the witness and the need for brevity, he smiled and said, "Well, the Senator from Maine makes a good point. . . ."

I had seen fragments of classified information which revealed that the Joint Chiefs of Staff were far less sanguine about this treaty than they declared publicly. During my ten minutes of questioning, I tried to secure an admission for the record on certain key issues that I knew had been discussed in private memoranda. At the same time, I did not want to disclose that I had seen any of the classified documents. I was in a stronger position to secure the truth if they only suspected that I had more information than I actually had. Finally, in the second round of questioning, I decided to use an exact expression employed in one of the documents. The Chairman of the Joint Chiefs lost his composure. Anger could be seen rising in his throat like mercury in a thermometer. I was told later that a member of the White House staff was overheard saying, "We'll get Cohen for this."

JULY 30, 1979

SECRETARY OF STATE CYRUS VANCE, Ambassador Ralph Earle (chief U.S. negotiator for the SALT II treaty), and General George Seignious testified before the Armed Services Committee today.

Vance projects an essential decency and integrity. He is direct and straightforward in his testimony. But he is not as adept as Defense Secretary Harold Brown in dealing with tough questions. His face tends to flush under pressure.

Scoop Jackson applied pressure quickly. He unveiled a scale model of the Soviet ICBM force currently under development. The size differential between our one projected new missile and that of the Soviets is visually dramatic. The missiles stood like large, grotesque phallic symbols—black missiles for the Soviets, white ones for the United States.

Jackson is a master at reducing complex theories to a raw kind of calculation that the average person can comprehend. Launch weight, throw weight, circular error probability are the esoterica of SALT negotiators and votaries. A visual display of the comparative size and numbers of the most destructive military weapons ever devised by the human mind conveys a very blunt message. It is a punch to the solar plexus calculated to shake your comfort and complacency.

After Jackson finished his tough questioning of Vance, he started to walk out of the Committee room, smiling with obvious self-satisfaction.

Jackson was elected to Congress in 1940—the same year that I was born. During his long career of public service, he had developed a reputation as a "Cold Warrior," a reflexive hard-liner who seeks a confrontation with the Soviet Union instead of areas of cooperation or accommodation. He is perhaps best known as the major architect of the Jackson-Vanik Amendment, which prohibits the United States from granting "most favored nation" trading status to the Soviet Union as long as it maintains a repressive emigration policy toward Russian Jews. His voting record, however, is not nearly as hard as his rhetoric or reputation.

What strikes me as unique about Jackson is that he has retained his essential vigor and enthusiasm for the political process. Each day he steps into the arena relatively unscarred and still optimistic that we are masters of our destiny, that perhaps during a hearing in the course of the day he can land a few ideological or evidentiary blows that will make a difference.

What is even more impressive than his enthusiasm for political life is his complete lack of vindictiveness. Most people I know who swing as hard as Jackson carry a lingering sense of anger or bitterness which wells up and spills out in the quiet, unguarded moments of congressional camaraderie. I have never heard Jackson, in private, attack anyone personally or speak maliciously about an adversary. He is a man of passion and, uniquely, one without poison.

He leaned over toward me and said, "Come on, now. Keep up the pressure on these guys. Bill, follow up on the verification questions. I'm the only guy who's being tough on them. . . ."

He smiled as he exhorted me and the others. He relished the battle and the sparks he was generating. No article appeared on the SALT hearings without a reference to the hard-line questions of Scoop Jackson.

"Okay, Scoop, we'll give 'em hell," I said.

"Bill, I'm not trying to tell you how to handle yourself, but these guys are getting away with murder. . . ."

Jackson was both right and wrong. The Administration witnesses, when pressed, could not justify the weakness in the agreement and were usually left resorting to the ultimate escape hatch: "Senator, I'm sorry. I cannot go into that subject further in open session. I'll be glad to meet with you and the Committee in Executive Session, but this is a very sensitive area and highly inappropriate to discuss publicly. . . ."

Not all Senators, however, are equal in their talents. I prefer to parry with a witness. Scoop is at his best when he is trying to bury one.

JULY 31, 1979

THE DAY WAS consumed with more testimony on the SALT treaty. At the end of the day as I was leaving the Senate Caucus Room, mind-weary with megatonnage and MIRVs, I was approached by a man who had been sitting in the audience. He introduced himself, but neither his name nor his face was familiar to me.

"When are we going to have a chance to get together and talk?" he asked.

"Well, not tonight," I responded in a puzzled and annoyed tone. "It's already after six, and I've been sitting here since nine this morning. I've got a dinner engagement that I'm committed to tonight. . . ."

"What about tomorrow?" he persisted.

"No, I'm sorry, but I'm going to be tied up with hearings all week. It's really a bad time."

With that declaration, I shook his hand, turned away and walked back to my office.

The next day, I received an angry handwritten letter from the man I had snubbed. He and his wife had contributed $1,000 to my campaign on the word of one of his friends that I would be a good Senator, and he felt that he was entitled to more than a cold handshake from me.

My initial reaction was one of sheer impetuosity. I called Tom Daffron and said, "Tom, check with the campaign treasurer and find out how much money we have left from the campaign. I'm going to return a contribution."

Tom just laughed at me. "Come on, Bill. The campaign doesn't have any money. As a matter of fact, we still owe about $10,000. Look, I think the letter you received was a little strong, but he did have a point. . . ."

Tom was absolutely right. I could huff and puff all I wanted, but the fact was that I didn't have any money to return, and I wasn't justified in running a banner of moral outrage up the flagpole in any event. The man wasn't after my honor, just some of my time. Several days later, I called him and invited him to meet with me the next time he came to Washington.

AUGUST 1, 1979

LATE IN THE AFTERNOON, a memorandum was handed to me by my staff. It was more bad news. Ten days ago, on a Saturday, I returned to Maine to attend the annual Aroostook County Potato Blossom Festival—an event that I had attended each year since 1972. Senate Majority Leader Robert Byrd had threatened to hold a Saturday session, but since he had cancelled one scheduled the week before, I concluded that he was bluffing once again, and I was not going to cancel my plans to return to Maine just because he enjoyed playing a cat-and-mouse game with the members.

I guessed wrong. Not only did Byrd carry through with his threat, but he scheduled for debate a bill in which I had an active interest. The shoe companies throughout New England were being devastated by foreign imports. The producers of hides were shipping them out of the country, thereby creating leather shortages for our domestic industry. I had cosponsored a bill to curb the export of hides and had pledged to take an active role in trying to secure its adoption.

Howard Baker was not in Washington on Friday when I left for Maine, but I had made it clear to the Republican leadership that I wanted the vote on the issue postponed until Monday if at all possible. Apparently Ed Muskie, who offered the amendment on Saturday, was unwilling to postpone the vote because he thought the number of absentees on Saturday would result in an advantage to the shoe manufacturers. He lost on the vote, 48 to 36. My absence was noticed by someone in New Hampshire, who was now threatening to write to every shoe worker in Maine stating that I had deliberately avoided the vote as a payoff to the Cattlemen's Political Action Committee, which had contributed $100 to my campaign. It was a preposterous "conspiracy theory," particularly in view of the fact that the shoe manufacturers had contributed heavily to me. But a shoe worker who was out of a job wouldn't be able to distinguish fact from fiction. It is one of the axioms of politics that "A lie will run halfway around the world before truth can get its pants on."

AUGUST 5, 1979

AT MIDNIGHT, Diane and I joined eighteen private citizens from Maine at Logan Airport in Boston. We were scheduled to depart on a ten-day "mission" to Israel that had been organized by Joel and Linda Abromson. Congress was in recess for the entire month of August, and so we had decided to take advantage of the opportunity to visit a country that has been one of the major focal points of our foreign policy for more than three decades.

We had rarely enjoyed ten full days alone together during our entire marriage. The prospect of spending fifteen hours a day for ten days with a group of our constituents was somewhat intimidating. Our apprehension evaporated during the long flight to Zurich. After the initial formality, we were able to take off our official titles and simply relax.

About twelve hours later, we arrived in Tel Aviv. For the first time since I had been a member of Congress, I was traveling in a foreign country without protocol or protection. Diane and I stepped outside ahead of the group. The air was warm, but less humid than that of Washington. It was dark. A large crowd waited outside the David Ben-Gurion terminal building for arriving passengers. For a fleeting moment, I felt fear rush through my pores. We were in a country that lived under the hair trigger of violence, of bombs in airports or trash cans. It was a time of terrorism, and we were standing alone in a forest of dark-skinned faces wondering if violence would come from one of them. I realized for the first time that the sense of security we take for granted on official congressional trips to foreign countries was missing.

Diane and I were joined almost immediately by the rest of the group and ushered to a waiting bus. But the memory of that moment when anxiety walked across my mind remains vivid.

AUGUST 7, 1979

MORNING IN TEL AVIV. From the terrace of our hotel room, we could look out into the Mediterranean Sea. The sun was lifting its red eye over the horizon. On the beach below, early joggers were already engaged in their physical ritual. A few people waded to their knees in the green-blue sea. Some just sat in the sand and watched the waves lick the shore.

Following an early (and typically heavy) breakfast, we boarded our bus and headed down the Jaffa Road toward the Gaza Strip. Tel Aviv is a busy city, a new city with no visibly unique sense of history.

A short time later we arrived in Gaza and met with the Governor—an Israeli general who was responsible for maintaining military rule in the community. We toured the refugee camps that have become so controversial in the eyes of the international community. They were not as bleak or barren as I had expected, but they were not up to standards that the Western world would consider acceptable for its own people. What seemed to break the curse that is stamped on the foreheads of the victims of war was the hundreds of children we saw. As our bus went wheeling through the narrow streets of the camps, young Palestinian children ran out to wave at us. Their eyes looked like liquid pools of chocolate syrup, their smiles as white as the petals of lilies opening to the morning sun.

After lunch with some of the crack Israeli pilots at Eitan Air Force Base (which Israel had agreed to give up), we wound our way back to Tel Aviv.

It was an incredible experience to see gardens rising up in the desert. The Israelis had undertaken a massive irrigation project in parts of the Sinai. The endless sea of sand anointed with water had turned green and bore fruit.

For the next four days we careened up the west coast of Israel, over to the Golan Heights, down the West Bank to the depths of the Dead Sea, where we floated in the salt-heavy water that felt like a green oil slick. We went to Masada, King Herod's retreat on a mountaintop where a thousand Jews later committed mass suicide rather than surrender to a Roman legion that had held them surrounded and under siege for more than three years.

It was all quite extraordinarily beautiful, but it was not until we came to Jerusalem that we first truly felt the depth of passions that have moved people over the centuries. The sight of the Old City, the walls that have endured so many assaults, the rocks and relics of the past scattered on the hills like dinosaurs' teeth that have gone yellow in the sun were simply breathtaking. Here the three great religions of the world converged and stood star-crossed, powerful, poignant and destructive. In Jerusalem, biblical stories and names climbed like ivy on the heart. At night, you could stand by the walls of Solomon and in the silence, hear voices from another age. Crucifixion, Crusades and Holocaust took on a deeper significance than we had ever known. At Yad Vashem, the memorial to the Holocaust,

we saw evidence of a brutality that surpassed the limits of human imagination. But for me, it was not the horror of the ovens being stoked with
living corpses that clutched my throat, not the masses of skin-covered
skeletons being bulldozed into uncovered graves like so much refuse. It
was the sight of a young boy wearing a cap and a short coat that covered
just the top of his knees. He reminded me of John-John Kennedy watching the caisson carrying his father's body past him on Pennsylvania Avenue. But this boy was standing with his hands raised above his head while
a Nazi soldier held a rifle behind his back. In that young boy's eyes I
could see not terror, but all the brown sadness that man has ever known.
That photograph remains an indelible tattoo in my mind.

AUGUST 16, 1979

PRESIDENT CARTER HAD BEEN busy lobbying on SALT during my trip to
Israel. Approximately one hundred leading citizens from Maine had been
invited to the White House to be briefed by President Carter, National
Security Adviser Zbigniew Brzezinski, and Secretary of Defense Harold
Brown. The owners of a large newspaper in Maine were among those
invited to the White House, and they came away fully persuaded that the
SALT II treaty—to which I was opposed—should be ratified. Two hours
at the White House and all doubts had been removed. Such is the power
of the office.

AUGUST 17, 1979

I CAUGHT a 7:10 A.M. flight to Maine. I was suffering from jet lag and had
a severe case of intestinal flu. I had lost seven pounds in two days and
my head felt as if someone had slammed it in a car door. But my schedule
had been set, and I had no choice but to contain my curses behind
clenched teeth.

   During my speech to a local chamber of commerce, my mouth went
completely dry. The medication I was taking to soothe withered bowels
turned my vocal cords into strings of dry rawhide.

   I struggled through a series of speeches and press conferences for
the next week, commenting about the furor caused by Andrew Young's
resignation as Ambassador to the United Nations. He had violated a long-
standing U.S. policy of refusing to negotiate with representatives of the

Palestine Liberation Organization, and then misled Secretary of State
Vance on the nature of his activities.

Jesse Jackson and other black leaders declared that they wanted a
meeting with the PLO and Jewish leaders. Young tried to calm the storm
that had erupted, but the news media were acting like bloodhounds that
have taken the scent. They were baying in bold headlines about wiretaps
and skullduggery. The Andy Young who had been the object of so much
scorn and satire for two and a half years was suddenly being canonized.
Young was now described as a courageous leader who could not count
the slow cadence of diplomacy. His impatience had driven him to take a
chance, but his goal was noble and selfless.

AUGUST 29, 1979

I FLEW to Boston and after a three-hour layover, finally boarded a small
aircraft for Presque Isle. My plane was an hour and a half late in arriving
at the Presque Isle airport. A local television news team was waiting. I
anticipated the questions. "What about Loring Air Force Base? Have
you changed your mind about Dickey-Lincoln? What are your objections
to the SALT II treaty? Will there be heating fuel for Maine and New
England this winter? . . ."

It is an hour's drive to Fort Kent. Seven years ago, I walked over
650 miles from the New Hampshire border to Fort Kent. Seven and a half
weeks on angry, blistered, swollen feet. Each summer I go back to the
St. John Valley—a traditional stronghold of the Democratic Party—to
reinforce my friendships and the fact that I remain accessible to them.

The St. John Valley includes Fort Kent, Frenchville, St. Agatha,
Lille, Madawaska, and Van Buren—communities that run the length of
the lower part of the spectacular St. John River in northern Maine. The
people are mostly of Franco-American heritage. They are proud, independent, open, gregarious, and lovers of the land. They endure—no, embrace—the long winters. Snow is a friend rather than an enemy in their
lives. It comes as early as October and does not loosen its bond in response to the spring rains until April or even May. Then the floods begin.
A newly constructed dike protects the downtown merchants in Fort Kent
this year. Private homes along the riverbank receive the floodwaters like
an unwanted baptism. The people do not move. They rebuild or repair.
Perhaps next year, the river will not run as wild.

The leaves are already turning from green to burnished gold. In less than three weeks, the potato fields will be filled with mechanical harvesters turning the rocky soil, shaking potatoes loose from their dark beds of earth. Families will take to the fields in force and fill the wooden potato barrels. It has been a dry summer. But two weeks of rain may cause the potatoes to spurt in growth and split—or rot. . . .

The sun was shimmering on the St. John. It moved in sheets of light like a school of silver fish just below the surface. There was a brief chill in the air which yielded to the last hot breath of August as the sun climbed in the sky. The hunched shoulders of the sloping hills looked like those of a weight lifter who had grown strong holding up the heavens. There was no talk of SALT II out there on the highway, only the sight of men chopping and stacking wood for the winter. The people cannot afford oil at $1 per gallon. The temperature will drop at times to −20 degrees or even −40 degrees. History repeats itself, or at least swings on the arc of the pendulum. A century ago wood was the primary source of heat. It yielded to coal, and coal, in turn, to oil. Now the chock of the axe blade is back. A cord of firewood (be sure to check the size of the load if it is not split—allow 15 percent for shrinkage) is selling for $35. Nearly double that in central and southern Maine. It can be expected to go up as demand increases. The people are still friendly. They have an indomitable will to survive the rigors of the long, cold winters—and they do it with a joy unmatched anywhere else.

Complaints from merchants are common. Americans buying gas in Canada. Customs regulations that favor Canada, and so on. They are apprehensive, but undaunted.

I walked only two or three miles before the rain started. I returned to the home of friends to rest before going to the annual Lions Club chicken dinner. The rain did not deter the people from turning out. A birthday cake had been baked. This was my eighth consecutive walk through the St. John Valley—a place of "unspeakable beauty." I always celebrate my birthday here—even though I arrived a day late this year.

AUGUST 30, 1979

WE HAD fresh trout for breakfast. The meal prepared by Carl and Lena Savage was so sumptuous that my walking schedule fell off its designated start by nearly an hour.

I stopped at the Kent Factory, a pajama manufacturer. Three ladies from the Town Office brought coffee and doughnuts on their break.

By 1:30, I had walked only twelve miles along the highway before a blast of cold air started to blow at my back. My shirt began to flap and flutter. Over my shoulder the sky was turning dark. A deep rumble rolled across the St. John from Canada. In minutes, a violent thunderstorm erupted. My walking tour was over for the day.

I secured shelter in a staff follow-up car and drove the eight miles to Madawaska to meet with the students at the high school to answer their questions on SALT, energy, Dickey-Lincoln and legalizing marijuana.

SEPTEMBER 1, 1979

THE NEWS HEADLINES CARRIED the story that Soviet combat troops were in Cuba. I had received advance notice from my office and had considered firing off a letter to the State Department protesting this latest piece of evidence of Soviet adventurism. I decided instead to wait until I returned to Washington to get more details before answering any questions from the press.

SEPTEMBER 3, 1979

TODAY WAS LABOR DAY, and I took Diane and the boys to see the latest James Bond movie, *Moonraker*. We were crammed into a 1966 Volkswagen Beetle that I had just purchased to replace my beloved Porsche—which was down and out with a broken rear torsion bar.

Just as I was taking smug satisfaction in the VW's trouble-free simplicity, the passenger compartment began to fill with smoke. An electrical fire had crackled along the wires from one of the headlights, forcing us to abandon the car for the night.

SEPTEMBER 5, 1979

A STACK of newspapers nearly two and a half feet high was sitting like a giant paperweight on my desk. I spent the morning culling the papers for items of interest that I might have missed during the August recess.

Usually when Congress returns from a long recess period there is an air of excitement and an urge to move ahead, to produce. This time, however, languor seemed to be the only thing in the air. The recess period had provided members with an opportunity to listen to the views and needs and complaints of constituents. As usual, there was a consensus in the abstract—"do something about energy" or "we're in a mess"—but what to do specifically depended upon the geographic region and the economic straits of the constituency: upper-middle income—deregulation; middle and lower income—freeze prices and stop letting big oil rip us off. In some areas, members even found their constituents hostile to helping the Vietnamese boat people.

Ten years ago, we would have been the first to extend the hand of help and humanitarianism. Inflation and a deepening recession have overshadowed our charity.

Two other events contributed to the darkness of the mood: the presence of Soviet troops in Cuba and the movement of Hurricane David, heading into the Washington area.

SEPTEMBER 6, 1979

SECRETARY OF STATE CYRUS VANCE'S statement demanding "clarification" from the Soviet Union as to why it had troops in Cuba was regarded as too vapid and weak a response by most of those on Capitol Hill. It was seen as the first step in an ultimate backtrack that would culminate in an assurance to the American people that the troops constituted no threat.

On the subway car, heading for a vote on the Senate floor, one of my freshman colleagues said, "This is the first chicken-shit vote that I've cast all year."

Another seasoned veteran said, "Yup, this is a chicken-shit vote, but I'm running against a demagogue in this election and I don't want him to charge me with Washington fever."

The vote pending on the Senate floor was to eliminate the complimentary tickets that the Kennedy Center could distribute. The amount of money involved was not the major point being argued by the proponents of this budgetary drive, but its symbolism—we could not continue to ask the American taxpayer to subsidize extravagance at any level, not even the cultural. But opponents of the amendment saw it as a petty and partisan attempt to embarrass the Carter Administration—the principal beneficiary of the tickets. The amendment was defeated 66 to 23. More than two hours was devoted to this debate—more time than matters that we pass with little discussion and ten times the appropriation. It was hardly a matter of high priority on the legislative agenda, but priority (and symbolic significance) is allowed to reside in the eye of each Senator.

Earlier in the day, Bob Dole had indicated that he was giving consideration to offering a resolution, as an amendment to a bill scheduled for debate, that would postpone any SALT II treaty consideration until the Soviet combat troops were out of Cuba or unless the President certified to Congress that their presence did not constitute a threat to the United States.

Majority Leader Byrd took great affront that any Senator would have the temerity to challenge his authority to call up any legislation, including the SALT II treaty, for debate. Byrd is one of the Senate's most skillful debaters. He took more than a half hour to make a point that I thought could have been made in five minutes. It reminded me of what Macaulay once wrote about an Oxford historian given to prolixity: "He employs more words in expounding a truism than any other writer would employ in supporting a paradox."

I spent the evening on my hands and knees cleaning up the mud in the basement level of our house—the last remainder of Hurricane David.

SEPTEMBER 7, 1979

FRESHMAN SENATOR LARRY PRESSLER, reacting to a story that Paul Tsongas of Massachusetts was the poorest member of the United States Senate, put out a press release that his net worth was actually several thousand dollars less than that of Tsongas. Apparently, poverty (at the higher levels of income in America) had become a badge of political honor.

The floor debate for the day focused principally on an amendment offered by Dale Bumpers of Arkansas to the Federal Courts Improvement Act of 1979. Bumpers wanted to abolish any presumption before a court of law that a federal regulation was consistent with congressional objectives and intent. The abolition, he argued, would put the federal government and private citizens and consumers on an equal footing. The argument has the surface appeal of equity and fairness, but if the amendment were adopted, it would reverse thirty years of administrative law and judicial precedent. The Bumpers proposal was pending before the Governmental Affairs Committee, and ordinarily the full Senate would have deferred action on the amendment until the measure had been fully debated in Committee. But the antiregulatory mood in the Senate was running like a swollen river against bureaucracy by any name. Logic and custom were swept away with little argument and no regret. The motion to table the Bumpers amendment was rejected by a 2 to 1 margin. I voted to table the amendment out of deference to the Governmental Affairs Committee, on which I served, and also because of a fear that Congress was shucking its own responsibility for checking excessive and unwarranted federal regulations and diverting it to the judiciary.

SEPTEMBER 9, 1979

AT 8:30 A.M. I flew to Boston and then boarded a private single-engine plane for Auburn, Maine.

The air was clear and cool. Fall had arrived. The purpose of my trip to Maine was to run in a five-mile race in Auburn to help promote a new small business—a private development that hopes to ignite the downtown urban-renewal program.

I was not enthusiastic about the race. I had run five miles only once in my life—about a year before. Most people assumed I was a runner because I campaigned in 1972 with a vigorous walk across the state and wore the crown of athlete on my head. The crown weighed too heavy today. At the three-and-a-half-mile mark, the fist pounding in my chest shifted to my right side. My shoulders ached. Thighs felt heavy. I just looked at the pavement going up the hills and tried not to think of the distance I still had to go. When I finally saw the finish line, I sprinted. I finished 73rd, with a time of thirty-nine minutes.

I ate some yogurt, received an honorary award, showered, changed and then went to the neighboring city of Lewiston, where four hundred runners covered a course of 6.2 miles. I handed out some certificates and returned to Portland to catch a flight to Washington.

The pain in my muscles was so severe that I could not sleep. Around 2 A.M., I finally got up from bed and went down to our den. I decided to use the time constructively and wrote an article on the subject of SALT and the presence of Soviet troops in Cuba that was published several days later in the *Washington Star*.

SEPTEMBER 10, 1979

THE TELLICO DAM WAS back on the agenda for a vote today. The hydro-electric project was controversial because, even though it was 90 percent complete in its construction, it had been judged to be in violation of the Endangered Species Act. The tiny snail darter had been elevated nearly to the status of being the national fish of America.

Howard Baker, a strong supporter of the dam, which is located in the state of Tennessee, was locked into battle with John Culver, one of the original architects of the Endangered Species Act.

The last time we voted on Tellico in May, I walked up to Culver just as the vote started and said, "John, how can you be against the construction of Tellico when it's ninety percent complete, and yet you're in favor of constructing Dickey-Lincoln in Maine and not a spadeful of dirt has been turned?"

Culver turned to me, cracked a wide smile and said, "Bill, that's what makes politics so interesting."

I had always voted against construction of Tellico in the past, principally because it was in violation of the Endangered Species Act and partly because it was considered to be economically cost-inefficient. That day, in a moment of pique over what I considered to be the hypocrisy of the Administration, I voted with Baker. He had helped me in opposing the Dickey-Lincoln dam project in Maine. Besides, I reasoned, if Culver was not concerned with consistency, why should I vote in support of his position?

Today, I returned to my position of opposition to the dam and voted against the Tellico project.

As the Senators responded to the bells that rang in their offices announcing that a vote was in progress, I noticed that Ted Kennedy looked slimmer than he had in the past. The press had been speculating that he was running for President on the basis of the fact that he had cut ice cream from his daily menu. He wanted to be lean and trim for the coming campaign against President Carter.

There is an aura that hangs over Kennedy. His large head appears even bigger because of his thick, shag-cut hair. The curls lie in layers that bring to mind a marble statue of a Greek hero that one sees in a museum. His face has a reddish hue and a healthy look to it. He is wide-shouldered and wears a back brace that helps to slim him somewhat. He wears dark suits and keeps his jacket buttoned, which gives him an Incredible Hulk appearance. And then there is the perpetual smile on his face when he is talking to his colleagues—a boyish enthusiasm and vigor that blows away any dark clouds of ominous preoccupation which might hang over his colleagues. Or so it seems.

Al Simpson approached: "I got on the subway and there were five television cameras following me. . . ."

"Yes," I interrupted, "and you turned around and saw Ted Kennedy sitting next to you."

"Bill, it's the damnedest thing the way he attracts the media."

"Al, just be sure to sit next to him at all times and you'll never be in the shadows."

CHAPTER 14

SEPTEMBER 11, 1979

THINGS HAPPEN QUICKLY in politics. There can be a long drought of action on the Potomac and suddenly a flash flood erupts and sweeps down everything in its swirling rage. The revelation of Soviet combat troops in Cuba swelled into a torrent of anger almost overnight and threatened to shake the SALT pact from its diplomatic foundations.

Frank Church, the Chairman of the Foreign Relations Committee, a strong supporter of SALT, was in serious political trouble in Idaho. In August, at a press conference, he had planted his feet firmly in the cement blocks by saying that the Soviet combat troops must be removed from Cuba or the Senate would not consider SALT II.

Some Senate members were grumbling privately that this was a "setup" or "deal" for Church so that he could claim credit for chasing the Russians out of Cuba. Shades of John F. Kennedy. Others complained that Church was placing his political interest above that of his country. Perhaps the brigade was not a threat to the United States. Perhaps the Soviets would not back down on this one. What would the Chairman of the Foreign Relations Committee do then? Hold the SALT treaty hostage for political reasons?

From the conversation that dominated the corridors of Capitol Hill, it was clear that Church had hurt himself. One is tolerated or forgiven for practically any vote on an issue if personal survival is at stake. But when an issue is larger than the political fortunes of an individual (usually, in the eyes of the beholders who are not candidates), a measure of respect is irretrievably sacrificed. The SALT II treaty was such an issue.

Frank Church was out on a limb. The Administration could not crawl out after him. The Soviet Union might very well resist making any concession for fear of losing respect in the eyes of the Cubans or its other satellite countries. The United States had not complained about the presence of MIG-23s or Soviet submarines. Why the outrage over 2,500 soldiers who had no ground or sea-lift capability and posed no threat to the United States?

Without a reduction or elimination of the combat unit, Church could not support the SALT II treaty. If the reduction were cosmetic only, it would not satisfy those who had grown doubtful about the desirability of the treaty.

Bob Dole had a resolution to postpone SALT until the troops were out or the President certified to Congress that they presented no danger to the United States. Majority Leader Byrd objected to what he perceived as Dole treading on his turf—the setting of the legislative agenda. It occurred to me that Byrd might, in light of recent events, allow the measure to be offered and thereby provide the Administration and SALT supporters with an "out" from their dilemma. The legislative process can be an intellectual minefield. One is never quite sure whether a sure step today will explode in your face tomorrow.

SEPTEMBER 12, 1979

ANOTHER DAY of trauma—not on Capitol Hill but at home. Away from the keen eye of his mother, I helped to shave the whiskers of our younger son, Chris. His brother had not begun shaving until his fourteenth birthday. Chris wanted to beat that record, even though I thought he was pushing the matter a bit.

SEPTEMBER 13, 1979

THE SENATE SELECT COMMITTEE ON AGING HELD hearings to determine how we could help the elderly, many of whom were facing the choice of going without food or without heat this winter. The price of fuel had doubled, inflation was raging at double-digit levels, and there was no relief in sight. The cold finger of fall was already touching the topsoil in many parts of the country. Could Congress take action? Could the bureaucracy move? The opening statements of the members of the Aging Committee and those who testified before us indicated that there were as many opinions on the subject of appropriate legislative solutions as there were problems.

At 11:30, I left the hearing to attend a press conference that John Chafee, Bob Stafford of Vermont and I were holding to announce our support for Howard Baker for President. We each made an opening statement, and then Baker opened up the session for questions from the press. The conference lasted a full hour. The questions covered the total range of issues from SALT and the presence of Soviet troops in Cuba to inflation and the decontrol of oil prices. At one point, Baker was asked, "If Kennedy is a candidate, do you intend to make Chappaquiddick an issue?"

"No," Baker responded, "it is not an issue. It is not relevant to his qualifications as a presidential candidate. Politics has become so mean and nasty that unless we return some measure of civility to the process, no one is going to want to run. I will do everything in my power to see to it that none of my staff or supporters raise it as an issue. . . ."

That evening on the major networks, not a word was mentioned about three New England Senators endorsing Baker's candidacy. The only reference to the conference was a brusque and cynical editorial comment:

"At a press conference today, in a well-rehearsed statement, Howard Baker said that he would not make Chappaquiddick an issue if Senator Kennedy becomes a candidate."

The implication was that Baker had raised Chappaquiddick as an issue and then piously declared that it would have no place in his campaign.

SEPTEMBER 15, 1979

TWO YEARS AGO TODAY I had announced my candidacy for the Senate. Today I flew back to Bangor to see my parents and address the State of Maine Credit Union.

President Carter made the mistake of entering a grueling six-mile footrace. He had to drop out on his doctor's orders after running 4.2

miles. He was exhausted, but said, "I feel great." One did not need a vivid imagination to foresee the editorial-page cartoons that would fill the magazines and newspapers. The symbolism of an earnest President undertaking a task clearly beyond his abilities would not be lost on the public. Moreover, many would question why he was engaging in such a physically stressful activity when he should be devoting all his energies to the crucial matters of state. President Carter did not seem to realize that he is long past the point where the public would admire him for daring to be different. To have failed so visibly only seemed to underscore the risk in the use of symbols; they so often are translated into a meaning quite opposite of their intent. (Congressmen who engage in similar physical endeavors do not enjoy or suffer the dramatic notoriety of the President.)

Diane had wanted to come to Maine this weekend, but I was running heavily into debt on my credit cards. Her car needed a new transmission ($800), my two cars were both being repaired ($500) and I could not afford her air fare this month. Her disappointment hung in a shroud of silence when she drove me to the airport.

SEPTEMBER 16, 1979

AN AFTERNOON RECEPTION WAS held for me in Piscataquis County, a beautiful but economically undernourished rural area of Maine. I spoke for forty-five minutes on SALT, national defense and energy. I also defended Israel as an important ally. Apparently, this did not meet with universal approval. One woman called my aide at 1 in the morning to complain about my statements.

Following the reception, I stopped by a golf course to meet constituents who were playing in the annual tournament. Finally, I drove to Bangor to address the annual Israel Bond Sale. My parents could stay only for the cocktail hour, since my father had to be at work by 11:30 P.M. My great-uncle, who was ninety-nine years old, came to hear me speak and stayed for the evening.

SEPTEMBER 19, 1979

MUCH OF TODAY WAS devoted to a debate on the 1980 Budget Resolution. Ed Muskie, Chairman of the Budget Committee, fended off every attempt to amend the budget and won the grumbling admiration of his colleagues.

Joe Biden of Delaware and I were talking while one of the votes was being tallied.

"You know," Biden said, "you've got to give him credit. He's got a quick temper, and that's probably the one thing that kept him out of the White House, but damn, he's competent. . . ."

Ed spotted the two of us talking and looking in his direction. He walked over toward us wearing a smile of satisfaction because he knew he had just beaten back the last challenge to his budget. As he approached, I said, "Ed, we were just talking about what an SOB you are."

He was tired after being on the Senate floor rising to defend his child, the budget process, but he just laughed at us. Later, we had a chance to talk alone.

"Bill, I don't know how much longer the budget can survive under the pressure."

"It will survive as long as you're Chairman, Ed. Beyond that, maybe we'll learn to discipline ourselves."

"I don't know what's going to happen when Henry Bellmon retires. God, he's been a pillar of strength. I've never worked with a better human being. Of course, he'll still be here next year, but after that, I don't know. . . . You know, it's the fellows on this side [Republicans] who've really been holding tight on this thing. . . ."

"Ed, Joe and I were talking about you earlier. We were admiring your ability."

Muskie turned and said, "Thank you. That means a lot to me."

SEPTEMBER 20, 1979

TODAY A GOVERNMENTAL AFFAIRS SUBCOMMITTEE BEGAN hearings on a bill to eliminate the exemptions that Congress had written for itself into the laws applying to the general public. We have our own pension plan and therefore do not have to pay a Social Security tax. We have the right to hire and fire members of our staffs with virtually no recourse for them, although we have imposed the Equal Employment Opportunity Act upon federal agencies and those in the private sector. The Occupational Safety and Health Act (OSHA), perhaps the most criticized federal legislation, does not apply to Congress. Even though the repeal of the exemptions for Congress had little likelihood of ever being passed by the Senate, today marked the first time we were even willing to discuss and debate the double standard at a public hearing.

Late in the afternoon, my secretary, Cindy Whiteman, returned a call to a constituent for me. Apparently, his ninety-one-year-old grandmother, who was in a nursing home, had not received a birthday card from me this year for the first time since I was elected to Congress. She was heartbroken. I sent a belated one, explaining that I had been in Israel during August and had simply overlooked the date.

SEPTEMBER 21, 1979

SAM NUNN HAD requested a closed session of the Senate so that he could call to the attention of the members the results of a military mobilization effort that had been conducted, called "Nifty Nugget." The operation revealed serious deficiencies in our mobilization plans in a time of war, including manpower and equipment shortages. Nunn is genuinely concerned about our state of readiness and is adamantly opposed to the all-volunteer Army, which he considers a social experiment that is undermining the quality and spirit of our military. That view is shared by an increasing number of Congressmen. Today's session served the purpose of preparing a foundation for the need to return to a system of face-to-face registration of young males and, ultimately, the draft.

I wanted to be present for the entire presentation on "Nifty Nugget," since I had been asked to rebut some of the underlying assumptions that placed the blame for our deficiencies at the doorstep of the volunteer Army. But a group of Maine Republican legislative leaders were waiting in my office. I was under the impression that they wanted to meet with me to discuss the status of energy legislation in the Congress and what assistance the people in Maine could expect from Washington this winter.

Instead, I was greeted with a measure of hostility. They felt that I was not giving them enough information on legislation or programs I was sponsoring. In addition, they wanted a copy of my schedule whenever I returned to Maine, so that I could integrate local officials and the party organization into my schedule.

I missed the most crucial part of the Senate discussion and returned to a virtually empty chamber.

SEPTEMBER 23, 1979

PRESIDENT CARTER SCHEDULED a Sunday party on the South Lawn of the White House tonight. A cool nip was in the air. The peak of the Washington Monument, with flashing red eyes, rose in the distance like a giant head sheet of the Ku Klux Klan. The flags at the base of the Monument cast eerie shadows along its floodlit height. Large jets took off and landed at National Airport every three minutes, the roar of their engines filtering through the conversation. The talented composer-pianist Marvin Hamlisch was performing tonight. With him were Lucie Arnaz and comedian Robert Klein. They performed a stand-up routine from their current Broadway musical production, *They're Playing Our Song*.

Round tables covered with yellow floral cloths were spread across the South Lawn for the members of Congress and their wives. Seafood, vol-au-vent and watercress salad was served buffet style. The women wore mink or fashionable wraps. Ted Kennedy and Speaker Tip O'Neill were noticeably absent.

President Carter looked fully recovered from his disastrous footrace in the Catoctin Mountains last week. Rosalynn stood stern-faced and unsmiling by his side. Carter spoke briefly from a flatbed stage that had been erected in the southwest corner of the lawn.

"Tonight is the first majority that I've had in Congress in quite a while. It's also a night that required no computer analysis to compose a guest list [a reference to reports about Carter's decision to become more selective in who receives invitations to White House functions], a night when nobody loses, a night when everybody gets rewarded."

I left our table and returned to the buffet to get coffee. Reporters from the *Washington Post* and *Star* approached me. I tried to say something inconsequential.

"Senator, what do you think of President Carter?"

"Well, it's been said by others that he's a tough fighter. He's not out of it yet."

"He seems to have a majority of Congress with him tonight. It may be for the first time."

"Well, it's probably due to the presence of Marvin Hamlisch rather than the President," I suggested jokingly, not wanting to give the impression that I or many of my colleagues were attending the function to show our support for Carter.

Although the reporter to whom I said this was not taking notes, my comments appeared verbatim in *The Washington Post*. The lightness of my intent was lost in the flat letters of ink.

SEPTEMBER 25, 1979

NEWS ITEM: Freshman Senator Larry Pressler announced that he was a candidate for the Republican nomination for President. His program emphasized youth, gasohol and a fresh face. Most of his colleagues thought the announcement a bit premature.

President Carter accused Senator Kennedy of legislative impotence and said that he (Carter) had never panicked in a crisis. The press was off and running. "Panic" and "crisis" were unconcealed code words for Chappaquiddick.

SEPTEMBER 28, 1979

REPUBLICAN SENATOR BILL ARMSTRONG of Colorado was on the Senate floor leading the effort to oppose increasing the national debt limit to $879 billion, a $49-billion increase. Armstrong is a tall, thin young conservative who has the deep, mellifluous voice of a radio announcer (he owns a radio station) and the serious tone of a schoolmaster. But his obvious sincerity and genuine concern for and deference to the views of his colleagues soften any surface appearance of rigidity.

Today, he argued that the increase in the debt limit (which is always called temporary, and always remains permanent) was a vote for more inflation. A number of fiscally conservative colleagues joined in Armstrong's crusade. To the untrained eye, it might have appeared that the debt-ceiling increase was in trouble, as few Senators rose to defend our alarming drift toward a trillion-dollar national debt. But the simple argument that has been made year after year—"If we incur the debts, we have to pay the bills"—prevailed. The vote was 49–29 in favor of the increase.

Much of the day was spent waiting for the House and Senate conferees to reach an agreement on the budget appropriations bill for fiscal 1980, which began on October 1. There were two major stumbling blocks preventing any rapid accord. The House had imposed stringent restrictions on the availability of federal funds for abortion and had also voted for a 5.5-percent increase for all members of Congress. The Senate wanted to retain current law on the federal funding of abortions—permissible if the mother's life was in danger, if the pregnancy was due to rape or incest, or if there was a danger of long-term injury to the mother—and was opposed to the pay increase. The conference committee worked until the early hours of the evening, but the deadlock remained.

At 8, I went to the Republican cloakroom, just off the Senate floor, to await further word on what the House would do and watched an evening of professional boxing that was capped by the Ernie Shavers–Larry Holmes heavyweight contest. What started out to be a boxing match turned suddenly, in the seventh round, into a brawl. Shavers unloaded a right hand that put Holmes on the canvas. Although Holmes recovered and managed to win a TKO in the eleventh round, both men were so exhausted they stumbled all over each other in the ring.

The brawl in the Las Vegas ring somehow spilled over onto the Senate floor. The House had unloaded a surprise roundhouse to the defiant and protruding jaw of the Senate. The Senate conferees believed they had reached an agreement—the Senate would yield on the pay-raise issue and the House would accept the Senate's language on abortion. The House conferees had returned to their chamber, however, and urged the full House to hold to its position. By a voice vote, it voted to uphold the House position and then adjourned for a ten-day recess!

This left the Senate in the position of either accepting the House position on abortion and the 5.5-percent pay raise or rejecting the entire Conference Report. If this occurred, the wheels of government might come to a screeching halt, since there would be no authority for any federal agencies to operate and no money with which to function. In addition, under existing law, all members of Congress, federal judges and

22,000 top federal employees would receive a 12.9-percent raise automatically unless we voted to impose a 5.5-percent cap. While we could roll back the congressional raise at some future date (the public would lead a charge up Capitol Hill to make sure that we did), under the Constitution we could not roll back the 12.9-percent raise for judges once it took effect. The House assumed that we would not dare reject the Conference Report and be forced to explain how we had permitted such a turn of events.

Senate Majority Leader Byrd tried to persuade the members to vote to pass the Conference Report itself and then vote on the abortion and pay-raise issues separately.

Like Larry Holmes, the Senate members picked themselves off the canvas and fought back. Republican Minority Whip Ted Stevens said he favored the 5.5-percent pay raise, but he would not trade that for depriving a woman of her right to have an abortion.

Other members who supported the House's provision on abortion were opposed to the pay raise.

Byrd tried to reason with the members and called for calm. But fury had taken hold of pent-up exasperation, and anger blew out the candles of restraint. The Senate voted 55 to 9 to reject the entire Conference Report and let the House carry the burden of running the federal government without authority or money.

At the conclusion of the vote, Byrd adjourned until 12 noon the next day with the suggestion that if the President invoked his authority and called the House members into session, he would find the Senators on the job, ready to move into the next round of the fight.

OCTOBER 1, 1979

PRESIDENT CARTER ADDRESSED the nation on the presence of Soviet combat troops in Cuba. In essence, he said that the Soviets refused to yield any ground on the propriety of the troops' being in Cuba and therefore the United States had no choice but to increase our personnel at Guantánamo and upgrade our intelligence and surveillance measures.

The reaction in the Senate was predictable. Supporters of the President praised him for his restraint and ability to place the Soviet troops in proper perspective. Critics charged that Carter had walked up the hill to face the Soviet challenge, turned around and walked down again. The "status quo" that Carter had claimed to be unacceptable three weeks earlier was now acceptable. The United States had the growl of a papier-mâché tiger.

OCTOBER 5, 1979

I ATTENDED a breakfast meeting with President Carter's omnicompetent representative, Bob Strauss. He had just returned from a mission to the Mideast and wanted to give us an update on his progress. In his typical mule-skinner manner, he reviewed the positions of the Egyptians and Israelis, and offered some prophetic observations about the Reverend Jesse Jackson's return to the United States. The essence of his report was "Gentlemen, I've got some good news and some bad news. There have been some positive developments, but they are still sixty percent apart on the autonomy issue."

I returned to my office to sign some mail and discovered a request to donate 50 cents an hour to a dance-contest benefit for Multiple Sclerosis. I receive hundreds of requests during the course of the year to donate money or personal items. Several months ago, I wrote a gentle letter to one constituent who wanted me to help buy carpets for his church. The reply I received was not wholly unanticipated. He expressed his regret about having voted for me and promised never to do so in the future.

OCTOBER 11, 1979

THERE WAS nearly full attendance for the Herman Talmadge debate. Members do not enjoy sitting in judgment on a colleague. The resolution before the Senate was to "denounce" Talmadge for his gross negligence in the management of public funds—the reimbursement for funds that were never expended and were diverted into a secret bank account by his administrative assistant. Some believed that Talmadge actually should have been censured for conduct that brought the Senate into dishonor. But the majority of the Senate members were sympathetic to a colleague who had fallen on hard times. Talmadge had lost a son, suffered a bitter and public divorce battle, had a bout with alcoholism and had to endure an intensive public scrutiny of his personal finances and habits. While some of the revelations concerning his spending practices were not reconcilable with claims of innocent neglect, the record against him did not rest on a foundation of specific and provable facts of criminal misconduct. Underlying the public statements and somber mood of the day were the gnawing doubts among the members about their own failure to exercise control over their office accounts. The fact is that most members of Congress delegate bookkeeping responsibilities to staff members, and they rarely have the time or the inclination to serve as watchdogs over their employees. We place blind trust in our staff members, at our peril. We take credit for their excellence and remain vulnerable to their errors or intentional misdeeds. Whatever doubts the members of the Senate had about Talmadge's claims of innocence, few felt comfortable or secure in pointing the finger of righteous piety at the accused.

The Senate verdict was received with general scorn. Our apparent timidity was translated into the stamp of a double standard of justice—one for the powerless, another for the privileged.

Late in the afternoon, John Glenn asked me to join him and Sam Nunn for a meeting with representatives from the State Department. We met in Robert Byrd's elegant office just off the Senate floor. The State Department officials advised us that the Administration was becoming increasingly concerned about South Korean President Park's oppressive measures to silence any opposition to his rule. They feared Park would strengthen the resolve of his opponents, spark open clashes, and undermine stability in the region. They did not want to run the risk of undermining Park (as it was charged we had undermined the Shah of Iran through our espousal of human rights and equivocal support for his policies) by publicly criticizing or rebuking him. On the other hand, they believed that unless he received some indication that we did not support the trend of his policies, he would see no benefit in moderating them and might become even more extreme.

The three of us had met with Park during our return trip from China last January and had filed a report that urged President Carter to suspend the unilateral withdrawal of troops from South Korea. President Park held us in high regard, so it was suggested that a diplomatically worded private letter indicating our strong support of his presidency and our concern over reports of oppressive measures taken against his opposition might serve a useful purpose.

I was not enthusiastic about sending such a letter, which I thought was bound to become public at some future date. But I agreed to consider signing the letter after we saw the draft and approved its language. The letter, however, was never drafted or sent. We were never told why.

OCTOBER 15, 1979

A VOTE WAS in progress on Jacob Javits' amendment to the Department of Interior appropriations bill to provide emergency fuel aid to the poor and elderly. Ed Muskie had led the opposition to Javits' amendment on procedural grounds—asserting that this was not the proper bill to which to attach this amendment. I was persuaded by the merits of Ed's argument about the need to protect the integrity of the Senate procedure and that there would be another opportunity to consider emergency fuel aid. It was a tough vote politically. Nearly every New England Senator was voting for the Javits amendment. Opposition to the amendment would be interpreted as callous indifference and disregard for those in desperate need of assistance. The public would never understand the need to maintain "procedural integrity." I wanted to give Ed some support so that he would not be standing alone in the "No" column.

After voting "No," I discovered that Robert Byrd was going to offer a nongermane amendment as soon as the Javits amendment was disposed of and that Muskie had agreed to support him. I was going to vote against Byrd for the same reason I had voted against Javits: procedural integrity. The irony was that I would have been more concerned about consistency than Ed and have cast a vote against the interests of my region in the process. I switched my vote to "Aye" on the Javits amendment, which lost by a narrow 43-to-47 margin.

OCTOBER 16, 1979

I FLEW to Bangor to attend the funeral of my former law partner Errol Paine. He was forty-one years old and at the peak of his career as one of the finest criminal trial attorneys in the state. Over the weekend, he had been hauling firewood for a neighbor with his tractor. He lost control of the tractor momentarily and was thrown from the seat as the tractor flipped over. One of the tractor's large wheels crushed his head against a rock.

In the flick of an eyelash, one of my closest friends was dead. The news reports said only that a prominent Bangor attorney had been killed in a "freak accident."

I wrote a letter to Errol's father telling him what his son had meant to me. I thought of Al Simpson's question at the Senate Prayer Breakfast —"Why do we always wait until our friends are dead before we tell them that we love them?"

OCTOBER 17, 1979

THIS AFTERNOON confirmation hearings were being held for a number of military appointees, including the new Secretary of the Navy, Edward Hidalgo, and the new head of Selective Service, Bernie Rostker. Everyone was confirmed except Rostker, on whom Chairman Stennis deferred a vote on the ground that more information had to be furnished by the nominee before the Committee could give him full consideration. The fact was that no additional information was needed. The opponents of the volunteer Army had been conducting guerrilla warfare and waiting for an opportune time to launch a sneak attack on Rostker. Rumors were circulated that he planned to appoint a number of subordinates who were associated with some amnesty group. Stennis wanted a full report on these rumors, so that the members of the Armed Services Committee would not be caught by surprise.

Delay could only work to the disadvantage of Rostker. Selective Service was under a mandate to report to Congress by the end of January 1980, and to provide a viable program for meeting the nation's mobilization needs.

The longer Rostker was denied a position of authority with which he could carry out the mandate, the lower the odds that he would be able to meet the deadline with anything resembling a thoughtful program.

When I learned that the Rostker nomination was not going to be considered, I left the hearing room without voting on the other nominations in order to register my objection with the Chairman.

OCTOBER 19, 1979

WE HAVE an unlisted telephone number at our home in McLean. For the past two months someone had been systematically dialing our number and then hanging up as soon as Diane or I picked up the receiver. There had been a number of break-ins in the neighborhood recently, presumably by the notorious Silver Gang. I surmised that the pattern and persistency of the phone calls was part of an effort to determine in which periods during the day our house was most likely to be vacant. Today I had our telephone number changed. The phone calls started again almost immediately after the number was changed, and we received a flyer in the mail asking us why our number was unlisted and offering a security system for our house.

I thought today's events were too coincidental for comfort and decided to call the police. Through a special procedure arranged with the telephone company, I agreed to have our line monitored. By a simple turn of a switch, the phone company could determine the exact origin of each incoming call.

OCTOBER 20, 1979

I FLEW to Hampden-Sydney College with Gary Hart and Richard Burt, a reporter for *The New York Times*. I had agreed to substitute for Jake Garn of Utah in a scheduled debate with Hart on the subject of SALT II. Burt was to serve as moderator.

The debate went well enough, although I tended to oversimplify the alternatives open to our European allies if SALT were rejected. Hart implied that NATO itself might start to unravel in the face of our lack of leadership. In response, I suggested that our allies could visit the Berlin Wall so that their leftist forces could be reminded of the choices available to Soviet-dominated societies. Gary jumped on me for proposing such a simplistic solution to a very sensitive situation. He was right. I made the error of responding to what I considered to be an irresponsible argument (NATO unraveling) with an even less responsible counterpoint.

On our return flight to Washington in a twin-engine Cessna, I made another error. I opened a can of Coca-Cola that the college had supplied to us, along with cold-cut sandwiches, as we left the airport. The high altitude and the lack of a pressurized cabin in the plane produced a Yosemite-like spray—all over the slacks and sport coat of Hart, who was on his way to a law-school reunion in New York.

OCTOBER 25, 1979

AT 4:30 P.M. I boarded a familiar "flying submarine" at Andrews Air Force Base. I had been appointed to serve as a delegate to the North Atlantic Assembly conference being held in Ottawa. We arrived one hour and seven minutes after takeoff and boarded a bus bound for the Hôtel Château Laurial.

I worked on a preliminary draft of a speech and then joined Ted Stevens, Scoop Jackson and Fritz Hollings of South Carolina for dinner. Following dinner, I spent an additional two and a half hours refining a speech that could not exceed five minutes in its delivery. It always takes me a long time to write a short substantive speech. In this case, I learned that it was unlikely that I would even be allowed to deliver it. The official proceedings were not going to commence until 11:30 A.M. the next day. Two hours would be spent prior to that listening to formal speeches by Canada's Prime Minister Joe Clark (who has since been ousted and replaced by Pierre Trudeau) and the chairman of the conference, Paul Thyness. I had to leave for the airport no later than 12:15.

OCTOBER 26, 1979

JOE CLARK STOOD before the Canadian Senate to address the Conference delegates. He is a young man with a soft face and was dressed in a modish dark blue suit, off-white shirt and red tie. His attempt at humor fell somewhat flat in his opening, but he delivered his remarks articulately and bilingually.

I sat next to Congressman Bill Whitehurst of Virginia and a member of the British Parliament, who spoke glowingly of the wit of Winston Churchill. I exchanged my prepared speech for a recitation of his handwritten notes.

On the wall opposite me were four large murals depicting scenes from what appeared to be World War I—men in barracks, cities blasted by bombs, women and children with faces warped with anguish and despair.

At 11:15 a meeting of the Senate delegates to the Conference was convened in the "control room." Hell broke loose. Henry Jackson wanted the delegation to support a change of two words in the proposed resolution that the Conference would debate and then vote on. Jackson wanted to delete the words that called for an early "ratification of" SALT II, and substitute the words "decision on."

Pro-SALT Senators objected.

"The Assembly wants to say yes to ratification of the treaty, and now you want to change yes to no. Well, I can't support you. . . ."

Jackson countered: "Look, this is interference with the internal affairs of the United States. This is the first time any such roll-call vote on an issue like this has ever taken place. The Assembly is going to put itself in a position of voting on a measure before the Senate over which we are divided. There are twenty-seven amendments pending already, and there are going to be a lot more, and yet they are telling us to ratify without amendments at a time when the majority of the Senate delegation here at this conference are opposed to the treaty in its present form. . . ."

Another Senator who was opposed to the resolution jumped into the fray.

"Listen, if this resolution passes as it's worded, it's telling me to vote for ratification of the treaty. I don't know how I'm going to vote, but if I'm forced to vote against this resolution, it will appear as a vote against the treaty. I don't want to do that, but they're going to force me to do it. . . ."

He was interrupted: "Were you chosen to come here, or did you ask to come?"

"I asked to come, and I've been coming as a delegate to the Conference for eleven years."

"Well, I've been coming for twenty-two years, and you don't have to vote. You can abstain. . . ."

The air was charged with emotion. Jackson stepped back into the center of the ring. "Listen. I've served in the House and Senate since 1940, longer than anybody else in this room, and I've never seen a conference handled like this one. The State Department has been up here all week working this thing. So has ACDA [the Arms Control and Disarmament Agency]. No one contacted us or asked us how we felt about the resolution that you people had in mind. It's just never been done before, and the delegates are now in the position of placing themselves at odds with a majority of the delegates here from the United States Senate. . . ."

An apology was offered for the failure to confirm the resolution's wording with the full delegation. Jackson was not deflected.

"I'm not asking for any apologies; I'm just stating the facts."

At this point, "Dickie" Fosdick, Scoop Jackson's national-security-issues adviser, slipped into the room and whispered to me.

"Bill, I've got about forty members of the press waiting across the street in the conference room of the Convention Center. What should I do—tell them to come back at noon?"

Dickie is a diminutive woman who, standing on her toes, might reach four feet ten inches. She wears her gray hair in a French-poodle cut. Her rosy cheeks and bouncy manner give her a youthful zest that belies her years. She's been with Scoop during his career in Washington politics, and she shares her boss's love for a brawl.

"No, Dickie," I said. "Tell them we're on our way."

At that point, I motioned to Fritz Hollings and we got up and left the room. As we started for the elevator, Rhett Dawson, the chief counsel to the Republicans on the Senate Armed Services Committee, asked, "Why are you leaving? I think you guys were starting to get through to them."

"Rhett," I said, "they are not going to budge—not after spending the week persuading the delegates to adopt their language. Jackson has dropped a great big rock in the water, and now is precisely the time to leave, while emotions are running high. If they think there's going to be a brawl on the Convention floor, they might be a little more open to change. . . ."

Hollings agreed. "Yep. Let's git over to that press conference and give 'em something to write about."

Fritz Hollings is one of the most striking men in the Senate. He is tall, wide-shouldered, white-haired, and strides with a confidence that says, "If you pick a fight, I'm ready." He is a man who seems slightly out of place in this slice of the twentieth century. Whenever I see him I think of him on a large white horse, wearing knee-high leather boots (with spurs) and a wide-brimmed hat, leading a charge over some hill with a razor-sharp sword held high in the air. . . .

He is regarded as one of the toughest debaters in the Senate, not given to fancy oratory or rhetorical flourishes. His newsletters reflect the idiom in which he speaks. "Keep your eye on the doughnut, not the hole." "There is no educational value in the second kick [the first kick was SALT I] of a mule."

No one, however, should be deceived by his charm or Southern lyricism into thinking that he is cotton fluff, mint julep and jasmine.

While we were waiting for Scoop Jackson to arrive at the press conference, a reporter asked Hollings, "What is your reaction to our Prime Minister's statement this morning that strongly endorsed ratification of the SALT II treaty?"

It was a tough question and required a diplomatic answer that would not be construed as a slap in the face of Canada's highest elected official. Hollings broke into a broad grin and said, "Well, now. We're guests here in Ottawa, and we have great respect for your Prime Minister's views. I just wish he had used the same force of logic when he saw through Mr. Brezhnev's offer to NATO for what it was—a locking in of NATO into a position of inferiority. Yes, sir, I wish he had applied the same insight to the SALT treaty as he did to Mr. Brezhnev's policy. . . . Now, let me add that we South Carolinians love Canada, got some forty thousand Canadians who visit us down home, and you be sure to tell them that they're always welcomed there. . . ."

Jackson walked into the room and launched a broadside against the proposed resolution as an interference in our internal affairs. Ted Stevens stressed the importance of including the Soviet Backfire bomber under the treaty, as it could strike Prudhoe Bay from the Soviet Union and clearly had the range of a strategic weapon. Orrin Hatch waved a stack of twenty-seven amendments that he was prepared to offer to the SALT treaty itself. I stated that our allies were engaging in a very dangerous game by suggesting that the modernization of their theater nuclear forces would be conditioned upon the Senate's ratification of SALT:

> "To our fellow NATO parliamentarians who say, you must ratify the SALT II treaty or the NATO alliance will unravel, our efforts to modernize NATO's theater nuclear forces will fail, I say we do not see the logic of your argument.
>
> "First, I do not believe that any European leader would act to weaken NATO or would acquiesce in its dissolution because of actions taken by the United States Senate to strengthen it. Secondly, the Senate cannot be deterred from its Constitutional responsibility by such arguments. We cannot take seriously the linkage of SALT to long-range theater nuclear force modernization because to accept such linkage would be to conclude that our allies are not fully dedicated to their own defense.
>
> "Let me suggest that among the critics of the treaty are to be found some of Europe's greatest friends, and our criticism is motivated by a genuine concern over the impact of this unequal treaty on the strength of the alliance.
>
> "Our commitment to our European allies is firm. It will not vary

if SALT II is accepted or rejected. But to suggest that NATO will fracture, dissolve or seek accommodation with the Soviet Union unless the treaty is ratified without change, may set a test that cannot be passed and suspend the alliance over an abyss from which it cannot retreat or cannot be rescued.''

I had to catch a plane back to Washington and regretted that I could not stay to witness the debate. We would lose the vote on the proposed resolution, but Jackson and company were not going to make it easy for the Administration to wave the Conference resolution as an untattered flag of victory.

It took me six hours to return to Washington via commercial flights. I was on standby all the way.

October 29, 1979

TODAY, Chuck Percy led a group discussion on the fiftieth anniversary of "Black Tuesday"—the day of the stock-market crash. I decided not to participate in the colloquy, since I had no more than a secondhand familiarity with the Great Depression and was not completely sure that I had the right answers to today's economic woes.

I was preoccupied with some ominous clouds hovering over the citizens of Maine. The House and Senate conferees were due to meet on the Military Construction Bill, and it was unclear whether I could sustain the amendment that Ed Muskie and I had drafted and whose passage we had secured in the Senate. If we failed, the economic difficulties of northern Maine would dip deeper than they already were.

I wanted to be appointed a conferee, but John Tower was out of town, and Chairman Stennis was unlikely to add my name to the list if I made such a request. I put a "hold" on the naming of conferees (a request by any member of the Senate to delay action on a matter is usually honored as a senatorial courtesy), which upset Chairman Stennis.

On the Senate floor, I spoke with Ed Muskie and asked if he had heard rumors that the Administration was going to announce its support of Loring's staying open. Ed said he had been doing some negotiating behind the scenes.

"Bill, I told them we would be willing to accept a change in the language of the bill that they object to provided they make a clear and unequivocal commitment to spend some appropriated money to upgrade the facility. Otherwise, even if we win, the Defense Department could simply refuse to spend money for the base and then cite its deterioration as a reason for its obsolescence. I won't know for twenty-four hours whether they'll strike a compromise. I know that Lucien Nedzi [Chairman of the House Military Construction Subcommittee] wants to get Secretary Brown's advice on the issue, so I decided to give Secretary Brown a little of my own advice. Now, there are some who might say such a gesture is a little political on the part of the Administration, but I suggested that now just might be the right time to show a little interest in our part of the country. . . ."

Ed was smiling now with satisfaction at the thought that he was giving the President a little Down East political advice which might boost the President's popularity in a region that could well go to his challenger, Ted Kennedy.

"Ed, they can use a little practical advice. I won't say anything until I hear from you tomorrow. There'll be enough credit to go around if the Administration agrees to accept your suggestion. If they don't, we've still got a chance. I've called all of the Republican conferees and most of the Democrats. We still might be able to pull it off. . . . I'm frankly more concerned now about Maggie's [the Chairman of the Senate Appropriations Committee, Warren Magnuson] latest move to spread the shipbuilding contracts for the frigate program to the Todd shipyards in Washington and California."

"I just finished talking with Maggie," Muskie said glumly, "and he's being totally unreasonable. He's running scared and he doesn't give a damn about his proposal being legislation on an appropriations bill or that Maine has been the low bidder on four ships. He's going to use his position as Chairman of the Appropriations Committee and there aren't going to be many Senators willing to vote against him. We'll have to be prepared to fight him on the floor, but our prospects are not bright. Everybody I've talked to says that Maggie is wrong on the merits, but merits aren't going to count on this one. . . ."

I left on that dark note and started contacting the Republican members of the Appropriations Committee to see if I couldn't persuade them to buck the Chairman. Maybe if Magnuson saw that he was going to have to fight this one on the floor, he might agree to some compromise instead of just trying to steamroll over us.

OCTOBER 31, 1979

I HAD breakfast with Henry Kissinger and several Republican Senators. Kissinger described the 1980s as a period of crisis and asserted that any Republican candidate must run on a platform of "Churchillian" scope and power. In Europe, our stock had never been lower. Our European allies deal with the Administration on a day-to-day basis, but no one took this Administration seriously anymore.

"The Soviets are trying to split Germany from us with offers and will continue to make such offers with each ally.

"It must be remembered with respect to TNF [theater-nuclear-force modernization] that the missiles will not be deployed for four years. European allies have no idea what the Senate will do with the protocol that is currently in the SALT II treaty."

At this point, Jake Garn interrupted Kissinger and said, "Henry, you are too depressing. I haven't recovered from Brussels yet." *

Kissinger, breaking into a wide grin, responded, "I really shook them.

"In Morocco, I'm not sure how long the King will last. In San Salvador, we are encouraging the overthrow of a military government just as we did with Somoza. If this takes place, Mexico will inevitably be affected.

"Nineteen eighty-one is going to be a period of radical crisis. If Sadat has a heart attack, I wouldn't know where to begin to put together a peaceful solution in the Mideast.

"With Cuba, I am disappointed with the handling of the entire matter. The perception of being frivolous and starting a crisis and then craven in ending it will cause us difficulty for a long time to come. We confronted the Soviet Union and they said to go to hell. Call it a training center if you want. The fact is that they are not training anybody but themselves.

"The King of Morocco may be next to fall. We send arms and then say settle the conflict. One day, we have got to encourage someone we are arming to beat someone armed by the Soviets.

---

* Kissinger had delivered a speech in Brussels advising our allies that they could no longer rely upon the "nuclear umbrella" of the United States or the doctrine of "massive retaliation" as a deterrent to a nuclear strike by the Soviet Union and its Warsaw Pact allies. He urged the NATO countries to upgrade and modernize their theater nuclear forces to counter the Soviet Union's expanding nuclear capability.

"If Morocco falls, the Saudis will conclude that the United States is totally impotent. The question will be, could we keep the Sixth Fleet in the Mediterranean. . . ."

At this point, Kissinger started to outline his reservations about the SALT II treaty and expressed his lack of support unless we could correct the protocol by specifying that theater nuclear systems must be reduced, commit ourselves to a substantial increase in defense spending over the next five years, and append other amendments upon which he had elaborated in his testimony before the Foreign Relations Committee and the Armed Services Committee.

I had to leave at 9:30 to attend a meeting with Ed Muskie and could not stay for the balance of Kissinger's remarks.

I arrived at Ed Muskie's office at 9:45 and reviewed the statement that he was going to make before a press conference scheduled at 10. We called the Save Loring people in Aroostook County and advised them that we had achieved our goal of keeping Loring Air Force Base open in return for our agreement to drop the amendment that Muskie and I had succeeded in having adopted by the Armed Services Committee and the full Senate.

At 10, we met the Maine press and spent the next forty-five minutes outlining the contents of the proposal from the Department of Defense and our analysis of this agreement's prospects.

I returned to my office to call various radio and television stations in Maine to announce the decision by the Department of Defense.

At 11:30, Scoop Jackson brought me up to date on the status of our frigate program. Magnuson was so angry over yesterday's donnybrook that he would not talk to Ed Muskie. Jackson said that Magnuson had the votes for an even split of two ships for each of our shipyards.

"But, Scoop," I said, "Maggie's always complaining how we can't have legislation upon appropriation and this would be legislation upon appropriation."

"Bill, it's already been clear that this will not be ruled as being legislation on appropriation."

What Jackson was saying was that Magnuson had the matter wired if he could ever get the vote out of committee, and he had the proxies in his pocket to do exactly that. Jackson said he was working on a compromise that would help preserve at least three ships for the Maine yard, which would be consistent with its current production schedule. This would avoid a floor fight which we probably could not win.

Scoop also said that he would hold tight on the language that would

be included in the conference report to protect Loring Air Force Base
and that he would not back away unless it was cleared with me.

NOVEMBER 2, 1979

HENRY KISSINGER WAS the featured speaker at a banquet in Portland,
Maine, held for delegates to a Republican mini-convention. There were
1,400 in attendance at the dinner. Kissinger was the biggest draw in the
history of Maine Republican politics. Three years ago at the Republican
Convention in Kansas City, his name was not even mentioned by President Ford or challenger Ronald Reagan. The word "détente" had been
expurgated from the lexicon of foreign policy.

I had the responsibility of introducing Kissinger to the audience and
took the opportunity to use some purple prose and a bit of hyperbole. I
wanted to accomplish two goals. First, to pay our guest a high compliment for his intellect and achievements and express concurrence with his
views about the need to revitalize a solid and consistently applied foreign
policy that was predicated upon military and economic strength rather
than the good intentions and unilateral restraint of the United States.
Secondly, by expressing my approbation of Kissinger, I hoped that I
might be able to transfer some of Kissinger's obvious popularity to Howard Baker—the man I had endorsed for President and would be introducing to the convention the next day. It was my hope to deliver a plurality
of the delegates to Baker.

But a political campaign is every bit as complex and treacherous as
a military one. Following fundamental rules does not ensure victory, but
ignoring them can guarantee defeat. Howard Baker's campaign effort, of
which I was the figurehead, was a classic case of how to snatch defeat
from the jaws of victory.

The first rule in politics is that the candidate should not take any
election for granted or convey to the voters the impression that they are
being taken for granted. He must see the race as tight at best or assume
that he is slightly behind but gaining momentum. The press may attempt
to dismiss this as so much balderdash or blatant posturing. But such
speculation is far preferable to press confirmations of a confident candidate who is sure of victory. Confidence runs too close to the line of
arrogance, and voters are quick to take offense—and retaliatory action
with their ballots.

We violated this rule. Somehow the press jumped to the conclusion that because he had my active support, Baker had the straw vote in Maine locked up. David Broder, the Pulitzer Prize–winning journalist for *The Washington Post,* wrote that Baker had the support of the state's most popular politician and implied that victory was well within reach. Other reporters accepted Broder's analysis as gospel. Martin Schram of *The Washington Post* wrote a piece on the value of a political endorsement, and while concluding that its value was in fact limited, he gave mine a score of 8 on a scale of 10.

Rather than putting out a different version of how things looked in Maine—"Ronald Reagan still has broad support; John Connally is well liked; George Bush is a summer resident and has strong Maine ties and the support of the Republican leadership in the State"—we allowed the front runner seed to stay planted in the press. Supporters of the other candidates then raised the value of my support beyond the bounds of reason. "If Baker doesn't win with at least fifty percent of the vote, it will be a loss." They complained that I was putting pressure on, calling in IOUs and twisting arms—all contrary to the fine traditions of Maine politics. I had in fact been calling key people throughout the state asking for their help for Baker. But there is a very broad line that one never crosses in Maine: treading on the independent judgment of Maine people. You can ask for help; you cannot demand it. Charges that I was twisting arms were designed to raise antagonism toward my personal telephone calls.

Howard Baker's campaign personnel started to believe the press clippings. Victory seemed so certain that they recommended that he move the date of his official announcement as a candidate to November 1, and then bring a planeload of national reporters to Maine to witness his first triumph on the campaign trail.

So sure did victory seem that Baker's staff scheduled him to visit four states in two days with Maine getting the least of his attention. He arrived at the Holiday Inn during Kissinger's speech, but waited until the very end of the evening to be called to the podium to be introduced to the guests. John Connally did the same and practically embraced Kissinger at the head table.

A hospitality room had been arranged for Howard on the top floor. Rule number two in politics is that people are more likely to vote for you if they have met you personally and have a chance to make a firsthand assessment of your character. A handshake and a few moments of conversation can compensate for a lot of campaign deficiencies. Tonight,

Baker's staff allowed him to stay only a half hour at the reception room and then hustled him off to another hotel to get some rest. He had to be up early to travel to Vermont for a morning of campaign activity. More than seven hundred people waited in long lines at the elevators and hallways to meet Howard. They went away that evening disappointed.

NOVEMBER 3, 1979

AT 7:30 A.M., I looked out the window and felt my skin go cold. It was pouring outside, and a heavy bank of fog was hanging over Portland harbor. It occurred to me that if Howard was able to fly out of the Portland airport to Vermont, he might not be able to land back in Portland later in the day. He was scheduled to address the convention at 2:30 P.M., thus having the edge of being the last speaker of the day, just before the voting started.

I picked up the *Portland Press Herald*. In a front-page news story was a quote attributed to Baker that he was so confident of victory that he was leaving to go to Vermont for the morning. My pulse quickened. I knew that statement would hurt.

I went to the convention hall and started meeting with those delegates who were still undecided. For four solid hours, I spoke with delegates in groups of 15. I spoke with over 350 delegates until I started to lose my voice. Supporters of George Bush cried foul and complained to the press that I was engaging in back-room politics. I was working harder for Baker than I had ever worked for myself. But the fact was that the people wanted to hear the candidate, not from me.

From the convention hall I could hear the roar that went up each time John Connally thumped the lectern and talked of a time for toughness in our foreign and domestic policies. He stood on the stage with the aura and confidence of a Mississippi riverboat gambler—tall, tough and competent. I thought he was going to run away with the vote.

George Bush was just starting to address the delegates when Howard entered the building. He was wet and looked a little weary. He had already delivered two speeches today. I told him that he had better dig down and pull up his best speech because John Connally had them standing in the aisles.

He had only twenty minutes to collect his thoughts. His aides were giving him conflicting advice.

"Be sure to stand at least a foot away from the mike, or they'll never hear you out there. The acoustics are terrible."

"No," said another, as we began the long walk under the convention floor to the back of the hall, "stand as close to the mike as you can and speak directly into it. . . ."

Howard's speech proved to be his undoing. He gave a lecture that was too academic. The delegates wanted red meat—nothing too heady or intellectual, just a recitation of the virtues that Republicans believe will lead the nation back to a position of power and prestige in the world. To make matters worse, he stood back from the microphone and only a few people could hear what he was saying.

I sat on the stage with one of my top campaign strategists, Chris Potholm. We looked at each other's ashen faces during the twenty-minute ordeal and knew that we were about to suffer a major loss.

When the votes were tallied, Bush edged out Baker by 20 votes. The news ripped across the nation. "Bush upset winner in Maine. Baker suffers humiliating defeat." For weeks reporters in Maine wrote columns about how I had overestimated my political support within the Republican Party or how my heavy-handed tactics had backfired. At the national level, no story on Baker was complete without a charge that he did not have first-rate organizational talent or that he even managed to lose the state of Maine to the emerging moderate candidate of the Republican Party, George Bush. There are very long knives, as well as heat, in the political kitchen.

I wrote a letter to the chairman of Baker's committee in Maine, thanking him for his tremendous effort. I added a postscript: "Does the bleeding ever stop?"

Several weeks later, to my dismay, the postscript appeared in the bold print of two nationally syndicated columnists—Jack Germond and Jules Witcover. The question contained its own answer.

NOVEMBER 7, 1979

THREE DAYS after the country was shaken by the news that the American Embassy in Teheran had been stormed by Iranian militants, I attended a briefing given by Secretary of State Cyrus Vance. Vance was gray and ashen and held his jaws firmly clenched throughout the introductory remarks. He advised us that 60 Americans from the Embassy and 500 civilians were all at the mercy of fanatics.

"The Shah needs an operation. Our people may be in one or two buildings—we are not sure. We must remain steady in support during this difficult and delicate mission.

"The Iranians think that any statement made in the United States is made by the President himself."

Don Riegle was the only one who spoke up and said, "I'm not enthusiastic about the Shah being admitted to the United States, but what have we done to anticipate the consequences of such action?"

Although we had been told that this was a very special briefing, nothing said during this meeting was any different from what had appeared in *The New York Times*. In fact, one Senator pointed out that some of Vance's statements were completely contradictory to what an energy committee had been told during a briefing earlier in the day.

We were all personally requested to refrain from making any inflammatory or provocative statements because that might very well jeopardize the lives of the American hostages.

NOVEMBER 9, 1979

A SECOND BRIEFING WAS held on Iran. The situation there had not changed. What had changed, however, was the tenor of the questions that Senators were asking. Patience and restraint were being rubbed wafer thin by the demonstrations taking place in Washington.

One freshman Senator of strong liberal persuasion asked Vance whether he had cameras to take close-up shots of the demonstrators. Some conservative members smiled when the question was asked. Just a few short years ago, any Senator who advocated that the government take photographs of and compile files on persons demonstrating in the streets of the nation's capital would have been denounced as a fascist.

A flood tide of telephone calls and telegrams came pouring into our offices demanding that we take action to punish those "damned madmen."

NOVEMBER 12, 1979

IN ST. LOUIS, Gary Hart and I addressed a group of public relations agents of the major corporations of America on the subject of "Issues of the 1980s."

At 7 A.M. we were extracted from our rooms by several aggressive young executives so that we could have breakfast with the executive committee responsible for putting on the program.

At 7:30 A.M., before coffee or juice had been served, the president of the organization, an eager, hard-charging public relations expert, turned to me and said, "Tell me all the positive things we can look forward to in the 1980s."

I looked over at Gary, rolled my eyes back as if to say, "Oh, God, not this early in the morning."

"Actually, I didn't come here to tell you about all the positive things you can look forward to. I came to talk about the mess that we're in and hopefully suggest some ways to get out of it," I finally said.

He persisted, "You mean you can't tell me one good thing that America has to look forward to?"

"I didn't come here to tell you that things are going to be better. We are going to face some very hard times during the next decade. I came to discuss them and not to fill you with false hopes."

In retrospect, I should have been more diplomatic in my answer. An item appeared in one of the columns of a nationally syndicated journalist which said that two Senators ". . . left a rather large audience stunned the other day, simply by standing mute when they were asked to cite something—anything—that made them hopeful about the prospects for the 1980s."

On our way to the speakers' platform, Hart and I joked that we should hire ourselves out as a team. No matter what the subject, we would just argue opposite positions.

Our presentation to the audience was followed immediately by that of George F. Will, the Pulitzer Prize–winning commentator whose major deviation from his conservative philosophy consists of parting his hair on the left side of his head. His love for the world of ideas, philosophy and Kantian inquiries into the intellect is leavened by his love of baseball and a perverse adoration of the Chicago Cubs. Old dreams die hard for him.

Will describes himself as a man who sees life through the prism of 1895 Ohio pessimism—a time during which there were only two cars in all of Ohio and they collided. Though there are many journalists and commentators who carve words with the grace of an artist, he possesses an extra dimension of talent that enables him to string historical anecdotes lyrically through his message into a long strand of pearled insight and wisdom.

Following Will's presentation (we were grateful he did not precede us at the podium), Hart and I attended a press conference. One of the reporters walked across the line of objectivity into semi-hysterical advocacy.

"Just what are you doing about this crisis in Iran? The American people want action. All you keep saying is we've got to handle it diplomatically for the time being. How long do you intend to wait? The American people are losing face all over the world. When are you going to do something about it? . . . ."

No matter how much we tried to explain that military action would not save the Americans (that they'd be dead on our arrival), that we would take punitive action as soon as diplomatic channels had been exhausted, the reporter simply came back with more hostile questions like "What are you going to tell Joe Blow who wants some action?"

After the conference, we were informed that she had apologized for her tardiness in arriving at the press conference and the way in which she asked her questions.

Gary had shown remarkable restraint at her suggestion that we were contributing to the loss of America's manhood and said, "You know, I'm always amazed how willing some people are to shed someone else's blood." A half hour after the conference, we learned that President Carter had announced that we were shutting off all imports of Iranian oil. Carter was simply taking the initiative on the inevitable consequences of our deteriorating position in the world because of our overdependence on foreign energy sources.

On the way to the airport, we speculated that oil prices would shoot up, gas prices and lines would escalate and lengthen—and no one would know (or believe) that it would be because of the cutoff of Iranian oil.

I picked up a newspaper at the airport. A Denver teen-ager had been shot and killed by an Iranian who fired into a crowd of people who had thrown a rock through his window.

Violence was out of the box. President Park had been assassinated in South Korea; Lord Mountbatten had been slain by IRA terrorists; anti–Ku Klux Klan demonstrators were shot to death in Greensboro, North Carolina. Sixty Americans were being held in Iran with the sanction of a "madman who would be saint," and the American people wanted to declare war and bomb the hell out of Teheran.

As we started to walk toward our departure gate, I turned to Gary and said, "I wonder what you'd find if we started peeling back the layers inside our skulls to find out why we do this."

"I don't dare look," Hart said with a light smile.

"I know what you mean, Gary. Just slam the hatch shut so it won't come out of the dark hole and attack you."

"Bill, I think one of the reasons I stay in politics is found in the faces of all these people in the airport. They all look so bored. And I know I'd be just as bored doing what they're doing. I'm never bored with this job."

NOVEMBER 13, 1979

MIKE HASTINGS, one of my legislative assistants, called Ed Muskie's office to determine if he was going to make a floor statement praising the passage of the Military Construction Bill which contained funds for Loring Air Force Base. The response he received was curiously ambiguous. Mike came into my office and said, "I think Muskie is going to make a floor statement on Loring. He's been claiming practically all of the credit for saving Loring. We think you should make a brief statement on the floor just to remind people that you had something to do with keeping it alive and well."

I went to the floor and spoke about the importance of Loring to our national security and to the people of Maine. Minutes later, Ed came rushing into the Senate chamber and delivered his remarks. I surmised that his staff had heard my remarks over the "squawk box" and advised him to make a statement even if he had not been planning to do so.

At lunch today, Howard Baker held up a poster-size photograph that he had taken. It showed several young, long-haired Americans dressed in faded blue jeans and work shirts. They were riding in the back end of a yellow Toyota station wagon, holding up a bicentennial flag. They were participating in a demonstration outside the Iranian Embassy on Massachusetts Avenue. A few years ago, these same young men might have been burning the flag in protest against a war. Today, they were holding it up with defiant pride, suggesting that they were now ready for us to start calling up our troops for an invasion of Iran.

Cyrus Vance gave the Senate another briefing on Iran. He has the State Department–induced disease of qualifying every statement, whether it is critical or trivial. The members started to display their exasperation.

Senator: "Why can't you tell us what your contingency plans are?"

Vance: "We do not think that would be helpful. We have plans, but we cannot say what they are."

Senator: "I've got a CIA report on the things the Soviet radio has been broadcasting. It's the most provocative and inflammatory statement I've ever seen."

Vance: "It was not helpful."

Senator: "You said there were sixty hostages, but the figures you gave us do not total up to that number."

Vance: "I said about sixty."

At this point, a Senator leaned over to me and said sarcastically, "I knew the loss of those two [listening] stations in Iran would impair our intelligence."

Vance was asked if Mexico had agreed to take the Shah back. He grew visibly angry and tapped his pencil several times on the table while peering over his half-moon reading glasses. He seemed, for a moment, to consider not even responding to the question and then finally answered, "Yes."

November 21, 1979

THE SENATE WAS not in session. During the night, terrorists in Saudi Arabia stormed the holiest of shrines in Mecca. In Pakistan, mobs stormed the American Embassy and burned it; a twenty-year-old Marine was killed. The Ayatollah Khomeini blamed the takeover in Mecca on the United States. A radio broadcast in Pakistan was said to have set off the mobs.

Members of the Senate were no longer willing to hold back. Jackson warned of American retaliation if hostages were hurt. McGovern pledged military action. Kennedy said we would do whatever was necessary. Goldwater said we would either take over their oil fields or destroy them.

The confrontation was escalating daily. The Shah seemed nearly irrelevant at this point. Americans were not accustomed to being spat upon. There was growing pressure to fight—if not to restore order, then only to restore our wounded pride and honor.

November 27, 1979

The Permanent Subcommittee on Investigations held what appeared to be the media event of the month. We were investigating the entire subject of "chop shops"—clandestine establishments that cut up the carcasses of stolen cars and distributed the parts nationwide. It was a multibillion-dollar industry. The risk to those engaged in car theft of being caught was minimal, and the profit was astronomical. A masked witness testified today that he had made $150,000 to $200,000 a year tax-free before he was finally caught and sent to prison. Photographers clicked away at the hooded witness with the intensity of barracudas pursuing live bait. Every angle of his face was photographed. It seemed as if they were trying to dissolve his mask in the cyclopean eye of the camera with the hope that they might expose his identity.

December 4, 1979

At noon, five Chrysler dealers from Maine arrived at my office to discuss my position on the proposed legislation to guarantee $1.5 billion in loans to the Chrysler Corporation. Susan Collins of my staff had prepared a memorandum on the subject several weeks earlier.* I reviewed it shortly before my constituents entered my office.

> Memo to: WSC
> From: Susan Collins
> THE ISSUE
>
>   Chrysler Corporation reported a $207 million loss in the second quarter of this year and anticipates a third quarter deficit of approximately $410 million. Altogether, its total losses for 1979 are expected to exceed $900 million, and it has debts of about $1.2 billion.
>   To prevent its financial collapse, Chrysler has requested $1.2 billion in assistance from the federal government: $500 million in the

---

* To the extent that I am considered well prepared for committee hearings or debates on the Senate floor, I attribute it to the high quality and dedication of my staff, the majority of whom have been with me since I was elected to the House of Representatives in 1972. This memorandum is representative of the hundreds that are prepared for me during the course of the year.

form of immediate loan guarantees and an additional $700 million in contingency loan guarantees, to be repaid by the end of 1985. The company expected to be able to raise $900 million privately, bringing the total needed to sustain it to $2.1 billion.

ARGUMENTS FOR AID TO CHRYSLER

The chief arguments in favor of assistance to the corporation are that its problems are caused by factors beyond its control, that failure to save the company would result in widespread unemployment, and that there is ample precedent for federal assistance to private enterprise.

1. Chrysler argues that its cash shortfall is in part the result of having to spend billions of dollars on research and engineering to comply with federal mileage, pollution, and safety standards.

2. Chrysler has been particularly hurt by the shift in the market away from the more profitable large cars to smaller automobiles that has resulted from fears over gasoline availability, which is beyond the corporation's control.

3. As the smallest of the Big Three, Chrysler is unable to take advantage of the economies of scale efforded its bigger rivals, GM and Ford. Consequently, it is more costly for Chrysler to comply with government regulations.

4. The general economic recession has lowered the annual rate of U.S. car sales from 11 million units in the first half of 1979 to 9.8 million in the last half of this year (estimated). This overall drop in the market has undermined Chrysler's chances of recovery.

5. Chrysler has made significant efforts to reduce its fixed costs. For example, it has suspended all merit pay increases, reduced the salaries of the Chairman and the President to one dollar a year, closed one plant and cut back operations at several facilities, and hopes to reduce costs by $567 million a year. Chrysler has also attempted to reduce its huge inventory of unsold cars, which costs a considerable amount to store and maintain, by offering $400 rebates to stimulate sales.

6. One study has estimated that the bankruptcy of Chrysler would cost the nation's taxpayers $16 billion, including an increase of $1.5 billion per year in welfare and assistance costs and a loss of $500 million in income taxes. The company's failure could also mean a long-term loss of 200,000 to 300,000 jobs. (Chrysler now directly and indirectly employs over 500,000.) Unemployment in the Detroit area would increase to between 16 and 19 per cent from the present 8.7 per cent level.

In Maine, Chrysler employs directly and indirectly about 700 people. There are also 708 shareholders and 116,998 Chrysler vehicles in the state.

7. Because Chrysler manufactures tanks for the Army, its default would have defense implications.

8. Chrysler owners would have difficulty in obtaining parts and service for their cars, should the corporation fail.

9. Chrysler's share of the U.S. car market has averaged about 12 per cent for the period of 1976-1978. If the corporation fails, the auto industry will become even more concentrated, with GM, which now has about 60 per cent of the market, growing even larger. This is not in the consumers' best interest and would probably create anti-trust problems for GM.

10. Those who argue that a bailout would violate the free enterprise system ignore the fact that the federal government has become increasingly involved in business over the past three decades. Few sectors have been as subjected to government regulation as the automobile industry. Since the federal government has required corporations to meet certain standards, it has become more responsible for the welfare of these enterprises. In effect, we have exchanged more political control for less economic efficiency.

11. There is precedent for the federal government to provide aid to both large corporations and small businesses. During World War I, Congress established the War Finance Corporation to keep companies afloat during the war. More recently, Washington has provided loans to Lockheed and Penn Central. The federal government actually made money on the Lockheed loan guarantees. Also, the Small Business Administration frequently provides loans and other assistance to small businesses who need help.

12. Federal assistance to Chrysler would be only a temporary loan to enable the company to make the investment necessary to market new models to return it to profitability.

13. The charge that Chrysler manufactures only gas-guzzlers is not true. In fact, it holds the highest Corporate Average Fuel Economy rating of the domestic companies. Sixty-seven per cent of its sales are for compact and subcompact cars, such as the Omni and the Colt (made by Mitsubishi of Japan).

SUMMARY

To quote Secretary of the Treasury Miller, "In general, government financial assistance to private companies is neither desirable nor appropriate. But in the Chrysler case, there is a public interest in sustaining the jobs and productive capability represented by the Chrysler facilities and in maintaining a strong and competitive national automotive industry."

ARGUMENTS AGAINST FEDERAL AID TO CHRYSLER

1. Chrysler's problems are of its own making. Its managers refused to read the handwriting on the wall and gambled that the 1973

oil crisis was just an aberration and that the average family would find plenty of gas to fuel the large cars that Chrysler chose to produce. Only GM immediately started designing smaller cars and downsizing its big car lines. Industry analysts agree that the company was late in foreseeing the shift to smaller, more fuel-efficient cars, and when it did finally shift, it relied on Volkswagen for engines for its most popular cars, the Horizon and the Omni. VW supplies only 300,000 four-cylinder engines a year to Chrysler—an insufficient number to meet the demand.

2. It does not make sense to blame government regulations for the corporation's plight. Were it not for these regulations, Chrysler would be in even worse shape because Washington forced Detroit into making more fuel-efficient cars that are now selling well. Had this not occurred, domestic manufacturers would have yielded an even bigger share of the market to foreign competitors. Management mistakes have played a far bigger role in causing Chrysler's financial problems than have government regulations.

3. Analysis by Townsend-Greenspan, Inc. (headed by economist Alan Greenspan) indicates that a Chrysler failure would have little effect on the economy as a whole, at least in the long-term. Its economists dispute the claim that the corporation's bankruptcy would mean a net loss to the economy of 200,000 jobs. They argue that the demand for autos will be the same if Chrysler goes under, so the jobs will simply shift elsewhere in the industry, or its facilities will be acquired by other companies, domestic or foreign.

4. The main people who would be hurt by default would be Chrysler's shareholders and managers. And the stockholders could claim a capital loss on their tax forms, which would cushion the impact. A bailout would set the dangerous precedent of relieving the management, the board of directors, and the stockholders of responsibility for the company's good health.

5. Compared to GM and Ford, Chrysler manufactures a significantly smaller proportion of its own parts, which means that it makes little or no profit on these components in final sales. Sixty-eight cents of each sales dollar on a Chrysler car goes to its suppliers, compared to 61 cents for Ford and 50 cents for GM. Consequently, Chrysler has had traditionally slim profit margins.

6. A study by the Transportation Department implies that, even with substantial federal aid, Chrysler would remain in a precarious financial condition for many years. There would be no guarantee that Chrysler would not need further financial assistance in the future, particularly in another recession.

7. If the government rescues Chrysler, it may have to do the same for Ford in a few years since its cash situation is only slightly better than Chrysler's. Ford has its head above water only because it makes two-thirds of its money overseas.

8. A decision to help Chrysler violates a basic principle of the free enterprise system against government assistance for firms in distress. A corporation has the right to succeed and the right to fail. Without such reward and punishment, the discipline of the marketplace simply vanishes, as *Business Week* editorializes. A bailout would subsidize inefficiency and discourage potential new entrants into the automobile industry. In essence, the government would be keeping alive an inefficient corporation whose products the consumer has rejected. Government money would give Chrysler an unfair advantage over other products.

9. Britain provided more than $329 million in cash and loan guarantees for Chrysler's ailing British subsidiary four years ago to save 25,000 jobs. Despite this aid, the subsidiary and the rest of Chrysler's European operations were sold last year to raise cash for U.S. operations. We should not follow the expensive path that the British have pursued of pouring money into failing companies in a futile attempt to save jobs.

10. Companies that ask for government help are just encouraging more government control of the economy and a lessened role for the private sector. For example, UAW president Douglas Fraser has suggested that the government purchase a one-third interest in Chrysler. John Kenneth Galbraith argues that if the taxpayers are to invest $1 billion in Chrysler, the federal government should be accorded an appropriate equity or ownership position. Government aid means government control.

11. There are alternatives to federal aid. Congressman Sawyer has suggested that the seven states with the largest Chrysler concerns authorize a revenue bond sale for the firm. Bonds would give Chrysler more cash, at lower interest rates, and a longer pay back period. Congressman Stockman, who opposes federal financial aid, instead proposes that the federal regulations most costly to the auto manufacturers, e.g., the airbag, emissions, and fuel efficiency standards, be either repealed or delayed (a bad idea; Chrysler's solution is not going to be found in dirtier air or less efficient cars).

12. Chrysler has not helped itself enough. Although it suffered a net loss of $205 million in 1978, the company paid dividends on common stock totaling $52 million and on preferred stock of $12.8 million. Normally, companies strapped for funds stop making payouts to stockholders as soon as the directors are aware of problems. Belatedly, this year, the company's board of directors voted to omit the dividend on its common stock for the third quarter, but continue to pay a limited amount on preferred stock.

13. Many of Chrysler's efforts to save money have been largely symbolic. For instance, the pay cuts taken by its president, chairman, and top managers will save the company less than $3 million during the next two years. The UAW has rejected the corporation's request for a wage freeze, although labor costs amount to about 30

per cent of Chrysler's total costs. Chrysler has not tried hard enough to obtain help from its bankers, suppliers, and workers to remedy its situation. Its proposal for federal aid does not specify how it would raise the additional $900 million it needs for its cash flow.

SUMMARY

As the new Secretary of Transportation, Neil Goldschmidt, says, "There are thousands of companies, little businesses and large in the U.S., run by people who work like the dickens, that go bankrupt every year, and they do not come to the government to be saved."

The staff recommended that I make no final decision until the matter had been fully debated, but the tentative recommendation was a negative one based strictly on the merits.

I agreed with the recommendation on the cold and analytical facts presented, but they were exactly that—cold and analytical. There was no flesh and blood in the memorandum. In front of me sat five men who stood to lose their life savings and investments. They employed a sizable proportion of the more than 700 people in Maine who worked for Chrysler dealerships and repair-service departments. More then 138,000 Chrysler-made products were sold in my state. The owners of those vehicles would suffer a sharp drop in the value of their cars. State tax revenues would decline. . . .

I tried to explain the danger of setting this kind of precedent to the dealers.

"But if I vote to bail out Chrysler, what will I say to Ford when they come knocking on the Treasury doors two or three years from now? What do I say to U.S. Steel Company, which just laid off more than thirty thousand workers?"

They were not worried about precedents. They were concerned about financial survival.

"Listen, we give foreign aid to every nation in the world. The least we can do is provide a little relief to one of our major domestic industries. . . . By the way, why don't we tell Japan and Germany to start supporting their own armies? We'd have more money available to take care of our domestic problems."

"Of course," I responded, "I think they should bear a larger responsibility for defense, but don't forget, we are the ones who insisted that Japan not have a large standing army. Those were our conditions. . . ."

We talked for nearly forty-five minutes. I succeeded only in persuading them that I was giving serious consideration to all the factors involved and might support an acceptable compromise. They succeeded, if not in their primary mission to secure my support, at least in reminding me that political decisions are not only based on memoranda typed in cold ink. These were vulnerable human beings whose fortunes and futures would be decided by my vote.

Today we received an alert notice from Nordy Hoffman, the Senate Sergeant at Arms. A copy of a leaflet that was being distributed on the streets of Washington was attached. It called for the formulation of plans for inflicting violence toward officials of the United States government.

> Muslims in America can not any longer tolerate such arrogance by the U.S. and must now prepare to stand behind of Islam in warfare in the United States.
> However, Islamic guerrilla warfare in the United States must not be unplanned. Strategies must be thorough, e.g., targets must be chosen intelligently and realistically, weapons should be chosen in corrolation with targets/persons in mind, timing, nocturnal encounter considerations, personal safety, retreat methods, etc. But most importantly, it is not necessary for a Muslim to sacrifice himself or herself in such efforts.
> Muslims should not limit themselves to conventional guerrilla weapons, e.g., shotguns, handguns, gasoline bombs, but other weapons which can be utilized with a relatively no noise factor, e.g., daggers, razors, short solid steel clubs, etc. With a relatively no-noise factor involved in an attack, the Servant or Servants of Allah can vacate the location/scene of the encounter unnoticed or inconspicuous.
> Because U.S. foreign policies are made by individuals some targets may exist as high-ranking persons; although, any American citizen can be targeted. . . .
> Since zionists are influencial in U.S. policies the targeting of zionist females in America can be effective towards our cause if these continued guerrilla strategies are made known to the U.S. public and government. . . .
> May Allah bless our community, our members and may Allah give some of leaders more strength to be more publically outspoken and supportive of the Islamic World Movement, or may they be replaced.
> As-Salaam-Alaikum.
> (Community Instructions: Duplicate, Disseminate, Circulate.)

We were given an emergency phone number to call and cautioned about the visibility of our Congressional license plates.

DECEMBER 5, 1979

AT 11:30 A.M., at President Carter's request, I was escorted into the Oval Office to meet with him. He was dressed in a blue glen-plaid suit and wore a matching blue shirt. His hair was clipped much shorter than when he was running for the presidency (it was no longer layered over his ears). Today it seemed more white than reddish blond. He was thinner than the last time I had met with him, some nine months before.

We sat down in two large chairs that faced each other as a photographer circled around snapping shots of us shaking hands and exchanging pleasantries.

"How are you, Bill? How are you finding the Senate—any time to write poetry?"

"Mr. President, I'm really enjoying the Senate. I had decided that I could not run for another term in the House. But I'm not finding much time for poetry. . . . As a matter of fact, I gave a speech last night to a group of psychiatrists about the fusion of the poetic and political eye, and I recited the poem I wrote about Inauguration Day 1977. It was a memorable experience. . . ."

"You mean the one you sent to me?" Carter asked.

"Yes, that's the one. They enjoyed it very much. . . ."

The President spent about five minutes discussing the economic woes of Iran and the success we've been having with the United Nations and our allies.

"Mr. President, I assume that you want to talk with me about SALT, and I'd just like to say at the outset that I have never in my political career acted in a partisan sense on crucial issues facing our country. I am not running for anything. I don't owe anybody anything. No one is putting any pressure on me to vote one way or the other. In fact, there is no amount of pressure that could be generated that would force me to vote for or against it. I have strong reservations about the treaty. I don't like it. But I come to that judgment after making an intensive study of it. I know from some of your past statements that you think Republicans are out to turn this issue against you. I want you to know that I respect you and that I absolutely would be no part of any partisan strategy on this issue. In fact, if I was asked to do so, I'd probably vote for the treaty itself on that basis. I just want to make that clear before we begin.''

"Well, I appreciate your saying that, Bill. I want you to know that I've followed your career. I've watched you progress. I have a great deal of respect for you and think you've got a great career ahead in the Senate or even higher office. . . .''

I demurred on having a long political career.

"Well, I've got at least five more years in the Senate. I'm not sure about anything longer."

The President then said, "Frankly, I have read all of your public comments on the treaty, and I find them to be anomalous to what I would normally expect of you."

He then went into a long discussion of the merits of the treaty which I had heard many times over. I tried not to interrupt and simply kept my eyes fixed on his as I listened to his arguments. His voice seemed to become softer the longer he spoke. Finally, he came to the argument about the impact that a rejection of SALT would have upon our allies and our role in the world in discouraging the spread of nuclear weapons (he referred specifically to Iraq and Libya as being countries we might hope to persuade not to turn to nuclear weapons—the irony of which did not strike me until I learned in a briefing later that day from Secretary Vance that we had suspended operations in Libya for that country's role in planning or encouraging the sacking of our embassy a few days before).

"I'm not asking you to change your vote or alter your position on the treaty now. I only ask that as you consider and debate the treaty, that before you cast your vote, that you consider yourself in my position now or at some future time, and think about the consequences of rejecting the treaty and trying to stop the proliferation. . . .''

He had never seemed more vulnerable than when he made that plea. I was touched by the pathos in his voice and the anxiety in his eyes, but I decided not to show any cracks in my resolve.

I raised questions concerning ambiguities in definitions and asked what we would have to bargain with for SALT III. For the first time the President revealed that we were contemplating a weapons system which would be disclosed to a few Senators within the next few months. Without saying that I was interested in hearing about it, I suggested it be disclosed prior to the conclusion of the SALT debate.

I mentioned that I was troubled by the reports that he had been advised not to disclose how good our satellite photography was for fear that the Soviets would take countermeasures to conceal their activities.

"I was not advised not to disclose this information."

"Well, I am only relying upon reports that appeared in the paper to that effect. But I mention it only to make the following point. If we are reluctant to disclose our capabilities for fear that the Soviets will take countermeasures, I maintain that we will be reluctant to reveal our weakness if they encrypt information we can't detect. The Joint Chiefs of Staff agreed that this was a problem but didn't want to discuss it publicly."

"But without the treaty," the President countered, "they could encrypt everything. They maintain that the treaty doesn't cover things such as accuracy of missiles or distance, and they should be able to encrypt this information. Without the treaty, which by the way is phrased so that they cannot encrypt information if it interferes with verification by national technical means, they could encrypt it all. . . ."

"Mr. President, it really doesn't matter whether we say they can't encrypt if it interferes with verification or they can encrypt provided they do not interfere with verification; the end result is exactly the same. And of course, if they did try to encrypt all the information, it would be extremely expensive and counterproductive to their testing. . . ."

"But if they encrypted information pertaining to the treaty," the President said, "we would file a complaint with the Standing Consultative Committee, and if we were rejected there, we could terminate the treaty."

We exchanged views without animosity or challenge to each other's intellectual integrity. I realized then why so many people were impressed with the President when he finished a SALT presentation. The average person (or indeed, average Senator who has not studied the material in detail) was simply not in a position to know that if the Soviets sought to put 40 warheads on the SS-18, it would be counterproductive militarily. The limit of 10 sounds like a major achievement in the face of a capability of 40, just as the right to totally encrypt sounds ominous as compared with the right to encrypt only that information not covered by the treaty.

During the latter part of our discussion, we were interrupted on two occasions by aides who handed him notes. I knew we were running out of time and apologized for taking so long. "No, no, that's all right. I'm interested in hearing your views."

We finally broke at 12:17 P.M.—our meeting nearly twenty minutes longer than had been scheduled. We parted on a cordial basis. He thanked me again for the poem. I thanked him for the opportunity to talk with him.

As I rushed back to the Hill to attend a working lunch being held in the security room in the dome of the Capitol, I thought about the savage force and unpredictability of the tide in American politics. Two months ago, I did not give President Carter a prayer of receiving the renomination of his party or of being re-elected if he did. He was being attacked by wild water rabbits, retreating to Camp David, and dropping out of uphill footraces. Today, he was born again politically. His approval rating was shooting up, while the once invincible Ted Kennedy was in a sky dive. Kennedy had tripped over a Roger Mudd interview on the subject of Chappaquiddick and had gone tumbling into a free fall when he began to criticize Carter for not shipping the Shah back to Iran so that we could secure the release of the Americans being held hostage. Jimmy Carter no longer had to mention the words "panic" or "crisis." Kennedy's desperation to climb back into page-one coverage in the daily papers served to widen the cracks in the feet of a legendary colossus. But presidential politics was a ride on a roller coaster. President Carter's present popularity could plummet tomorrow.

I arrived at the luncheon in time to be briefed on a new laser weapon system that was straight out of *Star Trek*.

DECEMBER 12, 1979

CHANCELLOR OTTO VON BISMARCK ONCE REMARKED that if one wished to retain his appetite for laws and sausages, he should not witness how either is made. A member of the general public who witnessed cartloads of cots and blankets being wheeled to the second floor of the Senate or weary-eyed Senators dragging themselves to their feet to debate the fine points of Senate procedure at 3 A.M. would have confirmed the wisdom of Bismarck's admonition.

The day began ordinarily enough. We had moved into the fifth week of debate on the so-called "Windfall Profits Tax Bill" on the oil industry. The House of Representatives had passed a tax bill that would have produced an estimated $270 billion in revenues to the federal Treasury between 1980 and 1990. The Senate Finance Committee had reported to the full Senate a bill that would produce an estimated $130 billion. That figure fluctuated almost daily as amendments to the bill were adopted and rejected during the long debate. The Senate had finally agreed to vote on a "minimum tax" on all oil that was produced, whether it was classified as "old oil" or as newly discovered oil. The vote was scheduled to occur at 11 A.M. I was sitting in the Republican cloakroom glancing at the morning newspapers as Jack Javits walked through the door.

"Jack," I asked, "how did you go on this one?"

"I voted in favor of the amendment—for the tax."

"Are you hanging out there alone?"

There was some peer pressure for the Republicans to oppose the amendment. I was going to support it, but still felt uncomfortable about breaking ranks once again. Javits did not even pause in his response or slow his pace toward the bank of telephones on the far side of the cloakroom.

"I don't know. I never bother to look whether I'm alone. I do what I think is right and don't worry about it."

The minimum-tax amendment passed 56–44 with only 5 Republicans supporting it.

Bob Dole, who was managing the bill for the Republicans, indicated that he had no intention of proceeding quickly to conclude debate. In fact, he suggested he was prepared to take a very long time discussing the consequences of the recent vote. This was code for a filibuster.

After several hours of debate which consumed the afternoon, Majority Leader Robert Byrd made a speech advising members that they should cancel their travel plans. We could expect to work through the weekend (possibly even on Sunday) and return to the Senate on the day after Christmas.

Lowell Weicker, who had supported the minimum tax, erupted into a blistering personal attack on Byrd.

"Why is it that the distinguished Majority Leader, having had a whole year to lay out his legislative schedule, plan his legislative schedule, to make certain those matters of priority are addressed by the U.S. Senate, has the MO [modus operandi], as the police would put it, of always running all the important issues up to the last minute, threatening the U.S. Senate with the fact that their privileges of being on vacation or recess will be withdrawn? . . .

"We can spend weeks on a hundred thousand dollars and not hear from the Majority Leader. But when you get into the billions-of-dollars category, be it oil, be it Chrysler or whatever, that is something that has to be resolved in a very brief period of time.

"Maybe the fault, then, really lies not so much in the nature of the issue or those who are trying to debate the issue, but in the nature of the leadership. As far as I am concerned, the leadership of the Senator from West Virginia has been lacking, not just in the last few weeks, but over a period of years. . . ."

Dole rose quickly to disassociate himself from Weicker's remarks.

I concluded that we were in for a very long night. I left the chamber and rushed home to pick up Kevin. He was being inducted into the National Honor Society. It was a highlight in his young life, and I wanted to witness and share the moment.

I returned to the Senate by 10 P.M. I had missed only one quorum call during my absence. The next major vote, that of cloture, was not to occur until 1 A.M. Under the Senate's rules of procedure,

> Notwithstanding the provisions of rule II or rule IV or any other rule of the Senate, at any time a motion signed by sixteen Senators, to bring to a close the debate upon any measure, motion, other matter pending before the Senate, or the unfinished business, is presented to the Senate, the Presiding Officer, or clerk at the direction of the Presiding Officer, shall at once state the motion to the Senate, and one hour after the Senate meets on the following calendar day but one, he shall lay the motion before the Senate and direct that the clerk call the roll, and upon the ascertainment that a quorum is present, the Presiding Officer shall, without debate, submit to the Senate by a yea-and-nay vote the question.

AT 1 A.M., the President Pro Tempore cut off Jack Schmitt of New Mexico from further debate. Ordinarily, a Senator cannot lose the floor unless he voluntarily yields his right to unlimited debate or inadvertently violates the complex procedural rules in a way that results in the termination of his right to speak. The vote on cloture is one of the few procedural mechanisms that take precedence over a Senator's right to speak until his mind and lungs are exhausted.

As we prepared for the vote on cloture, Majority Leader Byrd suddenly rose and raised a point of order against the vote. According to Byrd, the vote could not occur until one hour after the commencement of business the following day—which meant that the prayer and the following day's routine business must intervene before the vote could occur.

Republicans were furious. They rose to make "parliamentary inquiries" or "points of order." A series of Democratic Senators paraded to the dais to occupy the chair. Systematically they sustained Byrd's arguments on the propriety of his interpretation of the rules.

A number of Senators expressed outrage at what appeared to be a flagrant manipulation of the rules of the Senate. John Tower finally suggested that Byrd assume the chair and thereby eliminate the middleman. Byrd, in a moment of pique, did exactly that. After ten agonizing minutes in the chair during which he was forced to rule on the propriety of arguments that he had made from the floor, Byrd stepped down and resumed his position as Majority Leader.

At 3:34 A.M. we finally agreed to adjourn.

I was tired and decided to walk back to my office out of doors, hoping that the air might clear the cobwebs that were clinging to my senses. Malcolm Wallop and one of his staffers walked with me part of the way and then headed for the Russell Office Building.

Just then, we saw a car flick on its lights and start toward me. It had been parked along an unlighted access road between the Dirksen Building and the Capitol. Wallop yelled over, jokingly, "Bill, could be a hit man who's got a contract on you."

The car, a late-model Firebird or Trans Am, pulled up beside me. The driver rolled down his window and said, "Are you a Senator?" I looked into the car, first at the driver and then at the passenger in the front seat. I wanted to see if they were Iranian or Moslem supporters who had been reading the literature advocating violence against members of Congress. The tone of the driver was nonthreatening, but I knew they weren't looking for autographs at that hour of the morning. I decided not to take any chances. "No," I replied, "I'm not a Senator."

The driver rolled up the window and sped off.

DECEMBER 13, 1979

TODAY at an Armed Services Committee hearing, Secretary of Defense Harold Brown presented the Administration's preliminary five-year defense budget. Sam Nunn had been exerting maximum pressure on the Administration to significantly increase the defense budget. Nunn was crucial to Carter's securing enough Senate votes to ratify the SALT II treaty. Nunn's support would not guarantee ratification, but his opposition would certainly defeat it.

Brown denied that the 3.8-percent increase (above inflation) for 1981 and 4.6-percent increase in the four succeeding years was part of any "SALT-selling" to the Senate. Certain Senators had said that they wanted to see the President's budget before they voted on SALT, and the Administration was simply accommodating those Senators with an early presentation. Brown's statement did not have the ring of credibility.

At the end of the meeting, John Tower pressed Chairman John Stennis to set a date when the Committee could debate or vote on a Committee report to the Senate. Stennis refused to set any date. Finally, Stennis just stood up and stepped quickly back from the large hearing table in the Senate Caucus Room. The meeting was over.

DECEMBER 15, 1979

CHUCK PERCY OFFERED an amendment to the Windfall Profits Tax Bill to extend investment tax credits to coal producers. A motion to table the Percy amendment was made. As the vote was about to conclude, the Democratic leadership began to put pressure on Democrats who had voted with Percy. The tide was turning rapidly against Percy as time ran out on the vote. Percy was walking up the aisles asking Republicans who were opposed to his amendment on the merits to support him on this procedural vote. I stood up and asked, "Mr. President, how am I recorded?"

"The Senator from Maine is recorded as having voted 'No,' " came the response from Bill Bradley, who was serving as President Pro Tempore.

A number of other Republicans followed suit. We were stalling for time until Percy could secure enough votes. Byrd finally expressed his displeasure at our resorting to this tactic.

"Why don't you just vote? I voted Aye."

We had stalled long enough. The motion to table failed by 3 votes, although it was clear that the amendment would fail by a wide margin on the final vote. It seemed to me that Republicans were taking a small measure of delight in annoying Byrd in whatever fashion could be devised. They felt that Byrd had been too cute by half in the way he had tried to write the rules of procedure on the cloture vote earlier in the week. If this vote could help Percy for the moment and sting Byrd as well, they were willing to be of service. I relished the prospect as much as anyone.

DECEMBER 18, 1979

A MEETING to consider whether the Armed Services Committee should issue a report was scheduled for today. Scoop Jackson and John Tower had forced the meeting by circulating a petition among the Committee members calling for a hearing. A majority of the members signed the petition. The Chairman of the Committee, faced with the embarrassment of being outvoted, or "rolled," by his colleagues, reluctantly called for the meeting. But those who wanted a quick adoption of a twenty-five-page draft report which concluded that the treaty was not in the national security interests of the United States and should be rejected unless it was specifically amended were disappointed.

Chairman Stennis circulated excerpts from some of his remarks delivered on the first day of our hearings in July. He maintained that a report had never been contemplated, and certainly no amendments to the treaty would be recommended.

Tempers erupted. Supporters of the report argued that our hearings, which were more extensive than those of the Foreign Relations Committee, were a complete waste of time if we did not file a report of our findings for the benefit of our Senate colleagues.

Opponents of the report maintained that we were without jurisdiction to issue such a report and that by trespassing upon the turf of another committee, we were inviting jurisdictional retaliation in the future. The debate continued for three hours and then broke up without a resolution of the issue and on a note of bitter recrimination.

DECEMBER 19, 1979

WHILE SOME MEMBERS of the Armed Services Committee were grumbling over the delay in resolving the dispute in the Committee, a filibuster was blooming on the Senate floor on the bill to extend a $1.5-billion loan guarantee to the Chrysler Corporation.

Don Riegle and Bill Roth of Delaware had been successful in securing adoption of an amendment to the bill which altered the terms of the bill reported by the Finance Committee. Lowell Weicker threatened to filibuster. Supporters of Chrysler were up against the clock. If a bill was not passed before the Senate adjourned for the Christmas recess, the aid bill would be academic. Chrysler was in need of an immediate infusion of funds. Without the loan guarantee, the corporation could obtain no credit.

Joe Biden approached Weicker's desk. Biden, at the age of thirty-eight, is one of the most refreshingly candid (some would say excessively self-assured and cocky) members in the Senate. He is quick on the verbal draw, possesses a well-honed intellect and loves to debate. He is one of the biggest attractions on the lecture circuit and is generally thought to be planning for a run for the presidency, possibly as early as 1984. Biden gathered a group around Weicker and jokingly got down on his knees and said, "Lowell, if you don't agree to let us out of here, my kids are going to hang a banner from the gallery that says, 'Please free my daddy in time for Christmas.' "

Weicker finally agreed to relent, provided the Riegle-Roth amendment was rescinded and that Richard Lugar, who had been the sponsor of the version of the bill reported out of the Finance Committee, was permitted to assume a major architectural role in constructing the legislation. The Riegle-Roth amendment was withdrawn. A new compromise was offered and passed overwhelmingly.

The entire process revealed the power of a single Senator who, when armed with the ability to hold everyone else's vacation plans hostage to his demands, can override the will of the majority.

DECEMBER 21, 1979

AT 10:30 P.M., the debate on the Conference Report on aid to the Chrysler Corporation began. Bill Armstrong raised strong objection to the procedure of bringing important legislation to the floor without giving the Senators an opportunity to even see the report, much less reflect upon its merits. It was a scene that has been repeated many times over the years. Members found themselves pressed up against the wall of securing travel reservations to their home states or vacation spots. The leadership warned the Senators to plan on cancelling their plans and returning to Washington on December 26 unless the legislation was passed. The members were bone-weary from several eighteen-hour sessions. Their combativeness (with a few exceptions) had been drained. They wanted the pain and exhaustion to stop. They finally succumbed. Laws were passed in the early morning hours with few members caring about the details of the legislation.

But Armstrong put the Senate on notice that we could not continue to perpetrate this kind of procedural irresponsibility upon the public. He cited a host of legislation adopted since 1972, when he was first elected to the House, whose unintended consequences had cost the taxpayers billions of dollars. We were still correcting the mistakes that we made in the 1978 Tax Reform Act.

Several pages in the Chrysler Conference Report were out of chronological order and made absolutely no sense. Armstrong wanted an explanation. He was told that it was merely a clerical error which would be corrected. He was not satisfied. He asked if it would be in order to ask "unanimous consent" that on all future conference reports the members be given twenty-four or forty-eight hours to review the legislation before it was considered for final adoption. Majority Leader Byrd said he would object to such a request. "Congress has been around since 1789. This matter will wait." Byrd suggested that Armstrong file a resolution to amend the rules and pursue it through the regular parliamentary procedure.

I was tempted to add some moral support to Armstrong, although he needed no assistance from me. Last month, I held hearings on the subject of "hurry-up spending"—a practice by federal agencies of spending an extraordinary percentage of their budgets in the final days of the fiscal year in order to exhaust the funds Congress had appropriated. According to former Secretary of the Treasury Michael Blumenthal, the abuse is so flagrant that agencies are practically shipping the money out of the Treasury in wheelbarrows. This mismanagement of time and resources had resulted in thousands of dollars' being wasted on unneeded goods and furnishings. But the greatest loss to the taxpayers came in the form of poorly negotiated contracts or sole-source and unaudited agreements.

I was praised by a number of Senators for finally focusing public attention on a perennial problem. And yet there seemed to be some measure of hypocrisy in being too critical of agencies that mismanage their time and resources. The Senate had spent several hours debating the issue of the Kennedy Center's giving complimentary tickets to the Carter Administration. Tonight we would spend less time reviewing the final provisions of a $1.5-billion loan guarantee.

But it was 12:30 A.M. The point would not have been productive. Bill Armstrong had raised the flag declaring he was going to seek a long-overdue change. I decided to wait until he had a resolution before the Senate to change the status quo. Chrysler was thrown a lifeline at 12:31 A.M. by a vote of 44–33.

The rescue of the Chrysler Corporation was not the final denouement of the first session of the Ninety-sixth Congress. John Stennis insisted upon bringing up the confirmation of a federal district court judge for Mississippi. Ordinarily, this would have been a routine matter disposed of within minutes. Tonight, however, was an exception to the rule. Judge L. T. Senter had been charged by some civil-rights groups with being a racist who had used the word "nigger" on several occasions in open court and whose children had once attended segregated schools. The charges were denied and contradicted by other witnesses. Jack Javits and Birch Bayh protested having the nomination brought up in the early hours of the morning with a hearing record that was full of inconsistencies concerning charges of racial prejudice that were in need of resolution. Paul Tsongas, the liberal Democrat from Massachusetts who had defeated the Senate's only black, Edward Brooke, in 1978, said, "I would only point out to my colleagues that this is the last vote of the Senate in this decade. It does not seem to me a proper way to end it."

At 1:45 A.M. the vote began. I heard Ed Muskie vote "Aye."

"Ed," I asked, "why did you vote to confirm Senter? As a favor to Stennis?"

"No. The evidence on racism seemed awfully thin to me."

"I agree. But what about the propriety of bringing this kind of controversy to the floor at this hour of the morning?"

"Well, you've got a point. Procedurally, you can justify a 'No' vote, if that's what you want to do."

I wasn't at all pleased with having to vote on such an important position at nearly 2 A.M. I was mindful that Stennis himself had postponed a nomination before the Armed Services Committee because questions had been raised about the nominee. I signaled to the Clerk, who was calling the roll, and voted "No."

On my way out of the chamber, I stopped and spoke to Thad Cochran, the junior Senator from Mississippi, who had voiced his strong support for Judge Senter.

"Thad," I said, "I voted against your man not on the merits but as a protest against the procedure of voting on an important position at this hour of the morning on the last day of the session."

"Bill, you do what you think is right. It's just a damn shame that these charges were made against him. He's a good man."

"But why not wait until January to call up his confirmation?" I asked. "Why do it now, at this hour?"

"Bill, if this nomination is delayed any longer, the intensity of the attacks is just going to increase. You know, I just don't understand those people in the House who are criticizing him. I told them that if I could vote for Abner Mikva to be a judge, then they should not object to my supporting Senter."

Cochran's last point caused me to turn around. Instead of walking out the Senate door and heading home, I returned to the well of the Senate and changed my vote to "Aye." Perhaps I was being a little too self-righteous about the procedural priority I was placing over that of substance.

Thad Cochran was a young, bright moderate-conservative. He had cast a courageous vote when he voted to confirm former Congressman Abner Mikva to the Circuit Court of Appeals in Washington. Mikva was a former colleague of ours from the House whose liberal voting record was anathema to just about every conservative lobby group in the country. Cochran had had absolutely nothing to gain by voting for Mikva except a lot of criticism in rural Mississippi. He had put his stamp of approval on Mikva's qualifications and was now putting it on Senter's.

I took him at his word and went home.

POSTSCRIPT

I CLOSE the cover on one year in the United States Senate with nearly the same ambivalence with which I began. The calendar sheets—gorged with red-lettered hearings, meetings, office appointments, luncheons, travel schedules, and telephone calls—are stacked in silence on my desk. I am not sure of their significance.

For the past year, I have been recording events without reflecting enough upon them. Perhaps that in itself is an appropriate statement about life as a politician. Days spent careening from appointment to appointment, committee to committee, speech to speech, crisis to crisis without the time to reflect upon whether we have simply doubled our deeds without fixing our destination.

In reviewing the year, I am tempted to summarize and refine, to round out events that now seem episodic, incomplete and unbalanced, to wrap it all up in a package and tie it with the twine of analysis. But the political process is not a neat parcel, and it resists my every attempt at compression and synthesis.

What I have described in the foregoing pages is not *the* true version of what life is really like in the United States Senate. I have only related what it was like for me to become a part of the institution. The events, the people and the personalities have been refracted through the prism of my biases and so have emerged broader, narrower or less clear than they might have from another source. There are 99 other versions of life in the Senate, each of which bears its own stamp of truth.

It is my hope that this account will help bring about a better understanding of the legislative process—how judgments are formed, decisions made and compromises reached—and that the American people may have a greater sensitivity to the noble aspirations and the human deficiencies of those idealistic or egotistical enough to pick up the heavy sword and shield of public service.

These thoughts come to me while on a return flight to Washington.

A passenger sitting two seats behind me suddenly thundered, "The worst thing in our country is the politicians. And next to them are lawyers. There are just too damned many of them in politics, and they are the cause of our problems. If we could pass a law preventing lawyers from becoming politicians, the country would be a hell of a lot better off. . . ."

I waited a few seconds before turning around to see the latest source of conventional wisdom, hoping that the red glow of my ears did not disclose my identity or occupation. A man wearing a thin gray beard and a matching gray suit picked up my head movement as if he were scanning the plane's passenger cabin with a radar gun. The photograph of Rockefeller on the wall of our den, the one where he is making an obscene gesture to an antagonist, bloomed like a geranium in the flower box of my thoughts.

For just a brief second, I gave consideration to knocking the chip off his shoulder—actually, plucking the cherry out of his Manhattan cocktail. The temptation vanished. Instead, I slipped down in my seat and looked out the window at the soft white clouds that rippled out to what seemed to be the curve of the earth.

I was happy to be heading home, just another passenger and an anonymous politician.

JANUARY 13, 1980

ACKNOWLEDGMENTS

KEEPING A JOURNAL about political life for a year and documenting the people and events that leave an impression in the tissue of the mind is similar to approaching a heavily-laden buffet table—there is the temptation to load up one's plate initially and leave little room for later morsels that might prove infinitely more delectable.

I found the editing of this journal considerably more difficult than the writing of it. To the extent that I have been able to achieve a semblance of balance between private thoughts and political realities, personal opinions and dispassionate observations, I am indebted to a number of people who gave me their advice and encouragement.

My greatest debt is to my wife, Diane, whose artist's eye caught shades and nuances that were either unintended or insufficiently illuminated. My editor, Jonathan Coleman, with his sensitivity to the essential, was so quick and precise in his cuts that the author remained comfortable and relatively free of pain. I am grateful for his skill. I want to express my sincere appreciation to my friend and literary agent, Bill Adler, who assisted me with this book from its conception to its completion.

Special thanks go to my Administrative Assistant, Tom Daffron, who left the staff of a prominent Senator seven years ago to join me in the House of Representatives and encouraged me to run for the Senate because it is "the best job in the world." His sage counsel made it possible for me to become a Senator. He was right about the reward of the effort. I owe a generous measure of appreciation to my secretary, Cynthia Whiteman, who spent many hours of her personal time typing the manuscript, and to all the members of my staff whose idealism and dedication are so energizing. I thank them for permitting me to stand on their shoulders so that I might better see where we are and where we ought to be.

Professor Richard Fenno of the University of Rochester, one of America's most respected scholars on the Congress, came to my office one afternoon and asked me what I thought about my first year in the Senate. I handed him a six-pound manuscript and, to my surprise, he read every word. His comments were most incisive and constructive. I am indebted to my attorney and friend, Ed Weidenfeld, for providing me with invaluable insight from his experience as a former counsel and staff director of a Congressional committee.

Finally, my gratitude goes to my sons, Kevin and Chris, who tolerated my quasi-presence at home on weekends with uncommon patience and grace. I was writing instead of watching them play baseball and soccer. I only hope that this book will prove more enduring to them over time. One day, perhaps, I'll grow that mustache.

W.S.C.

INDEX

Nunn, Sam (*cont.*)
  meeting with Teng Hsiao-ping, 48–49, 57
nuclear weapons, 113, 119–20

Occupational Safety and Health Act (OSHA), 279
Occupational Safety and Health Administration (OSHA), 214
O Congress (Riegle), 65
Off the Record Club, 88
O'Hare Airport, 161–62
Ohira, Masayoshi, 54
Ohira Hotel, 52–53
Olympic Games, 254
O'Neill, Thomas P. "Tip," 77, 215, 235, 280
Ottawa, 289, 292
Otway, Thomas, 164

Pacific Ad Hoc Study Group, 33, 72, 73
Packwood, Robert W., 74
Paine, Errol, 286–87
Paige, Satchel, 34
Pakistan, 305
Palestine Liberation Organization (PLO), 152, 224, 266
Park, Chung Hee, 55–57, 285, 303
Park, Tongsun, 184
Pearson, Preston, 164
Peking, 44–46, 50, 51
Peking Opera, 51, 85–86
Pell, Claiborne, 86–87
People magazine, 249
Pepperdine University, 162
Percy, Charles H. "Chuck," 18, 23, 74, 80, 293, 320
Perry, William J., 89, 167
Peterson, Russell, 202
Philadelphia Naval Shipyard, 149
Philippine Islands, 39, 40
  Clark and Subic bases, 37, 39, 42–43
Pink Panthers, 172

Pirsig, Robert, 160
Piscataquis County, Me., 277
Pork Chop Hill, 55
Portland, Me., 18, 212, 297, 299
Portland Expo Building, 212
Portland Press Herald, 299
Portsmouth-Kittery Naval Shipyard, 149
potatoes, 171, 212
Potholm, Chris, 227, 300
Powell, Jody, 68, 193
prayer in public schools, 174, 177
Presidential Palace, Manila, 39–40
Presque Isle, Me., 38, 112, 266
press, 20, 27, 28, 88, 161, 165
Pressler, Larry, 270, 281
privacy and the computer, 241
Proxmire, William, 128
Public Works Appropriation Bill, 172

radiation, 151
Railsback, Thomas F., 25–26, 83
Rather, Dan, 74
Rayburn House Office Building, 70
Reagan, Nancy, 74
Reagan, Ronald, 69, 73–75, 219
Reasoner, Harry, 17
Red Lion restaurant, Bangor, 17
registration and draft, 107–8, 137–38
  Senate debate on, 231, 232, 239, 279
Republican Party, 133
Republican Trust Fund, 209
Resor, Stanley R., 117
Reston, James, 181
Rhodes, John J., 245
Rhodesia, 231
Ribicoff, Abraham, 80, 128, 174, 192
Richardson, Elliot, 33*fn.*, 132–33, 140, 239
Rickover, Hyman G., 151–52
Riegle, Donald W., 64–65, 171, 188–191, 301, 321–22
right-to-life amendment, 111
Rockefeller, Nelson A., 84–86, 102, 168–69, 218–19, 327